# The Children
# of Abraham

# The Children of Abraham

Judaism, Christianity, Islam

A NEW EDITION

## F. E. Peters

With a foreword by John L. Esposito

PRINCETON UNIVERSITY PRESS

PRINCETON AND OXFORD

Fourth printing, and first paperback printing,
for the Princeton Classic Editions series, 2006
Paperback ISBN-13: 978-0-691-12769-9
Paperback ISBN-10: 0-691-12769-7

The Library of Congress has cataloged the cloth edition of
this book as follows
Peters, F. E. (Francis E.)
The children of Abraham : Judaism, Christianity, Islam
F. E. Peters.—New ed.
p. cm.
Includes index.
ISBN 0-691-12041-2 (cl : alk. paper)
1. Judaism—History—To 1500.   2. Christianity.
3. Islam—History—To 1500.   I. Title.

BM157.P47 2004
201'.4—dc22        2004040049

British Library Cataloging-in-Publication Data is available

This book has been composed in Janson

Printed on acid-free paper. ∞

pup.princeton.edu

Printed in the United States of America

5  7  9  10  8  6

For

*Edward Peter Fitzsimmons*

# Contents

# *Foreword*

Publication of the thoroughly revised and substantially rewritten edition of Frank Peters's *Children of Abraham* is important for two essential reasons. First, it signals the enduring significance of this groundbreaking volume. Second, I can think of no time when it has been more needed. In addition to the inherent significance of Jewish, Christian, and Islamic religious faiths, the realities of globalization and international politics in the twenty-first century make understanding of these three great faiths and the dialogue among them imperative.

The initial publication of *Children of Abraham* occurred in a world that acknowledged the interconnectedness of Judaism and Christianity by coining the term Judeo-Christian. This reflected the realities of post–World War II geopolitics and theology. However accurate and well meaning, this approach tended to perpetuate the failure to recognize all the Children of Abraham. Islam is also a great monotheistic tradition with origins in the Middle East and a long historical and theological connection to Judaism and Christianity. Yet Islam was grouped and studied with Eastern religions—Hinduism, Buddhism, Taoism, and Confucianism. Peters's book was part of a movement among some scholars to correct this oversight or distortion and thus alert students and scholars, religious leaders, and the general public to the fact that there is a Judeo-Christian-Islamic tradition.

The world and international politics have changed dramatically in the years since the publication of *Children of Abraham*. While Muslims were relatively invisible in the cognitive and demographic maps of the West only a few decades ago, today the landscapes of most cities and towns include mosques and Islamic centers alongside churches and synagogues. Islam has emerged as the third largest religion after Christianity and Judaism—in some places second only to Christianity. Indeed in some areas Islamic centers and mosques now occupy former churches. Muslims live and labor in our cities, towns, villages, and—regrettably—ghettos; they are professionals and laborers, and they are among the unemployed. Thus today, consideration of Islam and the West must be accompanied by an understanding of Islam *in* the West or the Muslims of the West. The major Muslim communities and cities of the world of Islam include not only Cairo, Damascus, Islamabad, Kuala Lumpur, and Khartoum but also London, Bradford, Paris, Marseilles, New York, Detroit, and Los Angeles.

One of the great ironies of the past and present is that despite our apparent development and sophistication, too often we are bound by our cognitive as well as spatial ghettos. As evidenced by the examples of Northern Ireland, India, Palestine-Israel, and elsewhere the fact that faiths coexist in the same country or area does not mean that they come to know and respect one another. Only a few decades ago, neighborhoods in many American cities were identified by the ethnic or religious group that lived there—Italian, Polish, Irish, WASP, or Jewish. Desire to preserve a religious or ethnic identity within the American "melting pot" had important positive aspects but also too often reinforced a cultural or religious isolation. People lived near each other, even worked side by side, but often knew little about the cultural or religious heritage of others. How many Christians or Jews really understood the faith of their fellow citizens? For that matter, how many Methodists understood Catholics, and vice versa?

Like ethnic Christians and Jews as well as other religious minorities, Muslims in recent years have faced issues of faith and identity, the choice of assimilation or integration. At the same time, their experiences have differed as a minority seeking to define itself within and over and against majority secular or Judeo-Christian societies of Europe and America. If some (Muslims and non-Muslims alike) have questioned whether Islam is compatible with the pluralism and values of Western culture, non-Muslims have themselves experienced the testing of the boundaries of their notions of liberalism and pluralism. They have been confronted by concerns ranging from equal acknowledgment of Islam in society and the workplace to specific issues like recognition of Muslim holy days, the right to wear a beard or a headscarf (*hijab*) on the job, and the claims of mainstream Muslims to have their pursuits distinguished from the acts of religious extremists.

Family in the history of religions, as in the ordinary lives of many, is a source of strength, nurturing, love, and security but also of conflict and violence. Biblical and Quranic stories such as those of Cain and Abel, Isaac and Ismail underscore this truth. Despite—some would even argue because of—close family resemblances, relations between Judaism and Christianity, Christianity and Islam, Judaism and Islam have often been characterized by tension, conflicts and persecution. The beliefs of each that it possesses the one true God's revelation and special covenant and, in the cases of Christianity and Islam, that it supersedes earlier revelations, have been stumbling blocks to religious pluralism and tolerance.

Religious pluralism and tolerance came late to Christianity. Christendom had no space for Jews, Muslims, and indeed other Christians who were regarded as schismatics or heretics. Islam did provide a space for Jews and Christians, recognizing them as People of the Book, those who had received God's prophets and revelation. As protected (*dhimmi*) people, they could practice their faith in exchange for payment of a poll tax. Though second class citizenship by modern standards, this ideal (though not always observed) was progressive for its times. The coexistence of faiths can be seen in the early dynamic development of the Islamic world as a civilization that flourished and eclipsed Western Christendom in its Dark Ages. Muslim accomplishments were the product not simply of conquest but of a voracious quest for knowledge and development that relied heavily on other cultures. Under the cosmopolitan Abbasid dynasty (750–1258) seated in Baghdad, relations between Christendom and the Islamic world were marked not only by conflicts of imperial expansion but also by substantial interchange: diplomatic, intellectual, artistic, and commercial. Christian and Muslim businessmen engaged in brisk and prosperous trade. Rulers like Charlemagne and Harun al-Rashid were in diplomatic contact; Muslim rulers employed Christian clergy who knew Latin on missions to Christian rulers. Christians, who served as administrators and bureaucrats, as artisans and craftsmen and as translators, played a major role in the development of Arab/Islamic society, science, and civilization.

Muslims translated the scientific and philosophical knowledge of the ancient world from Greek, Latin, Syriac, and Sanskrit into Arabic. It was the first stage in a process followed by a mastery and development whose contributions would come to be known as Arab or Islamic sciences (algebra, geometry, medicine, optics, astronomy) and philosophy. The fruits of this learning would be appropriated by the West as Europe, looking to the great learning and libraries of the East, reemerged and retrieved its philosophical and scientific roots. Europe's great philosophers, Albertus Magnus, Thomas Aquinas, Bonaventure, and Duns Scotus as well as European scientists and physicians were indebted to Arab and Muslim masters such as Avicenna, Averroes, and many others.

Andalusia (Spain) from 756 c.e. to about 1000 provides the most famous example of interreligious coexistence and tolerance (sometimes described as a *convivencia*, "living together") in history, an experience often idealized as a period of interfaith harmony. Tensions did exist between the Jewish, Christian and Muslim communities. But at the same time Christians and Jews occupied prominent positions in the court of the caliph in the tenth century, serving as translators, engineers, physicians, and architects. Social intercourse and tolerance prevailed at the upper levels of society. This example, though important, needs to be balanced with the knowledge that, overall, actual contacts between the general populations of Christians and Muslims were relatively limited. More important, Muslims showed less tolerance toward Christians after the tenth century.

Understanding and appreciating their shared beliefs and values has become especially critical for the Children of Abraham post-9/11. It is a matter no longer simply of interreligious relations and religious pluralism but of international politics. In the twenty-first century, engagement in interreligious or civilizational dialogue is no longer simply the preserve of religious leaders and scholars of religion but is now pursued by policymakers and corporate leaders, a subject of national and regional foreign policy and the agendas of international organizations like the United Nations, the World Economic Forum, and the Organization of the Islamic Conference.

Central to interreligious and civilizational dialogue is an appreciation of both differences and similarities, recognition not only of what divides us but also of shared beliefs and values that unite us.

Most Christians and Jews have been raised with some appreciation of the interconnectedness of the Old and New Testaments, Jewish and Christian common belief in God, prophets and revelation, moral responsibility and accountability. Few until recently have possessed that broader Abrahamic vision which recognizes the integral place of the descendents of Abraham, Hagar, and Ismail. Most are still surprised to learn that Muslims worship the God of Abraham, recognize God's revelations to Moses and Jesus, believe in the sanctity of life, and reject acts of illegitimate violence and terrorism. Instead, the faith and lives of the moderate mainstream are often overshadowed by the rhetoric of an extremist minority who follow a theology of hate and engage in acts of violence and terror. The words of some Western policymakers and political commentators, media coverage, and regrettably the statements of some religious leaders perpetuate misperceptions and stereotypes and risk promoting a clash of civilizations. These conditions make publication of the second revised edition of Frank Peters's *Children of Abraham* even more important and timely.

John L. Esposito

# *Preface to the New Edition*

Twenty-five years is more than middle age for a book these days, and so I was both delighted and a little apprehensive when Princeton University Press judged this small volume of mine healthy enough for at least a checkup and perhaps another couple of cycles around the track. Reading one's own earlier books is a bit like taking a middle-age physical: you hope for the best but fear the worst. And again like most physicals, the exercise never quite turns out as expected. I did find a lot to change. Some of the footnotes, with references to then current work on the subject, had aged beyond repair and so I took them out. The rest was sound, I discovered, although some of the emphases lay in places other than where I would put them today. In the sections on Jesus, for example, I was more concerned with what scholars thought, which interested me, rather than with what Christians thought, which was what the reader might like to know.

I was given only one caution—I was, after all, a guest in a publishing house, though I confess that after all these years it is beginning to feel like home—that I should not unpack *all* my luggage here. I had already done that twice and had been accommodated by the publication of the two volumes of *The Monotheists: Jews, Christians, and Muslims in Conflict and Competition*, some of whose material reappears in chapter 8 of the present work, and the earlier three volumes of *Judaism, Christianity, and Islam: The Classical Texts and Their Interpretation*. So I was kindly asked to keep this book reasonably short. I have done my best. I have quietly slipped in a new chapter, but otherwise I have rewritten, extensively in places, rather than expanded. I have referred the reader to my longer works when appropriate. This is very much a new book and, as befits a new edition, a better one.

I thanked a number of people in the first edition, and I'm still grateful after all these years: thanks, friends; you helped get me started. This time the matter is far simpler: this new *Children of Abraham* is purely and simply a labor of love.

Pla de Palau
Barcelona

# *Preface*

Judaism, Christianity, and Islam are all children born of the same Father and reared in the bosom of Abraham. They grew to adulthood in the rich spiritual climate of the Middle East, and though they have lived together all their lives, now in their maturity they stand apart and regard their family resemblances and conditioned differences with astonishment, disbelief, or disdain.

Rich parallels of attitude and institution exist among the three religions that acknowledge, in varying degrees, their evolution one out of the other. They have all engaged at times in reciprocal polemic of great ferocity, and sometimes pursued a more ecumenical course, but neither is the intention here. My purpose is merely to underline both the parallels and the differences, and to connect them to common origins and to a common spiritual and intellectual environment.

I have not attempted to write the history of the three religions; others have rendered that service to each. I have selected certain issues and institutions and laid them out in a manner that would invite comparison. The matter is sometimes complex, and so I have tried to be clear in the text and generous in the notes, where the reader is invited to pursue more deeply questions I have only touched on.

Judaism is the eldest of this family of three, and its extraordinary career stretches thousands of years before the Christian and Muslim eras, when these latter two normally reckon that "history" begins. The present inquiry begins at the very outset of the history of monotheism, when his god made a treaty or covenant with a certain Abraham. The story of monotheism is, in fact, the history of that covenant and its claimants. Where to close is somewhat more arbitrary, since after the seventh century of the Christian era we are discussing not one but three religious communities, each at a somewhat different stage of its growth, and each of which is still in existence, and apparently thriving, even today. I have chosen to close at the somewhat imprecise point at which I judged that the three religions had reached their normative expression, that is, when the chief institutions, codes, practices, and spiritual attitudes that in some perceptible manner continue to characterize them today were in place.

Thus this study ends in what we in the West commonly call the Middle Ages, and so ignores both the European responses to these religions and the great movements of reform and revival that have occurred in more modern times. I can offer in mild defense of this closing only my own competence, which extends no farther than I have written. It is perhaps far enough. All the issues of reform and all the wellsprings and mechanisms of revival are present in the place and period under consideration. Faith and reason, Scripture and tradition, understanding and enlightenment are all very old adversaries.

I have tried to write a useful book. The matter and reading grows thick where I thought that common knowledge runs thinnest. My intent in the notes has been to provide guidance rather than proof on specific points. I have attempted to call the reader's attention to accessible basic texts, useful introductions, or illuminating discussions at the point where the issue or topic arises rather than collecting them all at the end. I have also used many transcribed technical terms out of the conviction that the reader of these pages will certainly read further, and I would prefer he or she be introduced to this common vice by me rather than by other, less helpful hands. In any event, I have gathered all in a glossary at the end. Finally, I have reduced all dates to the Common Era (B.C.E/C.E.).

A brief personal note. These reflections are quite literally the product of the Kevorkian Center for Near Eastern Studies at New York University, where the comparative questions and issues raised in the pages that follow were once regularly and routinely discussed by faculty colleagues and students alike, and in the same spirit that they are offered here. It is difficult for me to imagine putting them on paper in any other atmosphere. For that I thank those colleagues, students, and others, past and present, particularly

Baruch Levine and Lawrence Schiffman for their patient *pilpul*; Linda Knezevich, Stuart Miller, Nadine Posner, and Peter Zirnis for their immediate and invaluable help and stimulation; the late and regretted Dan Urman of Beersheba University, my first Hebrew teacher, and Edward Peter Fitzsimmons, who first interested me in Torah and to whom this book is affectionately dedicated; Père Georges Anawati, O.P. of Cairo and now of the Kingdom of God; Rowland Mitchell and Anthony Manero for expanding my education; two, now alas one, Browne, one Green and one yclept Dean; Peter Paul and Mary.

# The Children
# of Abraham

# The Scriptures:
# Some Preliminary Notions

The three great faiths called Judaism, Christianity, and Islam were born of an event that each remembers as a moment in history, when the One True God appeared to an Iron Age sheikh named Abram and bound him in a covenant forever. Abram is the later Abraham, the father of all believers and the linchpin of the faith, and indeed the theology, from which the three communities of that God's worshipers emerged. The history of monotheism had begun.

## One God

The monotheists not only worship one god; he is the same god for all. Whether called Yahweh or Elohim, God the Father or Allah, it is the selfsame deity who created the world out of nothing, who fashioned humankind in his own image, who made the covenant with Abraham and his progeny, and who subsequently intervened in human history to punish his enemies and chastise his friends, and to send instructions, warnings, and encouragement to those who would listen. The divergent names are occasionally troublesome, however, most notably the persistence of the untranslated "Allah" in Western languages, and some Jews and Christians, and even some Muslims, appear to think that they are worshiping different gods.

There are even more profound dislocations. Though historically and ontologically the divinity worshiped by Jews, Christians, and Muslims is one and the same, his portrait, which is more often than not a self-portrait, is quite different in the various books they call Scripture. The biblical Yahweh is not only majestic; he is often homely, at times familiar and even regretful on occasion. His providence for his creation is universal but his interventions in the affairs of humankind are often specific and concrete. The Quran's Allah is equally majestic, equally omnipotent and provident, but he is also supremely transcendent; he walks not among humankind. His ninety-nine quranic attributes—he is the compassionate, the merciful—are pronounced, rehearsed, listed in the Quran, but they are rarely experienced there. The Bible is dramatic, expository, and descriptive; the Quran is hortatory and assertive; and their portraits of God differ accordingly.[1] As for Christians, God the Father, though conceptually identical to his biblical prototype, has receded into the shadow of his celebrated and equally divine Son.

## People of the Book

Jews, Christians, and Muslims are all "People of the Book." God's covenant with Abraham was recorded and collected in a book that contained not only the contract but also, in the book's varying parts, the working out of the covenant in history. They call this record simply "The Book" or "The Writing" (Scripture), or, more descriptively, "The Good News" or "The Recitation." These Scriptures, all purporting to be in some sense the words of the One True God, are by no means identical, nor are they thought to be such by the three communities. That there is a Book, all agree, but whether that Book is the present Bible, or the New Testament, or the Quran is precisely the point that separates Jews, Christians, and Muslims.[2]

In the Jewish—and Muslim—view, God gave and Moses wrote down a distinct and discrete multipart book, the Law or Torah. But although the Torah holds pride of place in Jewish revelational history, God's direct interventions were in one manner or another continuous between Moses and Ezra, and thus the Jewish Bible is a collective work that includes, under the three headings of Law,

Prophets, and the miscellany called Writings, all of God's revelation to his people.

This was certainly the Jewish view in Jesus' day, and there is no reason to think that Jesus regarded Scripture any differently. He in turn produced no new Writings or Book of his own, and so Christian "Scripture" is formally quite different from what the Jews thought of as such. The Gospels are accounts of Jesus' words and deeds set down, in approximately a biographical framework, by his followers. In the eyes of Christians, Jesus did not bring a Scripture; he was himself, in his person and message, a revelation, the "Good News." His life and sacrificial death sealed a "New Covenant" that God had promised—it is foreshadowed in the Old Testament—and so the Gospels and the accounts of the deeds and thoughts of the early Christian community recorded in the Acts of the Apostles and the letters of various Jesus followers came to be regarded by Christians as a New Covenant or Testament to be set down next to the Old, that recorded and commemorated in the Jewish Bible.

Muhammad may have had only an imperfect understanding of this somewhat complex process. Though he commonly refers to the Jewish revelation as *Tawrat*, the Prophet of Islam was certainly aware that there were other Jewish prophets, and so possibly revelations, after Moses. But he never mentions a New Testament; his sole references are to "the Gospel," in Arabic *Injil*, and he seems to have thought of it as a sacred book that Jesus had brought or written, much as Moses had the Torah.

Muhammad had a strong sense of the prophetic calling and of the line of prophets who had created the Judeo-Christian tradition, and after some brief initial hesitation, he placed himself firmly within that line. He too was a prophet, and now in these latter times, when God's earlier revelations had become distorted at the willful and perverse hands of the Jews and Christians, Allah had given to him, no less than to Moses and Jesus, a revealed Book. Or so it was in its final, codified version. What God himself had instructed Muhammad to call The Recitation, in Arabic *al-Quran*, was in fact a series of messages delivered to Muhammad by the angel Gabriel over a period of twenty-two years. Each part was already identified as Scripture during the Prophet's lifetime, and the Book was finally closed only with Muhammad's death.

## Three Sacred Books

Thus there came into being three sacred books, each in some sense the Word of God; each regarded as a complete, final, and authoritative statement regulating the role and conduct of humankind vis-à-vis its Creator; and each a birthright and charter for a community that had not existed before. And each community lived in the conviction that God had spoken to it for the last time: the Jews, for the first and final time; the Christians, for the second and final time; the Muslims, for the third and final time.

As already remarked, the Bible, New Testament, and Quran, though looked on as emanating from the same source, are very different works. The Bible is a composite and varied blend of religious myth, historical narrative, legal enactments, prophetic admonitions, cautionary tales, and poetry composed over a long period.[3] The time span of the New Testament is considerably shorter, a half-century perhaps, but it too has a very mixed content of quasi biography, community history, letters, and an apocalyptic Book of Revelation. The Quran, as already noted, is absolutely contemporary to its revelation, twenty-two years in the lifetime of the Prophet.

There is nothing but God's own Word in the Quran, as Muhammad himself could assure the community of believers. In Jewish and Christian circles, however, there were assuredly circulating other writings that had some claim to being God's Word but are not found in the Bible or the New Testament.[4] Both these Scriptures represent, then, a deliberate decision by someone to designate certain works as authentic Scripture and to exclude others from the canon.[5] That decision was essentially theological, and the exclusion of the noncanonical writings, generally called Apocrypha, from the Jewish or Christian Scriptures does not render them any less interesting or important from a historical point of view. The Books of Maccabees never made it into the Jewish canon, for example, nor the Gnostic gospels into the Christian, but each tells us something of the events and attitudes of the time that produced them.

## On Translation

It is notable that where once sectarian differences among Jews, Catholics, and Protestants created marked discrepancies in their respective translations of Scripture, the differences have presently narrowed to so few words or passages that it is possible for Jewish and Christian scholars to collaborate in such translation projects.[6] There is no need and no urgency toward collaborative translations of the Quran, however. On a few occasions in the past Shiite Muslims have accused Sunni Muslims of tampering with the text of the Quran, but the theme is muted in Islam and the overwhelming majority of Muslims are convinced that the present text of the Book is the uniquely authentic one.[7]

Muslims, like many Jews, have a strong sense of Scripture as the *ipsissima verba* of God, enhanced, in the Muslim instance, by the absence of any intervening notion of author: Moses may have been the author of the Pentateuch, but Muhammad merely repeated the Quran verbatim. The Quran itself underlines this claim. Do you doubt the divine origins of this Book, it asks. Then you try to produce another like it (Quran 10:38, etc.). The doubters did not, of course, and, in the later Muslim view, could not. Islam has few dogmas, but one, surely, is the intrinsic inimitability of the Quran, a conviction that makes all translations of the Book problematic.

The Quran has been translated, but those efforts have been relatively slow in coming—the earliest known translation was into Latin in twelfth-century Spain for Christian missionary purposes—and often by non-Muslims. But Islam no less than Christianity is a missionary faith, and belief in the Quran as the Word of God spreads far more quickly, and eventually more widely, than knowledge of its Arabic. There finally did appear, reluctantly and tentatively—sometimes transparently disguised as paraphrases—Muslim translations of God's words for the benefit of Persian and Turkish speakers, and then for the growing number of converts in western Europe and the Americas.[8]

The Bible, Old and New Testament, has long been available in English, and early on in a version that shaped the English language itself, the so-called King James version of 1611. But it is more than familiarity that makes both Bible and Gospels better served by their translations than is the Arabic Quran. God's message to Muhammad was delivered in the highly charged, affective images of the sacred poet. It is allusive rather than explicit, a great body of warning, command, injunction, and instruction delivered against a background as barren to our eyes as the steppe itself. We feel Sinai and Canaan in the Bible; Palestine, its houses, mountains, rivers and lakes, its towns and cities and the people who inhabited

them are all present in the Gospel narrative. In the Quran, however, we search without success for Mecca, for the profane but
vividly commercial life of the Quraysh, for Muhammad's family
and companions. In its pages there is only a voice, the voice of
God alone. When it was heard, it overwhelmed hearts, as it still
does in its written form, but it leaves the historian attending
vainly, and deafly, for context.

# CHAPTER ONE

# The Promise and the Heirs

The Bible begins absolutely, "In the beginning . . . ," with the creation of the world. The Quran speaks of it as well—not by following in the biblical tracks, but allusively, touching the creation story here and there as suits its own highly moralizing purposes. The Bible's opening book, Genesis, introduces the first of our kind, Adam and Eve, and their fall from the Creator's grace; we read the same, again with somewhat different nuances, in the Quran. We learn of Noah and the catastrophic flood that nearly destroys humankind. It is not until the eleventh chapter of Genesis that Abraham rather abruptly enters the narrative and the history proper of monotheism begins. Abram, as he is still being called at this point, is the head of a small tribe, an extended family really, just one of many leading a marginal living along the fringes between the Middle Eastern desert and the sown. He had originated in what is today Iraq—"Ur of the Chaldees"—and wandered across the Fertile Crescent before coming to rest in the south of what would later come to be called Palestine. During his trek and on several occasions before his death and burial in Hebron, the god worshiped by Abraham appeared to him and promised the patriarch and his descendants plentiful offspring and a land of their own, the very land in which they were now living.[1]

It is from this simple but astonishing act, a deity making contact with a paltry sheepherder on the margins of the Fertile Crescent, that the entire history of monotheism flows. That same deity has been worshiped by millions beyond the counting as the

One True God, and his devotees have dominated, as Jews, Christians, and Muslims, the most profound sensibilities of humankind for the length of recorded history. What was happening in these scenes recorded so simply and almost matter-of-factly in Genesis? It is not so much a command as an offered contract, whose simple terms were the exclusive worship of this god and the signal circumcision of all the males of the community—which was, in fact, Abraham's extended family.[2] Abraham, it appears, was already a monotheist. He had earlier rejected the heavenly deities worshiped by his father and ancestors in Iraq, as the Quran's account (6:74–83) makes clear.[3] What his god was requesting here was a pledge of continued fidelity, for which he and his descendants would be rewarded.

There is an extended and familiar dialogue between Abraham and his god through the subsequent chapters of Genesis. The issue, it appears, is the inheritance. Abraham and his wife Sarah had no children and they, or at least Sarah, was far beyond the age for bearing them. It was Sarah at any rate who suggested to Abraham that he might father a child with his Egyptian slave-concubine Hagar. The attempt was successful—there is no hint of a miraculous intervention—and Hagar bore him a son. Abraham named him Ishmael and in obedience to the Lord's command, he circumcised him on the eighth day after his birth. Almost immediately Sarah regretted her suggestion and demanded that Abraham turn mother and child out of the camp, a sentence of almost certain death.

Neither the child Ishmael nor his mother perished, however. God intervened to save them and further promised that Ishmael, though no longer the heir to the promise, would himself be the father of a great nation. Mother and son wandered off into the Negev, out onto the fringes of the biblical account—but not out of history. A later generation of Jews, and then the Christians after them, thought that the Arabs were the descendants of Ishmael— they noted the similarities of Arab culture and practice to that of the Hebrews—and "Arab," "Ishmaelite," as well as "Saracen," with a fanciful etymology  that connected it with Sarah, were interchangeable terms for long stretches of Middle Eastern and European history.[4]

This was not so in Arabia, however. Without any explanation, the Quran (2:125) identifies Ishmael along with his father, Abraham, as builders of the Kaaba, the stone building in the midst of Mecca that Muhammad's ancestors and the Prophet himself identified as *Bayt Allah*, the "House of the God." It was left for the next generation of Muslims to explain how Abraham and his firstborn could have gotten from Palestine to Mecca, but there is no sign whatsoever that Muhammad himself thought that Ishmael was the father of the Arabs, much less that either he or his followers were blood descendants of Abraham.[5]

To return to the Bible, Abraham had a second son, Isaac, this time miraculously by Sarah, and it was through him that the pledge of a Chosen People and a Promised Land would descend to succeeding generations. The Covenant has to do with worship, but with Isaac, a new motif appears: obedience or "trust." ("Belief" in the One God is a more modern and less accurate view of what was unfolding in Genesis.) His Lord called on Abraham to sacrifice his sole heir, the young Isaac. It was a terrible act, a perverse command in the light of the just concluded Covenant, but Abraham undertook to fulfill it without question or demur. Only at the last moment did his god stay the patriarch's hand: Isaac was unbound and a fortuitous ram substituted as the sacrifice. God was pleased, the modern reader is perhaps appalled, but countless generations of Jews, Christians, and Muslims—the Quran (37:102–113) does not make it clear which son was being sacrificed, Isaac or Ishmael— have regarded the "binding of Isaac" as a supreme example of human obedience to God.[6]

The account in Genesis proceeds, first with its focus on Abraham, then on his son Isaac and his grandson Jacob, whose name is changed to Israel. *Benei Israel*, in English "Children of Israel" or Israelites, his offspring called themselves: they descend in tribal units from Jacob's twelve sons. They were lured into Egypt, enslaved there for a number of generations, and finally led forth to freedom by the oddly Egyptian-named prophet Moses.[7] According to the Bible's second book, aptly called Exodus, it was Moses who led the twelve tribes of Israel to safety in Sinai; who received from God on a mountain there the highly detailed terms of the Covenant in the form of a law, in Hebrew, *Torah*; and who guided them, with God's frequent miraculous intervention, across the wilderness to the very borders of the promised *Eretz Israel*, a Land for Israel. It was left to his successor Joshua to lead them into their inheritance.

So end the five biblical books credited to Moses' authorship and called simply Torah or the "Five Pieces" (Pentateuch), as well as the following book, ascribed to Joshua, which describes the conquest of the land of Canaan. In the books called Samuel and Kings the Bible moves forward in the manner of a history chronicle, which in fact it now is, with an eye chiefly on the rulers of Israel who, beginning with Saul, are recognized as kings. The reign of Saul, and especially of his successors David and Solomon, were periods of expansion, growth, and even modest opulence for the new kingdom of Israel.[8] Jerusalem was taken from the local Jebusites and David made it the capital of the realm. He brought into the town the chief totem of the Israelites' religion, the Ark of the Covenant, a gold-fitted portable cask-shrine decorated with semimythical cherubim on its lid and containing mementos of the Sinai experience and the tablets of the law given to Moses by God on Mount Sinai. Jerusalem thus became both the political and the religious center of the Israelites.[9] Solomon consecrated this event by constructing atop the eastern hill of the town a splendid temple to "house" the Israelite deity who had no image or icon—a remarkable fact in human religious history—but whose "presence" or "glory," as it was sometimes called, had an unmistakable spiritual and at times even sensual reality for the Israelites.[10]

The Bible presents no sunshine history of Israel.[11] After Solomon, the kingdom began to disintegrate into a northern and a southern realm—Israel and Judah as they were known—and their kings led and the people followed into rank idolatry. The Covenant lay in tatters and God's justice was visited on his Chosen People in the impotence of their leaders in the face of their more powerful neighbors, Egypt, Assyria, and Babylon. Above the smoke of idolatrous sacrifice and the din of war could be heard the voice of Yahweh delivered through his prophets, Isaiah, Jeremiah, and Ezekiel, now threatening, now warning, now hopeful with the promise of a new age and perhaps even a new Covenant.[12]

Christians and Muslims have little interest in the post-Pentateuchal books of the Bible as such. The prophets reappear in the New Testament and the Quran, though shorn of their poetic grandeur, in the first as proof texts for a promised Messiah and in the second as exemplary figures to illustrate the price of disregarding God's warnings. There is, moreover, a notable difference between the Christian and the Muslim reception of these books.

The Bible was a profound element in the culture of Jesus' earliest followers, who were, of course, all Jews, whereas for Muhammad's audience, for whom its contours and contexts remain unexplained, the Bible is simply an earlier Book whose figures are occasionally, and sometimes opaquely, adduced by the Quran.[13]

In the late seventh century B.C.E., the northern regions of Solomon's royal enterprise, now the kingdom of Israel, were overrun and its inhabitants dispersed by the Assyrians; the fate of Israel's ten tribes that dwelled there remains unknown. In the early sixth century the remaining Israelite polity, the southern kingdom of Judah, fell into ruin. The Babylonians from across the Fertile Crescent took and sacked Jerusalem, plundered Solomon's temple—the Ark of the Covenant was among the disappeared spoils of war—and carried off the best and brightest Judeans into exile in distant Babylonia.

## A New Beginning

The dispersal of Israel's political and religious elite might well have signaled the end of what would have been nothing more than a curious experiment in monotheism, a somewhat longer Palestinian version of Akhnaton's ill-fated Atun adventure in Egypt. But it was not so. The Israelites kept intact their national and religious identity—perhaps they were identical at that point—during those two or three generations in Babylonia. And when a regime change occurred in Mesopotamia and the more relaxed Achaemenian Iranians gave their Judean subjects leave to depart, there were enough Israelites with conviction and energy to return to Palestine and attempt to rebuild on that sacred soil not the kingdom of Israel, which would have been impossible under the circumstances, but the people of Israel.

This was no easy endeavor. Resources were exiguous and others had occupied parts of the land. Judea after the Exile was a different place from what it had been before, as was the world around it. The older parochial empires had disappeared and new ecumenical political forms prevailed, accompanied by new social and economic institutions and a quickening of the intellectual life in the Middle East. Judaism too was different, as we can see now with the historian's hindsight. It both clashed and blended with the new world about it, and though it had done this from the beginning, the effects were now deeper, more volatile, and far more visible.[14]

Among the new neighbors of the Israelites—or rather, as they were now called, the "Judeans," a term that comes to rest, via Greek and Latin, in English as "Jews"—were the Hellenes or Greeks. These people had come to the Middle East with Alexander the Great in the 330s B.C.E. and stayed to found kingdoms, build cities, and spread their enormously attractive way of life among the indigenous peoples of the East.[15] Pre-Exilic Judaism had been, perhaps, farther up the ladder of religious evolution than the faith of the Philistines, Canaanites, and Phoenicians, and so could resist or assimilate those competitors with relative ease. But the Hellenes were not Canaanites and Caesar Augustus was not Hiram of Tyre or even Ashurbanipal. The new rivals of Judaism were at once more attractive and threatening, and possessed intellectual and spiritual resources little understood in a parochial Judea. Judaism did not simply react. It first refracted the incandescent energies of the new age and then slowly brought them into focus in a form that has survived with vigor into our own day.

In the course of that difficult process of self-transformation, Judaism proved remarkably fertile in new perspectives, some of which were finally rejected but proved nonetheless to have a vitality of their own. Christianity immediately and Islam somewhat more obliquely appear in certain lights like Jewish reform movements. At the very least they are growths from the same stock— post-Exilic Judaism—in a generative process that has no parallel in the varieties of human religious experience. We begin by laying out the chief stages of that process and how they are understood by modern historians.

## After the Exile

When the Persian shah Cyrus permitted the Jews exiled in Babylonia to return to Palestine in 534 B.C.E. and to restore both the temple cult and some small element of a national identity, a new chapter in the history of Judaism began. There were two obscure centuries of restoration and growth under Persian sovereignty, followed in quick succession by a cultural, religious, and political confrontation with the Hellenes, a war of national liberation, the restoration of a long-defunct Jewish monarchy, and finally the annexation of Palestine to the powerful Roman Empire, under whose sovereignty it remained for six centuries.[16] Many of the themes of this complex period in the history of Judaism appear under various comparative headings in the pages below, and so only general considerations are offered here. From the outset, one should speak more properly of the varieties of post-Exilic Judaism than of a single phenomenon. There were, almost from the beginning of this period, both a Palestinian and a Diaspora Judaism, and if our view of the latter is dominated and partially distorted by the immense preserved literary output of one man—Philo of Alexandria—we can make far more precise and radical distinctions in the Palestinian version.

The biblical books of Ezra and Nehemiah provide a portrait of a Judaism already facing both temple and Torah. Ezra himself, who was the chief architect of the post-Exilic restoration, was the perfect type of his age: he was both a priest (*kohen*) and a scribe (*sofer*). This latter was already a new office and function, a man learned in the Scriptures, a teacher certainly, and possibly a judge on matters of the law.

Though the older priestly and the new clerical Judaism were united in the person and philosophy of Ezra, that cohesion was not permanent. With the inroads of Hellenism and the affluence it brought to the urban centers of the Middle East, we can observe the natural evolution of the upper levels of the Jewish priesthood into a class of power and privilege that was drawn into the cultural and political orbit of the new Greek rulers of Palestine, whether they governed from Alexandria in Egypt as Ptolemies or, after 200 B.C.E., from Antioch in Syria as the Seleucids.

At first the Hellenic Seleucids of Syria granted extensive privileges—exemptions, actually—to their rather odd monotheistic subjects in Judea. Many upper-class Jews gradually assimilated to the new Hellenic ways. But they did so neither as rapidly nor as totally as their rulers in Antioch might have wished. And in a world where religion was normally a useful subaltern of politics, religious exceptionalism translated rather easily into political insubordination or, to put the precise point upon it, treason.

The Seleucids thought they scented treason in Judea and came down hard on the Jews and their "Mosaic constitution." To resist was perhaps absurd, but resistance there was. A new leadership arose out of the lower priestly ranks and from among those Judeans the class distinctions of Hellenism had disinherited in their native land. The Maccabees extended social and economic distress into the incendiary area of religion: they equated Hellenism with godlessness, and so brought into their camp all those pious groups (*hasidim*) and clerics of the law who were genuinely outraged by the new, alien, and irreligious style of the Jewish upper classes.

## *Jewish Parties and Sects*

The Jewish revolt against the Greek Seleucids of Syria in 167 B.C.E was a stunning political success—it reconstituted an independent Jewish state in Judea—but its sequel brought to the surface new factional strains in the community.[17] The Maccabees' coalition disintegrated over the twin issues of their own progressive Hellenization and their legitimacy as high priests in the restored kingdom. The earlier Hasidim reappeared as Pharisees, a group that was both a party and a sect in that they had a distinct religious position and were at the same time deeply engaged in political activity under the Hasmoneans (as the Maccabees were called in their new dynastic role).[18] Or so we suppose. We are not on very firm ground here, since we must rely for our information on the self-serving narrative of the Books of Maccabees and on the historical works of the Pharisee Josephus, who was writing with a special purpose of his own for a Roman audience. Josephus's *Jewish War* and *Jewish Antiquities* remain, however, our best entry into Palestinian Judaism.[19]

The authors of the Books of Maccabees were appealing to the sympathy and support of Jews outside Palestine as surely as Josephus was attempting to explain the somewhat arcane practices and convictions of his coreligionists to a baffled audience of Gentiles, and so neither was much concerned with either historical or theological accuracy when it came to the Pharisees. The Gospels likewise present a number of vignettes, generally unflattering, of Pharisees engaged in controversy with Jesus. The overall result is, not surprisingly, a confused and often contradictory portrait of the group. Making sense out of this mélange has exercised both Jewish and Christian scholars, with sometimes astonishing results.

The Pharisees have been regarded as everything from hidebound and frigid legalists to Jewish revivalists and social reformers on a Weberian model.

Research on the Pharisees does not encourage one to think that a consensus is about to emerge on the subject, since the critical link that connects the Pharisees of Josephus and the New Testament with the early rabbis cited in the Mishna has yet to be established.[20] But if we leave aside their political role in the history of the times, we can conclude with some assurance that the Pharisees were probably the spiritual descendants of the earlier Hasidim and that they were characterized as a group by (1) their detailed study of the Torah; (2) their acceptance of an oral legal tradition that enabled them to extend Torah precepts into new areas of behavior; and (3) their own strict observance of the laws of ritual purity, especially in matters of food. Their observance set the Pharisees off from most of the other contemporary Jews and led to a moral exemplarism and social cohesiveness typified by their meal fellowship (*habura*).

Linked by both Josephus and the Gospels to the Pharisees is another, somewhat dimmer group, the Sadducees.[21] Their name may have come from Zadok, a high priest at the time of David—the priestly hierarchy at Qumran was also known as "the Sons of Zadok"—and it seems plausible to identify the Sadducees as supporters of, if not identical with, the priesthood that presided over the Jewish temple liturgies in Jerusalem. They were almost certainly defenders of the legitimacy of the Hasmonean high priesthood, but Josephus was far more concerned to show their legal and theological positions vis-à-vis the Pharisees. The Sadducees were, on his testimony, literal interpreters of the law who rejected all Pharisaic appeals to the "tradition of the Fathers," and so could be at the same time stricter in their exegesis of scriptural prescriptions and more permissive where the Torah had not explicitly spoken. They were unwilling, for example, to accept, as the Pharisees did, the notion of an afterlife, since it had little or no scriptural attestation.

This portrait of the Sadducees is not a very full likeness, since none of their own writings is preserved, and after the destruction of the temple in 70 c.e. they had no spiritual progeny in Judaism, save possibly the Karaites, a sect that arose in the eighth century under Islam, and that shared the Sadducees' repudiation of an oral tradition. The same judgment of ignorance once prevailed with respect to a third group linked by Josephus (but strangely absent from the Gospels) to the Pharisees and Sadducees, the Essenes. They are portrayed, in Josephus's usual shorthand fashion, as an ascetic congregation who had separated themselves from the main body of the Jews. They lived in communities, were celibate, and possessed goods in common. Now, however, the Essenes of Josephus, Philo, and others have been identified, with only some hesitation, with a group about which we know a great deal, the sectaries at Qumran.

Since 1947, when their community center and writings were discovered at the northwest corner of the Dead Sea, the community at Qumran is better known by direct and contemporary evidence than any other Jewish religious group of its day. Their own writings have been published and translated, and their habitat and way of life studied by many scholars.[22] They were in fact much as Josephus described them, a highly organized community (*yahad*) who lived a life of strict asceticism, some of them celibates, apart from the rest of the Jews and read a more "catholic" Bible than the later canonized version of the Hebrew Scriptures. But what is now clear is the context of this life. The Essenes were a community of priestly dissenters who rejected the authority of the Hasmonean high priesthood in Jerusalem, and so did not participate directly in the temple liturgy. Instead, they awaited their vindication through a messianic return and a climactic and victorious war against the forces of evil. In the meantime, the community lived in a state of severe ritual purity and spiritual readiness for the eschatological battle that lay ahead. They were a purified people of a New Covenant who were elected for survival in wicked days.

## Apocalyptic and Messianic Judaism

The Dead Sea scrolls show a community living out two themes long familiar from the broad "Bible" of the post-Exilic period: those of apocalypse and messianic expectations. The sectarians' own writings are gloomy documents that decry the wickedness of the present time, whether that time is to be associated with the Hasmoneans or the Romans. It was probably a similar religious despair in the present that provoked other Jewish authors from

Seleucid times onward to console their brethren with the promise that this was merely the prelude to a great eschatological catastrophe out of whose ashes would emerge an Israel Triumphant.

The most common form of these meditations was the "unveiling" (*apokalypsis*), a vision of the horrors and glories of the End Time.[23] Their powerful message, though obscured in detail by the authors' preference for allegorical, parabolic, and symbolic expression, was nevertheless clear. A new age was close at hand. Its advent would be signaled by political and natural upheavals, but at the term of these cataclysmic events the judgment of history would yield to the judgment of God. The righteous would be glorified; the evil destroyed.

In the apocalyptic visions of Qumran, as well as those of the anonymous authors of Daniel, Enoch, and other documents of post-Exilic Jewish piety, a central figure of the End Time is that of the Messiah. This "anointed one" (*mashiah*)—*Christos* is simply the Greek translation of the word—is most often a priest-king of Davidic descent who will be God's instrument of restoration. On this there was general agreement, but a closer inspection of the texts shows a wide discrepancy of detail.[24] The Apocrypha on one hand, some of them pre-Christian and others possibly the subject of Christian rewriting, and the rabbinic sources on the other, all of them post-Christian and some of them certainly reacting to Christian claims, provide very different versions of the Messiah.[25] Again, at Qumran there was another, distinctly Essene anticipation of a Messiah.[26]

Some of these differences are doctrinally generated, but even if we confine our attention to unmistakably pre-Christian material, Jewish concepts surrounding the person and mission of the Messiah show considerable variations. The visions and parables of the apocalypse were obviously susceptible to widely differing interpretations. Most of the messianic passages may suggest, for example, a spiritualizing exegesis, but only if we divorce them, as they frequently divorced themselves, from the historical context of debates about Hasmonean legitimacy, Herodian oppression, and Rome's dashing all hopes for the restoration of an independent Jewish polity. Josephus's frequent references to brigands and insurrectionists who appealed to messianic expectations, and particularly the career of Bar Kokhba, whose politico-messianic claims were endorsed by as eminent a Pharisee as Rabbi Akiba,

are a sufficient clue that the Kingdom of God of messianic speculation was understood by many as an achievable political goal
here on earth.[27]

## Hellenistic Judaism

Since the sixth century B.C.E., Jews had been living in dispersion
(diaspora) outside Palestine and had encountered in the great
urban centers of the Mediterranean world the potent force of
Hellenism, that complex sum of attitudes, ideology, and style that
comprised the Greek and Roman way of regarding the universe,
society, humans, and God, and whose cultural conquest of the
Middle East had quite revolutionary consequences for Judaism,
Christianity, and Islam.[28] On the popular level the Greeks and
Romans were polytheists, worshipers of the multiple gods of the
Mediterranean basin and little different in practice and belief from
the other peoples of the Middle East. But beyond the practice lay,
in the possession of the intelligentsia, a theology, a speculative but
rational theory about the nature of god, a single transcendent
God, who created and ruled an orderly universe (*kosmos*). Theology was, moreover, a theory capable of explanation, defense,
emendation, and expansion. The natural theology of the Hellenes
and their Roman students and successors was a profound and
novel challenge to whichever Jews chose to pay heed, as it would
be later to Christians and Muslims. It acknowledged ignorance,
which was curable, but not mystery, which was not. It explained,
where revelation described; it argued, where revelation merely asserted. And its manner of proceeding, inductively up the chain of
creation or deductively from the first, self-evident principles of
reason, rendered the revelations of the monotheists not merely
otiose but, in some profound sense, an affront to the powers of
human reason.

Like many of his fellow Jews dispersed around the Mediterranean, Philo of Alexandria heeded the new science of theology.[29]
An unusual number of his works in Greek have been preserved—
chiefly because the Christians found them useful for their own
closure with Hellenism—and in them he unfolded his ambitious
and enormously influential project: to take his Hellenized Jewish

readers through the writings of Moses, showing them as he went that there was no incompatibility between Hellenic-style theology and what the Jews regarded as the Word of God. Moses too was a philosopher, Philo explained, whose intuitive grasp of truth was the equal of Plato's and who was in fact the superior thinker in that he was capable of converting abstract truth into concrete law, speculation into practice, understanding into observance. And, Philo added, as the crown upon the argument, Moses came before Plato, so if there was any borrowing going on, it was likely the Greek who had done it.

There was of course opposition to making Moses into a Platonic philosopher and to converting the primeval landscape of Genesis into an orderly Stoic cosmos. But it was shouted rather than argued: any real discussion of the issue would immediately concede the point since it had necessarily to be conducted in rational, and so Hellenic, terms. Rather, the resistance was political, and if Jewish resistance to political Hellenism, whether of the Seleucid or the Roman variety, was successful on occasion, it was in the long term doomed to failure: the descendants of the heroic Maccabees had invariably to be the desperados who threw themselves off the parapets of Masada. And the resistance was social, particularly in Jerusalem, where the mores of the Hellenically assimilated, their taste for theater and athletics and nudity, aroused the ire of the piety-minded. Pharisees and Sadducees waged a relentless war over the existence and authority of an oral tradition in the law, but they fought equally relentlessly about food, clothing, and membership in the city's Greek gymnasium.

A more ideological counter to Hellenism showed itself in the apocalyptic-eschatological stance adopted by many of the opposition pietists. Apocalypse and Torah, the latter now supplemented in some circles by the "tradition of the Fathers," were the two chief weapons invoked by those Palestinian Jews who regarded Hellenism as a fundamental attack on Covenant Judaism. The debate is described in lively terms in the pages of Josephus, whose own cultural Hellenization and religious Pharisaism show how complex the issue was in fact. The Gospels, for their part, present Jesus in a cultural and religious landscape that appears at first glance remarkably free of Hellenic notions and coloring. And yet many of Jesus' miraculous cures betray not only the acceptance of a

Hellenic system of magical belief but many of the techniques associated with that system. As we shall see, the very first conflict to trouble the nascent Christian community was between Hellenist and Torah Jews, both of whom had accepted the messiahship of Jesus but whose differing understanding of their own Jewishness was not transcended by that acceptance.

# CHAPTER TWO

# A Contested Inheritance

The Covenant was made with Abraham and its rewards were promised to his heirs. Who are the heirs? For many centuries and down to the present three separate communities—Jews, Christians, and Muslims—claim that they, and they alone, are the true inheritors of the promise, the authentic monotheists, the truly saved, redeemed, validated, justified. The promise of a land, fulfilled under Joshua, disappointed by the Romans, long expected across the centuries, and once more, perhaps, fulfilled for the Jews, has not taken a similar hold on Christians and Muslims, who between them have held sway over much of the planet.[1] It is rather the promise of a Chosen People, now parsed broadly to mean eternal vindication and salvation, that is contested among those who claim to be the Children of Abraham. Jews claim the Covenant as their own by reason of both their linear descent from Abraham via his son Isaac and his grandson Jacob, the latter also known as Israel, and their fidelity to its terms. Christians, for their part, contend that, as God had forewarned, the promise had been redrawn as a New Covenant and they were its heirs through their faith in God's son, Jesus, the Messiah. Muslims, finally, claim the inheritance not so much by supercession, as the Christians do, as by a return to the pristine form of monotheism, the original "religion of Abraham."

But before the Christians and Muslims began to assert their claims, there were serious disputes among the Jews themselves, indeed, among Abraham's own sons, and Isaac's, as to the inheritance, and the just-noted sectarian Judaism of post-Exilic times was at base the product of this same dispute. Some of those groups had purely political aims, but most were true sects, with a unique claim to be the faithful remnant, the True Israel.

## *Jesus*

Where does Jesus of Nazareth belong in this confusion of Jewish sects and parties, spiritual and political ideals and programs? First, it should be remarked that it has only relatively recently become apparent that Jesus belonged anywhere in this Jewish complex.[2] Portraits of Jesus were for centuries dominated by doctrinal considerations, and even when the "quest of the historical Jesus," as Albert Schweitzer's famous book described it in 1906, had begun in earnest, the overwhelming importance of Jesus' Jewish milieu was not often understood or acknowledged.[3] Parallels and antecedents were vigorously sought elsewhere, particularly in the surrounding and better-known (as well as more attractive) Hellenic tradition.[4]

Schweitzer's quest continues, and with increased energy, though with quite different emphases. His project of refocusing attention on a Jewish Jesus engaged by an urgent eschatology has been strikingly underscored by the discovery of the Dead Sea scrolls. These documents, which are absolutely contemporary with the birth of Christianity, have been closely examined for insights on John the Baptist, Jesus, and their followers.[5] The results have been suggestive rather than conclusive, but they point to one unmistakable fact, namely, that Jesus and his movement can be located within the spectrum of Jewish reform movements that swept Roman Palestine in the first century, this one, like others, with a strong eschatological and messianic character.

If we turn from the historians' uncertainties to the believers' convictions, we can affirm that the Christians' hope of salvation is based, as Paul often put it, on "faith in Christ Jesus," and, more precisely, on the belief that the same Jesus of Nazareth was raised by God from the dead since, again the phrase is Paul's, "without the resurrection our faith is nothing." The Christian debate over the nature, source, and effects of that saving grace elicited by faith in Jesus has been long and often acrimonious—so acrimonious indeed that it created a major schism in Western Christianity, the one that separated Catholics and Protestants in the sixteenth century and keeps them apart to this day. But all agree that, however they were understood, the foundations of the Christian faith are to be found in a body of documents called the New Testament.

The New Testament is the Christians' Scripture, and whatever Paul's understanding of Jesus—which the early Church obviously approved by including his letters in the collection—the New Testament opens with four Gospels or the "good news" (Gk. *euangelion*) of Jesus the Messiah. These are documents attributed to two of Jesus' inner circle, Matthew and John, and two second-generation Christians, Mark, a disciple of Peter, and Luke, a companion of Paul. Each Gospel purports to be a narrative of events that actually occurred, in short, history in the form of biography.[6] Hence, the life of Jesus, the "historical Jesus" as he would be more self-consciously referred to in modern times, was of crucial importance to the Christians from the beginning, an importance manifested in multiple different categories. Jesus' reported miracles, for example—his cures, his exorcisms, his restoring the dead to life—were all thought to be proof of his messianic claims, or of his authority, or even of his relationship with the deity—and since he was Jewish, that would of course be Yahweh—whom he often called his "father."

Jesus' teaching, which he often delivered in the form of parables, a curveball (*parabole*) of a story of everyday life with a provocatively unexpected ending, became the basis of Christian ethics and his life generally a paradigm of Christian virtue.[7] His enactments, like baptism and the Eucharist, became the basic institutions of the new Christian society, while his call and dispatch of his chosen followers, the "Apostles," was the foundation for a hierarchical authority for that society. Jesus' death was regarded as the sacrificial act that redeemed or ransomed humankind—the imagery is Paul's—from the sin of Adam and enabled it for salvation. Finally, his resurrection from the dead provided unmistakable proof of Jesus' divine nature and foretold the believers' own triumph over death.

The Gospel accounts of Jesus fall into three large narrative divisions.[8] The first, present only in Matthew and Luke, tells of Jesus' miraculous conception and virginal birth from Mary, the betrothed of a certain Joseph. It was said to have taken place in Bethlehem, the city of David, though the family was from Nazareth in Galilee and Jesus spent most of his life there. The likely date was 4 B.C.E.[9] The second section begins with Jesus' baptism in the Jordan at the hands of the ascetic doomsday preacher John the Baptist.[10] Jesus soon set out on his own, however, with his personally selected followers, "the Twelve," later called Apostles, "those sent forth." His ministry, almost exclusively conducted in the Galilean countryside, consisted mainly in the eschatological warning, much like John's own, to "repent, for the Kingdom (of God) is at hand" and in preaching an ethic of social justice and compassion. There were frequent clashes with the Pharisees over matters of the law. This phase lasted one or two years. Finally, and here the Gospels grow more detailed and specific, there is the narrative of Jesus' last days, which unfolded not in Galilee but in Jerusalem, and reached their climax on Passover, probably in 29 or 30 C.E., when he was executed by crucifixion on the orders of the Roman prefect of Judea, Pontius Pilate, but at the instigation of a Jewish high-priestly cabal, as the Gospels have it. His body was removed from the cross before the sunset that would begin the Sabbath—Passover fell on a Friday that year—and hurriedly buried in a newly hewn rock tomb nearby.[11]

The Gospel authors were now faced with an enormous paradox. The man whom his disciples thought might be the Messiah of Israel had died an ignominious public death. His followers were in despair. And yet, within thirty-odd years, perhaps sooner, that despair had given way to a kind of exaltation: it was *because* the Messiah had died on the cross that all humankind was saved. Jesus was none other than the "suffering messiah" foretold by Isaiah, the "despised servant" who had "given himself up as sacrifice for sin."[12] Between the crucifixion and the later readjustment of messianic expectations occurred the extraordinary event of the resurrection.[13] It was an event without witnesses, however. That Sunday morning, when the Sabbath was over and Jesus' followers could return to the site, they found an empty tomb. Not long after, Jesus himself began to appear, undoubtedly alive, undoubtedly in the flesh, and yet undoubtedly different from the man they had known before.[14]

Though the somewhat later Jewish historian Josephus (d. 95 C.E.) takes explicit though only passing note of Jesus and his death,[15] the rabbinic references from 200 onward are invariably oblique—it was neither a prudent nor a pleasant topic—and occur in the context of the Mishnaic treatise "Sanhedrin" dealing with judicial procedures.[16] The texts agree that Jesus, Jeshua ben Pandera, as he is often referred to, was tried before a Jewish court, found guilty, and put to death, either by stoning or hanging (on a cross?), "because he had practiced sorcery and enticed Israel to apostasy." There is no mention of Roman involvement in the matter. It was quite otherwise among the Muslims. The Quran's thirty-five references to Isa ibn Miryam show an extraordinary regard for Jesus, "the Messiah," as it frequently titles him, and it castigates both the Jews for claiming to have killed him—in the Muslim view Jesus was taken alive into heaven, where he will remain until his return on the Day of Judgment—and the Christians for worshiping this exalted prophet who was nevertheless, like Muhammad, merely a mortal.[17]

His followers later came to believe that Jesus' death and resurrection had ushered in not the End Time, as they had expected, but a new era, the breaking in of the Kingdom. With the passage of time and the absence of the anticipated cosmic apocalypse—an absence remarked on by Jews skeptical of Jesus' messianic claims—the Christians began to revise their eschatology as well. Jesus would not be returning soon, but when he did, his *parousia*, or "presence," would mark the cosmic End Time. In the meantime, the communities of the Jesus movement, which were progressively distancing themselves from the Jewish congregations where they had their origins, had to fashion for themselves an ongoing form of a Christian life. Thus, the teachings of Jesus and the early forms of worship, now detached from their Jewish context, were formalized and institutionalized to create the system called Christianity. The message of Jesus became the possession of the Church.

## The Parting of the Ways

Eventually the followers of Jesus constituted a religious community separate from the Jews, with lingering doubts over the schism on the part of the Christians and none, as far as we know, on the part of the Jews.[18] Paul's letters written in the 50s and the Gospels three or four decades later show the parting of the ways in its earliest stages. The "Messianists" (Gk. *Christianoi*) were harassed out of synagogues and congregations and were pursued and persecuted—Paul himself was part of that earliest effort, before his conversion—by the new Pharisaic leaders of the post-70 Jewish community.[19] Why? Judaism then as later was capable of accommodating diversity. And Jesus was certainly not the only Jew to be taken as the Messiah. Perhaps it was the progressively higher "Christology"—the titles of honor bestowed on Jesus—among his followers, who had taken to calling him not merely "Son of Man," a messianic title borrowed from Daniel, but also "Son of God." The latter sounds as though it should offend Jews, as indeed it eventually did, but only when read through the prism of Christian Trinitarian theology of the late third and fourth centuries, and only if one overlooks or underestimates, in the light of that theology, Jewish familiarity with "Son of God" and similar manners of speaking. Not only in Philo but in Jewish post-Exilic writing generally expressions like "Son of God" might still in the first century be understood in a manner not only acceptable but agreeable to Jewish beliefs and sensibilities.

Far more likely what cast the Messianists out of the synagogue and converted them into Christians was the issue of the Gentiles or non-Jews. Every Jewish scenario for the End Time included the Gentiles, sometimes by their acknowledging the truth of Israel or even being collected into it as worshipers of the One True God. The early followers of Jesus addressed the obvious interest in the Messiah on the part of the Gentiles, who were already a part of synagogue audiences throughout the Diaspora, in eschatological terms. It was in that same spirit of an eschatological ingathering of the Gentiles that a decision was made, after some hesitation and chiefly at the urging of Paul, to receive them into the brotherhoods without circumcision and with minimal Torah observance. We can only guess that it was this formal Jewish Christian inclusion of the Gentiles in the Covenant, and in growing numbers, that began to trouble other Jews. The approach of the End Time might explain or excuse the inclusion of Gentiles, but for many Jews—indeed, for most Jews—the End was patently not yet, and so the Messianists' embrace of increasing numbers of Gentiles brought about a rupture between the parent community and what had turned out to be a dangerously radical sect.

## Rabbinic Judaism

The double conquest of Jerusalem in 70 and 135 C.E. profoundly affected the course of Judaism and set it on its path from "politics to piety," as it has been aptly called.[20] Both temple and even the dreams of state were gone, and out of the doctrinal and cultic diversity of barely a century earlier survived only the Pharisees. The temple priesthoods were rendered moot; Hellenistic Judaism and its spirit of accommodation fell into increasing disrepute; militant nationalists were swept away by the Romans, and new messianic claims, whether pacific or militant, fell on deaf ears.

The Pharisees, as we have seen, are familiar figures from the New Testament and other sources.[21] It was long assumed that it was a simple step from the Pharisees of the first century to the sages of the second and following centuries of the Christian era, who produced the great literary and ethical structure of talmudic or rabbinic Judaism. To more critical eyes, that step is no longer regarded as quite so simple.[22]

For as long as there was a temple in Jerusalem, and for as long as the Torah was the foundation of Jewish life, the wardens of both were the priests (*kohenim*), the male caste of Aaron's descendants who had exclusive control of the temple and, through it, the ritual, legal, and, indeed, much of the economic life—the temple was Israel's chief corporation—of the community. Their progressive Hellenization after 300 B.C.E.—Hellenism's chief appeal was always to the social and economic upper classes—may have compromised the priestly authority, but whatever the case, we can note the presence, from the Hasmoneans onward, of another important institution, the Sanhedrin.[23] This was a mixed council of elders—priests served on it and, increasingly, Pharisees—and it was governed by collegiate heads, the senior *nasi*, who served as its president, and the junior *ab bet din*. This body took responsibility for the moral well-being of the community and adjudicated cases of law and conscience that fell within the general competence of the Mosaic law.

The later Jewish tradition recollected the holders of these two chief Sanhedrin offices as collegial "pairs" (*zugot*),[24] but is vague on the details of their functions and rulings until about the time of Jesus, when the *zug* of Hillel and Shammai filled the offices and developed what were recalled as distinctive attitudes toward interpreting the law. The "schools" of Hillel and Shammai dominate legal discussions down to 70 C.E., when the Sanhedrin had necessarily to leave Jerusalem and reconstitute itself elsewhere under the leadership of Yohanan ben Zakkai.[25]

These were difficult days for the Jews. Cultic Judaism, which had its unique center in Jerusalem since the days of David and Solomon, was no more after the debacle of 70 C.E., and the leaders of the community, most of whom appear to have been scholars rather than political figures or rich landowners at this point, had to rebuild a shattered community on new foundations. That new foundation was the law. It is obviously one of the oldest parts of the structure of Judaism, and since the time of the Exile was being promoted by many, the Pharisees chief among them, as a central concern of the Jew. Now, however, it became the unique standard of Jewish solidarity—or nearly so. In these new circumstances the Torah was supported, expanded, and explained by another document of growing authority, the Mishna.[26]

The Mishna is often presented as a redacted form of the oral law, the body of oral teaching referred to by the Pharisees as the tradition of the Fathers and thought by its advocates to go back to God's instructions to Moses on Mount Sinai. The contents of our Mishna do in fact appear to represent an oral tradition, edited, arranged, and set down in writing. But it is not, on the face of it, an oral Torah. The Mishna is constituted of neither laws embedded in a narrative in the manner of the Pentateuch, nor a law code in the sense of a general collection of statutes, nor even a commentary on the written Torah, to which it scarcely refers. Rather, it appears to be a discussion among lawyers about disputed questions in religious law, some apparently actual and contemporary and others just as obviously hypothetical as classroom exercises. Sometimes the discussants reach a conclusion, sometimes not.

The time, setting, and circumstances of the discussions are not specified in any convincingly historical way, but the lifetime of the authorities mentioned in the text stretch back to about 100 B.C.E.[27] Though the redaction of the final version is credited to Judah "the Prince" (*ha-nasi*) (ca. 170–217 C.E.), the Mishna is obviously a composite work that incorporated, under a generous, catholic perspective, what had developed as a kind of consensus within the Jewish community.

Many of the Jewish Diaspora communities were within the Roman Empire, but other important centers in ancient Babylonia dated back to the Exile and were still flourishing in the second to sixth centuries C.E.[28] With the redaction of Judah's Mishna, the scholars in these Iraqi schools joined their colleagues in Galilee in commenting on this now central text of the new Torah Judaism. Their commentary, written in Aramaic and called *gemara*, was joined to the Hebrew text of the Mishna. Together they form the Talmud: the Mishna with its Galilean gemara is called the Jerusalem or Palestinian Talmud; and with its Iraqi gemara, the Babylonian Talmud. Together they constitute the heart of rabbinic Judaism.[29]

The legal tradition was always strong in Judaism, as we shall see in discussing the Jewish sense of community, and there was always in post-Exilic Judaism an authoritative body, generally called the Great Sanhedrin, which both legislated and judged. Its head was the nasi, who both before and after the destruction of the temple possessed extensive legislative powers in his own right. Even after the Pharisees introduced the notion of an oral legal tradition whose validation went back to Moses, the nasi did not cease enacting positive legal prescriptions called *gezerot* and *taqqanot*. The first had, in fact, a Pharisaic justification in that such positive enactments provided "a fence for the Torah," that is, by surrounding the Torah with additional prescriptions, they guaranteed the observance of the Torah prescription (*mitzva*). But eventually *gezera* came to mean any legal enactment that was not a traditional rabbinic legal prescription (*halaka*), whereas *taqqanot* referred more properly to the creation of new institutions whose purpose was to improve the conditions of social, economic, and religious life.[30]

The legislative and judicial process was not confined to the nasi and his court. He could by "ordination" (*semika*) delegate his powers to individual rabbis so that they too could adjudicate disputes at law and issue binding enactments.[31] There was no such ordination among the Babylonian Jews. If some of the early Babylonian rabbis went to Palestine for ordination, the result was to strengthen the authority of the academies (*yeshivot*) where they taught, not that of the Babylonian exilarch (*resh galuta*), who was their nominal leader. With the disappearance of the Palestinian patriarchate in 425 C.E. under Christian pressures,[32] the Babylonian model began to prevail in Palestine as well: the rabbis could adjudicate and legislate on their own authority.

The rabbis have been described as "a relatively small group of religious virtuosi" who administered Jewish law for Jewish communities that were granted a certain degree of self-government by their political sovereigns, the Romans in Palestine and the Sasanians in Iraq. This law, like its later Islamic counterpart, had chiefly to do with personal status, and dealt with matters of marriage, inheritance, and the transfer of property. But the writ of the rabbis did not end there. In legal matters their word was law, but by their carefully cultivated prestige they influenced a broad range of religious and ethical matters.[33]

It is difficult to underestimate the rabbis' importance for the continuity of the Jewish tradition.[34] Judaism was precisely tradition, the handing down, in both spirit and letter, of the Covenant. The biblical account of that process smoothes over perhaps the enormous difficulties in both establishing and maintaining Jewish continuity. We have, however, graphic evidence of the difficulty when the Bible account ends and the historian can confront unedited testimony to the bewildering variety of Jewish sects and factions that prevailed in Palestine and the Diaspora in the years that followed the Maccabees, the Herods, and the Romans. The collapse of Jewish political expectations and the destruction of the Jews' unique place of liturgical worship were events of extraordinary magnitude in the life of the community. Masada is a modern myth; in the contemporary sources the taste of ashes is almost palpable.

Some Jews turned, as we have seen, to more radical expectations in this world or the next, to zealot nationalists or messianic claimants, to Gnostic reflexes of eschatological hope or historical despair, to the attractions of Hellenic assimilation. Not so the rabbis. Quietly, patiently, they rebuilt a shattered Judaism on the foundations of the law. The historian may cast a doubtful eye on their claim to represent an unwritten tradition going back to Moses himself, but that claim was accepted in the end by the great body of Jews, and the rabbis used its authority to expand, modify, and define the Torah for a new age.

Traditions calcify, and some later reform movements in Judaism have passed that harsh judgment on the Talmud. Whatever the truth of that judgment for the modern Jew, the Talmud, the men who composed it, studied, glossed, reverenced, and prayed over it, the rabbis who lodged it in the heart and practice of Judaism for more than three thousand generations of observant Jews, recreated Judaism. Though no Jew would be likely to put it so, the Talmud is the true New Testament of Judaism, and the rabbis, who quickly lost interest in such figures, were its veritable messiahs.

## The Origins of Islam

The lives of the Jewish founding fathers unfolded in such remote antiquity that they are by now irretrievable, and even the sages and scholars who contributed to the Talmud are represented by little more than disjointed utterances and judgments that provide flavor and personality but are poor makings for biography. Both Jesus and Muhammad are bathed, however, in a discernible historical light. If their careers are embellished with legend, we can also find in the narratives concerning them the traces of genuine biography: chronology, events, context.

The case of Jesus has already been discussed. For the Muslim, the Quran is not a historical document at all but an immediate and unconditioned revelation of God's will for humankind expressed in God's own eternal words. Western scholars have preferred to see in it not God's hand but the reflection of the interior life and religious mission of the man called Muhammad ibn Abdullah (ca. 570–632 C.E.),[35] and from it and somewhat more traditional biographical material they have constructed a life of the Prophet of Islam.[36]

The argument and critico-historical method of non-Muslim scholars may reflect modern Western attitudes toward reconstructing the past, but the early Muslims too had put together a biography of Muhammad, and out of much the same material available to the modern scholar: the Quran and the body of traditions (*hadith*; see chap. 4) that purported to report the sayings and deeds of the Prophet. Our earliest preserved example of such a biographical construction is the *Life* composed by Ibn Ishaq (d. 767) in Baghdad.[37]

Ibn Ishaq had predecessors, to be sure, in his biographical project on the Prophet, but all such work took place at least a century after Muhammad's death and only when Islam had moved outward from Mecca and Medina into an overwhelmingly Christian milieu.[38] This has suggested to some that the enterprise was undertaken as a direct response to the Christians' Gospels, despite the obvious difference in theological function of the two men and the two documents. For the Christian, Jesus was the Christ, the Messiah, whose redemptive act and teachings are authoritatively recorded in the Gospels. For the Muslims, Muhammad was a prophet (*nabi*), a human envoy (*rasul*) who delivered God's own words in the Quran but whose other words and deeds, though important for understanding the Quran and the direction of the Muslim community, are not immediate instruments of salvation.[39]

For all the uncertainties that modern scholarship finds in the Gospels, Jesus' life plays out against a Palestinian and, with increasing insistence, a Galilean background of which we have an ever more detailed and concrete understanding.[40] Josephus's works provide us with a near contemporary portrait of both the parties and the piety of Jesus' environment, and the Dead Sea scrolls have given us a privileged documentary opening into the sectarian Judaism of the day. Archaeology has uncovered the very streets of Jesus' Jerusalem and sifted through the sands around the Sea of Galilee.[41] Nothing remotely like this is available for sixth- and seventh-century western Arabia or for the town of Mecca in its midst. No contemporary Josephus has written its history, no Bedouin has found sealed scrolls in nearby caves, no archaeologist has turned over even a spadeful of its soil. We have only later Muslim recollections, or imaginings, of that time and place, the products of a different time and a different place— Baghdad—and of a different milieu—the cosmopolitan capital of a great political and religious empire called "the Abode of Islam."

We open the Quran and on almost every page there is material, from the "Garden of Eden" to the virginal birth of "Isa ibn Miryam," that can accurately be described as "biblical." The immediate and sensible conclusion is that some Jewish or Christian, or perhaps Jewish-Christian, influence was at work here. Muslims, equally sensibly, will have none of this. For the Muslim it is a matter of dogma that Muhammad enjoyed an absolute originality, remote from either texts or informants, and was in communication with God alone. But even if we grant that the Prophet delivered the Quran without any assistance from teachers or other people's books or stories, the same issue merely surfaces in a different form. How could his audience in early seventh-century Mecca have possibly understood the Quran's highly allusive and often opaque references to Abraham, Moses, Jesus, and the other prophets without some familiarity—oral, certainly, not textual—with biblical material and related apocrypha? And where and how would they have acquired such knowledge? We cannot readily answer our own question. Mecca is an almost locked book.

How, then, does the historian, Muslim or non-Muslim, proceed? Carefully, and with the Quran in hand. If the Quran came forth from the mouth of Muhammad, as it seems to have, then, whether God's word or Muhammad's own, it was uttered in terms comprehensible to a seventh-century Meccan and so may serve, with some basic adjustments, as a rough guide to the emergence of Islam. If we can credit it to Muhammad himself, the Quran may also reveal the evolution of the Prophet's spiritual life and his religious and political problems and strategies. The adjustment arises in the main from our present text of the Quran. As it now stands, and as it has for a very long time, the Quran is a composite work in which the revelations given by God through the angel Gabriel to Muhammad over the last twenty-odd years of his life are collected into 114 *suras* or chapters.[42] The suras vary greatly in length and are not arranged in chronological order; indeed, purely chronological considerations might invite one to read the book from its end to its beginning.

What we require, then, for our purposes is a rearrangement of the suras in something approaching the order in which Muhammad's audience heard them. This was attempted by Muslims fairly early on as they tried to connect individual revelations with events in Muhammad's life and so establish their context for both legal and pious motives, and was redone in the nineteenth century by non-Muslims for purely historical reasons. The results are not very different: we have a very rough idea of the chronological order of the suras, and if they are laid lightly and cautiously, like a template, on the earliest preserved biography of the Prophet, it is possible to sketch a life.[43]

## Muhammad, a Life

Though there is little else to recommend this exact date, the tradition states—a code expression meaning we are at the margins of reliability—that Muhammad was born in 570 C.E. in Mecca, a small settlement nestled in a wadi in the rising west Arabian highlands forty-five miles inland from the Red Sea. Later Muslim historians imagined the place as a major trade center whose paramount tribe, the Quraysh, controlled the rich caravan trade carrying the luxury goods of the East, chiefly spices, to the avid consumers of the Roman Mediterranean. The available evidence suggests otherwise; that Mecca was little more than a parched collection of mud-brick dwellings around a shrine, the cubical Kaaba and its surrounding taboo area (*haram*). The idols of the Bedouin had been set up in the Haram to attract nomads to perform the pilgrimage ritual known as the *hajj* and to trade under the protection of a sacred truce, all to the advantage of the Quraysh.

This was the religious and commercial setting in which Muhammad grew up. As an orphan he had little share in the local and very relative prosperity of the place, at least until he married a well-off older widow, Khadija, and went to work for her in trade. As with the life of Jesus before his baptism by John, we know little for sure about Muhammad's life up to and though his marriage. Then, in midlife—tradition makes him forty, again with no great conviction—he heard voices and perhaps saw visions of the type mentioned in sura 53. Disturbed and frightened, he sought counsel from someone who knew something of the Scriptures of the Jews and Christians. "You have received the Great *Namus*," he was told. The *Namus* was of course *Nomos*, the Greek for the Torah. Whatever the truth of this rather peculiar report, the Muslim historical tradition was locating the Prophet, as the Quran itself does, directly in the line of Jewish and, as it turned out, Christian prophecy.

The experiences continued. What Muhammad was receiving were messages for public delivery and, after some hesitation, he began repeating them before his fellow Meccans, likely in the immediate vicinity of the Kaaba. What the Meccans saw and heard was not Moses before them, however, but a more familiar figure, a poet-seer chanting a new message in an old style. No, Muhammad protested, he was not a poet; he was a prophet. His words came from God, the same familiar deity whose dwelling was before them in Mecca, the Kaaba. What was being urged on them was monotheism, that the Meccan High God, *Allah* in Arabic, was alone worthy of worship. Some few began to chant along with him, repeating his words—this "recitation" (*quran*) was liturgy as well as prayer—but most of the Quraysh at first paid little heed to what must have been one of many poet-chanters in the Haram. The message grew more threatening—God would reward the believers; the others would burn in the fires of Gehenna—and so too did the Quraysh. There was nothing less likely than that they would give up their gods, or their god business and the meager prosperity that had grown up around it.

Muhammad's career in his native Mecca was not brilliant. Jesus' ended after one or two years in a disaster rescued by nothing short of a resurrection from the dead. Muhammad continued his recitation-preaching for twelve long years in Mecca. The tone of the recitation was changing, however. The chants were longer, though his few followers continued to repeat and remember them, and they now included stories of other prophets in other times who had likewise warned a heedless people. Those older peoples had paid disastrously for their disdain of the prophets; now the equally heedless Quraysh who mocked Muhammad would pay. The Quraysh had finally had enough of the noisesome prophet and his fellow "reciters." When a boycott failed, violence was planned: Muhammad was to be assassinated and his followers killed or dispersed.

Some 275 inhospitable miles north and slightly east of Mecca was an oasis called Yathrib, later *Madinat al-Nabi*, the "City of the Prophet" or, more simply, Medina. Its Arab inhabitants were chiefly agriculturalists, though there was a notable Jewish presence there, some of whom were engaged in the small crafts of that time and place. The settlement was in crisis. Civil war had broken out between the two chief Arab tribes and the Jewish clients attached to each. In their despair they turned to a holy man some of them had heard during the hajj and market days at Mecca. Muhammad was invited to come to the oasis and he agreed—otherwise he would surely have perished. In 622 he and his followers slipped out of Mecca and they made their way to their new home. It was also the home and heart of the movement called Islam for the next forty years, and later Muslims marked the date and the event, the *hijra* or "migration," as the beginning of a new, and Islamic, era. There were conditions to this undertaking, Muhammad's as far as we can see, and they were formalized in the Medina Accords. All the area's inhabitants—pagans, Jews, and his own followers, the Muslims or "Submitters" as they were named on the Quran's own guidance—all agreed to accept uncontested the Prophet's decisions on matters of importance in the oasis.

Unexpected consequences began to unfold rapidly in Medina. Islam—"The Submission"—went public in its professions and prayer rituals, and the Jews of the oasis promptly rejected it and its prophet. More fatally, the Jews, who were coming to see the political bargain they had struck in religious terms, began to connive with Muhammad's still avid enemies in Medina. Muhammad, who had looked on the Jews as fellow monotheists, recognized treason when he saw it and struck out against Medina's Jewish tribes. Within five years they were expelled, enslaved, or killed. There was probably little political risk involved and the Jews' lands and possessions could be used to support Muhammad's own impoverished followers from Mecca. But what soon followed had the prospect of disaster. At a place called Badr Wells Muhammad and his Muslims ambushed a Quraysh caravan as it was making its way back to Mecca. It was a provocative and risky venture and could have been catastrophic in either execution or its retaliatory consequences. On the contrary, it turned out to be hugely successful— the Quran pronounced it a miracle—and, more consequently perhaps, highly profitable for the participants. The Muslims had become richer in one day than the other Medinese in a year of cultivating date palms. Next time, and there would certainly be a next time, there would be more volunteers, and more Muslims.

The ambush at Badr Wells was indeed a kind of miracle. Thenceforward the fortunes of the Prophet and his community never flagged. The Quraysh attacked Medina, as expected, were twice repelled, and then lapsed into what seemed like despair and then acquiescence of the fact that this son of Mecca, if not of God, was certainly not to be denied. When Mecca finally submitted to him in 630, it was almost an anticlimactic embrace of the inevitable. Muhammad ventured on ever more ambitious and far-reaching raids, most with gratifying results, rich with booty and the submission of tribes and the inhabitants of the settlements of western Arabia not only to the political overlordship of Muhammad but to the religious authority of his God: they became Muslims or *muminun*, "believers." Their conversion might appear minimal by some standards, but Muhammad sent out missions to instruct the new Muslims on recitation of the Quran, ritual prayer, and the paying of the *zakat*, the annual alms-tithe every Muslim owed the community.

The God-sent regulations of the Quran meanwhile continued to come forth from the lips of the Prophet, though now in a much altered style. The highly charged and boldly imaged rhymes of the Meccan era yielded at Medina to a more prosaic and didactic discourse. The object was no longer the conversion of the pagan Meccans but the instruction of Medina Muslims. The long Medina suras of the Quran—many of them doubtless composites, stitched together from separate pronouncements—explained to the new Muslims God's economy of salvation. Jews and Christians had distorted and debased the revelation given to them in the *Tawrat* by Moses and the *Injil* by Jesus. Now the Arabs were being summoned not to some revision or reformation of Judaism or Christianity but to the pristine form of monotheism, the "religion of Abraham," as the Quran itself calls it.[44]

Muhammad died, unexpectedly but not suddenly, in 632. By then he was the paterfamilias of many wives (Muslims were limited to four, if necessary, but the Prophet was quranically dispensed) and many female children (two males had not survived infancy), as well as both "Caesar" and "pope" of a community (*umma*) that was at once a "state" and a "church." "Church" and "state," "Caesar" and "pope" are all absurdly anachronistic in seventh-century Arabia, but the union of political and religious functions in the same community is unmistakable even there and has survived, in ideal if not always in practical form, down to the present day.

## The Legacy

Muhammad's legacy was first and foremost in the Quran, now, with his death, a closed Book, though not yet a finished book in our sense. Its suras or constituent parts lay scattered in the memories and perhaps notes—the literacy issue in Mecca and Medina is extremely complex;[45] neither the writing system nor the learning then in vogue leads us to believe there were many scribes in that place—of the Prophet's companions and had to be collected and arranged. The first two heads of the Muslim community after Muhammad are said to have tried to assemble the Quran, but the successful completion of the task is credited to the third of them, Uthman (r. 644–656). A standard text, we are told, was produced by a commission of experts and copies sent to the various centers of the growing empire with instructions that all variant versions were to be destroyed.

The effect of God's earlier revelations was, as Muhammad understood very well, the creation of communities, most notably the Peoples of the Book, the Jews and Christians. The Arabs, now in possession of a "clear Arabic Quran" (Quran 16:103), had become just such a community. But even during Muhammad's lifetime, his community achieved such remarkable political success that it had become in effect a state—a responsibility faced by Judaism and Christianity only at a considerably more advanced stage of their development. Thus Muhammad was not simply God's envoy; he was also, for much of his later life, judge, spiritual guide, and military and political leader, first of a community, then of a city-state, and finally of a burgeoning empire.

At base Islam is submission to the will of God and the recognition of the rights of the Creator over his creation. For one who had so submitted, the *muslim*—however revolutionary the internal spiritual consequences—there were few external, cultic obligations. From the initial profession of faith ("There is no god but the God and Muhammad is his envoy") flowed the obligation of prayer five times daily, with the noon prayer on Friday said in common; of almsgiving in the form of a tithe; of fasting and other abstentions in the month of Ramadan; and, if the circumstances were practical, of making a pilgrimage (*hajj*) to the "House of God" at Mecca.

These are mere bones, the ritual obligations of the Muslim, and though they became the point of departure of a vast body of prescription regulating Islamic behavior, they reflect neither the tone nor the urgency of Muhammad's message, particularly of the earliest revelations. The Meccan suras of the Quran have a dramatic eschatological emphasis, expressed now in commercial terms and now in the vivid images of Jewish and Christian apocalyptic. God who created the world will also be its judge. When the Day of Judgment comes, accompanied by chaos and confusion, the Lord of the World will open the accounts of all human beings and reckon each at his or her worth. For those who have gravely sinned or hoarded their goods out of meanness of spirit, there awaits a fiery Gehenna of extreme suffering. But the magnanimous individual who has submitted to God and committed his or her goods to the needy and the downtrodden will be rewarded in a garden Paradise of luxurious ease and splendor. Indeed, this is why the Prophet was sent, to warn humankind that the reckoning was close at hand.

Little can be said here of Islam's enormous and rapid growth from a state to an empire to a civilization.[46] By 750, a little more than a century after Muhammad's death, Muslim armies were fighting on the borders of China in the East and within striking distance of Paris in the West. Muhammad's successors ruled the imperial Abode of Islam first from provincial Medina, then (661–750) from Damascus, the venerable political and cultural center of Syria, and finally, after 750, from their own urban creation, *Madinat al-Salam*, the "City of Peace," better known under its village name, Baghdad. Other Muslim cities would rival even these in their splendor, wealth, and power: Cordoba, built on old Roman foundations in Spain; Cairo, a new creation next to old Fustat in Egypt; Istanbul, built atop imperial Constantinople and echoing its name; and the glittering cities that stretched like a string of pearls from Iran to India—Isfahan, Herat, Lahore, Delhi. Islam was a supremely urban civilization and so a scribal and literary one, and in those cities there collected, in the salons of princes, the arched *iwans* of the madrasas, and the privileged confines of Sufi convents, a vast array of artists, writers, scholars, scientists, and holy men. These pious Muslims extracted from the Quran, the life of the Prophet, the exploits of Muslim arms, the example of Muslim saints, and their own experience a staggeringly complex and detailed portrait of one of the world's great religious, cultural, and political enterprises.

This sketch has been all too brief, and perhaps even superfluous for those who know these traditions well. It is, in any event, merely preliminary to what follows, where the attitudes and institutions of Jews, Christians, and Muslims are examined side by side, not so much from the historian's perspective of tracing influences and borrowings, which there certainly were, as with the intent to illuminate how these three affiliated religions approached common issues on the ground that each of them had rendered holy.

# CHAPTER THREE

# Community and Hierarchy

Up to this point, Judaism, Christianity, and Islam have been spoken of in somewhat general descriptive terms without inquiring what gave each its unique identity. All three designations are abstract conceptual terms, of course, and it has often been remarked that there exist in fact only very concrete and individual Jews, Christians, and Muslims. But if "Judaism," "Christianity," and "Islam" are constructs, they were constructed not by social scientists looking for a manipulative handle but by the believers themselves, and very early on. "Judaism" appears in Maccabees and very explicitly and pointedly in Paul; "Christianity" was being used by Christians by the end of the first century; and "Islam" has the most exalted pedigree of all: it is God's own designation for the religion (*din*) to which he had summoned the believers.

The believers thus saw themselves in each case as members of an identifiable society, and they in fact organized themselves as such. *Benei Israel*, *ekklesia*, and *umma* each speaks, in its own context, of a community identity. Each of these religious associations derived its special quality from its having been founded by divine decree. The famous Covenant concluded by the One True God with Abraham was its founding charter and all subsequent claims of affiliation go back to it. Each has, moreover, a fundamental quality that sets it apart from other, simply human associations: its claims derive from God and they are absolute; they trump any merely human demands of loyalty, to the state, for example, or even the family.

# Benei Israel *and* Eretz Israel

Despite the confusions and overlappings in the biblical texts, and despite modern scholars' inability to settle on a chronology for the various pieces that were put together to compose the Bible, there is a unanimity of testimony that the creation of a people called "Israel" (*Benei Israel*) after its supposed tribal ancestor was the result of a covenant (*berit*) concluded between their god Yahweh and a people of his choice. They must submit to his will, as subjects to a sovereign, and worship him alone. If they do so, they will be rewarded, most notably by the possession of a promised "Land for Israel" (*Eretz Israel*).

Neither the provisions of God's will nor the exact boundaries of the promised land were spelled out at first; the small print would descend with Moses.[1] The actual implementation of the law governing the new Israelite manner of life had to wait on the conquest of Canaan. But one thing is clear: once there had been a people called Hebrews—perhaps simply "wanderers," a rather mixed bag of seminomadic herders—but now it was the Children of Israel who set up cult centers in Canaan in honor of Yahweh, who was now to be their God to the exclusion of all others, as he had requested of their father Abraham.

In what sense the Israelites were at the outset one people in Eretz Israel is difficult to say.[2] They were clearly organized along clan lines, and the fact of an association of twelve clans or tribes has suggested to some that the clans were united in a kind of confederation around a central shrine where they would periodically commemorate with ritual the covenant that gave them their identity. If so, the confederation was a loose one: there was no single leader and no apparent apparatus of central government. Individuals whom the Israelites generally called "judges" came forward when need or circumstances dictated.[3]

It was only with Saul and then David (ca. 1000–960 B.C.E.) that one of these "charismatic leaders" united the tribes of the Benei Israel into a somewhat unified whole, and only under David's son and successor Solomon (ca. 960–922) that a centralized and institutionalized monarchy of a familiar Middle Eastern type emerged. Cult center and liturgy were by then firmly established in Jerusalem, where Solomon's newly energized commercial enterprises financed the construction of a magnificent temple.

Thus Israel became a state ruled by a hereditary king, but its "constitution" was still God's Covenant. This latter had become increasingly explicit through the growth of a positive law whose provisions reflected Israel's conversion to a sedentary agricultural society. None of this was the king's writ, however, but rather "the Mosaic law," or even the "Mosaic constitution" (*politeia*), as it was known to some. Thus the evolutionary character of the community's laws was concealed beneath an appeal back to the original Covenant so that all that had occurred thereafter, whether through custom or design, was progressively incorporated into the charter of a still evolving Scripture.

Though God had promised that the scepter would remain in David's house forever, the Israelite monarchy proved ephemeral. Internal tensions between northern and southern clans shattered the fragile unity, and foreign cults began to make headway against Yahweh. Successive invasions by more powerful external enemies, and finally the carrying off of part of the population into exile in Babylonia left David and Solomon's political achievement in ruins. But the united monarchy and the Mosaic Covenant were not so closely identified that the destruction of the first necessarily signaled the end of the latter. New charismatic leaders, now prophets rather than earlier warrior types, arose in Israel to preach fidelity to the Covenant and, through it, the continuing identity of Benei Israel.

The Babylonian Exile is a mysterious period in the life of the Israelite community, since there are almost no sources to inform about life there, how the Israelites maintained their religious and national identity or even how they worshiped without a temple.[4] It was in Babylonia, we know, that they lost their maternal Hebrew and began to speak the ecumenical Aramaic of the Fertile Crescent. And when some of the exiles returned to Judea toward the end of the sixth century, others remained behind, though we cannot tell how many—enough at any rate for Babylonia to eventually develop into a great center of Jewish life and learning.

The returnees rebuilt Jerusalem and its temple and restored some semblance of liturgy and some degree of self-government there, though no longer as a kingdom but merely as a minor province, Judea, in the sprawling empire of the shahs. By Persian royal decree the Mosaic law was publicly promulgated by Ezra, who was, in the new order of things, neither a king nor a prophet but a priest (*kohen*), a member of Israel's ruling religious caste from the beginning, and a scribe (*sofer*), a new clerical office for a new clerical age. And, we guess, it was at this point in Jewish history that the Bible began to be assembled.

Post-Exilic Judea was, in the first instance, a temple-state under the general sovereignty of the Persian shah and later the Greek kings first of Egypt and then of Syria. It was ruled by a Crown-appointed governor who consulted on local matters with the hereditary high priest of the temple and a council of elders. But "Judea" was merely an administrative arrangement, and if it had within it the cult center of the Jews and was served by an official Jewish priesthood, there were also offspring of the Covenant in the other Persian provinces into which Palestine and the Transjordan had been divided, as well as even farther abroad, in "dispersion" (*diaspora*) in Syria, Egypt, and Babylonia.[5]

The Jewish Diaspora was not an exile, and those who lived outside the Judean temple-state did so by choice, not by constraint. In one sense they regarded themselves, and were taken by others, as one community, and the single name *Ioudaioi*, "Judeans," was applied to all, whether living in Judea or not. All Jews were bound to contribute a half shekel to the upkeep of the temple in Jerusalem, and many made pilgrimage there. In the larger centers of population abroad they constituted a "corporation," a Hellenistic notion that gave official sanction to a semiautonomous community of non-Greeks who had their own internal organization, guaranteed rights and privileges, and, very probably, their own formalized religious cult.

The Maccabean-Hasmonean insurrection of 167 B.C.E.[6] and the consequent restoration of a Jewish monarchical state in Judea had little effect on the Jewish sense of community except to underline a premise that had already been implicit in the first experiment in monarchy: a Jewish state, as the ancient East understood that latter term, was not identical with Covenant Judaism. And much as the prophets had made that point against the kings of an earlier day, so now others came forward to instruct the Hasmoneans. But where earlier charismatic preaching had been the chief weapon of the Covenanters against the monarchists, now the contest about an authentic Jewish life was waged in open political warfare. The Hasmoneans appear to have envisioned a peculiar hybrid state that was demographically Jewish but culturally Hellenized; their expansionist policies included the Judaizing of newly occupied lands, while they themselves became progressively more Hellenized in both their mode of government and their personal lifestyles. Finally, the Hasmonean head of state was eventually both Hellenistic king and Jewish high priest, the first in the history of Israel to have held such dual authority.

The prophets who opposed secularizing Jewish monarchs of an earlier day were rather isolated figures whose position as revivalists and reformers rested on charismatic foundations. Opposition to the Hasmoneans took the form of parties whose programs created neither revival nor reform in the first instance, but rather schismatic fissures in the Jewish community. The Sadducees, Pharisees, Essenes, and followers of Jesus were sects with sharply differing views about past history, future prospects, and what constituted a Jewish life. The Covenant that had once been concluded with the entire Benei Israel was now understood by many as a special covenant observed by a faithful remnant. The political question of a Jewish state had been rendered moot by Roman intervention, and although there were still those willing to die for its restoration, most of the community's spiritual energies were devoted to constructing new legal, ascetic, and eschatological canons to answer the question "What is a Jew?"

Many issues separated the sects from each other. One of them emerges, however, with singular clarity: that of table fellowship (*habura*). At stake was the extension of ritual purity, which everyone was required to observe within the temple and which was the special hallmark of the priesthood, to the everyday life of the Jew. Those who observe similar rules of purity, and they alone, may eat together, but no others, lest there be a defilement. Though a similar preoccupation can be observed at Qumran and among some of the early Christians, the strict enforcement of this ideal was at the center of the Pharisaic program. It set them off not only from Gentiles but from many temple-observant Jews and those "commoners" (*amme ha-aretz*) who totally ignored questions of ritual purity, though they too would surely have identified themselves as Jews.[7]

It was the Pharisaic answer to the question "What is a Jew?" that finally and uniquely prevailed well into the nineteenth century: a Jew was someone who observed the law, both the written Torah given to Moses and the unwritten law, the tradition of the Fathers, that went back to the same time and had the same sanction, and whose authoritative interpreters were the rabbis. After the disastrous insurrections of 70 and 135 only the rabbis spoke for Judaism. Temple and Qumran were gone, and the sectarian followers of Jesus of Nazareth had chosen or been forced to separate themselves from the parent body. More, the Romans accepted the Pharisaic disassociation from the insurrections, and chose to deal with the Pharisaic leadership as representatives of the Jewish Covenant, not merely in a religious but also in a political sense.[8] For their part, the Romans regarded the Jews as both an ethnic group (*natio*) and a religious community (*religio*) at whose head stood a single official, the *nasi*, "prince," or, as the Romans called him, the "patriarch."

If we review the powers and functions of the patriarchs from Gamaliel II (ca. 80–117) down to the abolition of the office in 425, we see that they not only presided over the chief religious court, the Sanhedrin, but announced the appearance of the new moon, which determined the date of Jewish liturgical festivals, among other things. The patriarch or his delegates (*shelihim*, "apostles") also collected funds from Jewish communities all over the Diaspora and determined and pronounced sentences of excommunication.

The expulsion or banishment of one of its members is a corollary of the very notion of community. Members may leave of their own volition, either by drifting away in the kind of silent attrition that affects all voluntary associations, or through a formal renunciation, which in a religious context is called apostasy and is viewed with extreme severity in all three monotheistic communities. Neither is the issue here, however, which concerns members of a faith community who were judged unfit or unworthy of continued association and so were banned.[9] As we shall see, the form among the Jews is to pronounce such a person *herem* or taboo. Early on such a sentence often and unmistakably meant execution, but in time it was mitigated to exclusion from the community. Though we cannot be certain how, why, or whether they were carried out on a regular basis, the grounds for a rabbinic declaration of herem can be reduced to worship of idols, contempt of God—through blasphemy, for example—and various sexual, social, and ritual offenses.

Once the norms of Pharisaic Judaism became, at least ideally, the norms of the entire Jewish community, the issue of excommunication becomes clearer. The earliest evidence for a formal procedure is perhaps the addition, sometime about 90 C.E., of three clauses to the twelfth of the eighteen benedictions of the synagogue liturgy. These are the so-called blessing over the heretics (*birket ha-minim*), which call down destruction on the Christians (*notzrim*) and sectarians (*minim*). There has been considerable debate over whether the minim were the Judeo-Christians who had accepted the messiahship of Jesus but continued to frequent the synagogue, or an entirely distinct group, a sect of Jewish Gnostics, for example.[10] But simply to cast this imprecation in the form of a regular and mandatory synagogue prayer made the curse its own effective fulfillment without trial or further process.

Under the rabbis there were other, more formal ways of distancing the offender. They ranged from a reprimand to a temporary ban (*nidduy*) to full expulsion (*herem*) from the community.[11] Many of the grounds are presented as disrespect for the rabbis, but this was probably interpreted in a formal rather than a personal sense, and included failure to observe the rabbis' legal enactments. The nasi and the courts could impose such bans, of course, but it is interesting to observe that any Jew could do the same if he or she observed a gross infraction of the law.

The nasi's political powers were created, in a sense, by the Roman authorities, who chose to deal with him as the official representative of the Jews of the empire, and all the evidence points to general Jewish acceptance of the nasi's acting as such. He was granted most of the honors accorded to a client king in the Roman Empire, and was exempted from various provisions of the Mosaic law to ease his necessary dealings with Gentiles.

At about the same time as the Romans were recognizing the nasi as patriarch, a parallel institution, that of the exilarch (*resh galuta*), was emerging under the Parthian dynasty in Iraq and Iran. Though the origins of the Babylonian office are somewhat obscure, it seems likely that about 70 C.E. the Parthians did formally recognize a single head for the various Jewish communities living in their Iraqi provinces, that the official in question claimed Davidic descent, and that, like his counterpart on the Roman side of the frontier, he had considerable power, including the disposition of a police force.[12] The Parthian exilarch differed from the Roman patriarch, however, in having powerful rivals in the

Palestinian-trained rabbis who staffed and directed the Babylonian *yeshivot*, sometimes styled "academies" but, more realistically, study circles collected around a group of sages. The relationship between the resh galuta and the rabbinic community in the Iranian empire was uneasy, and jurisdictional and political questions often divided them.

The institution that succeeded both the patriarchate and the gradually disintegrating exilarchate illustrates the triumph within Judaism of the yeshivot and their rabbis over all other competitors, social and political. When the Muslims came to power in the Middle East in the seventh century, they adopted the same kind of system favored by their predecessors: groups that constituted some kind of religio-social unity outside the Muslim community were treated as semiautonomous entities, which in much later Islamic times came to be called *millets*, and were permitted a considerable degree of self-regulation. Christianity, with its well-established hierarchical structure, presented few problems in this regard, but when the Muslims had to choose a representative of the Jewish community to the centralized caliphate, they turned to the prestigious "eminences" (*geonim*) who headed the two chief yeshivot at the towns of Sura and Pumbeditha in Iraq. Palestine had its own *gaon*, and he too was a rabbi who stood at the head of the Galilean study circles.

For many Jews, the passage from Christian to Muslim sovereignty must have seemed like a release.[13] The Jews were still minority subjects of a religious community that believed it had superceded them. They were still bound by certain religious, political, and social restrictions, as were the Christians who lived beside them in the Abode of Islam. But the Jews of Islam had at least escaped the particular theological animus that clouded, and sometimes bloodied, their existence in Christendom. In Muslim eyes Jews and Christians were precise theological equals, both of them privileged recipients of a divine revelation that each had wrongheadedly perverted. If Muslims regarded one set of their monotheistic subjects with greater suspicion, it was likely the far more numerous Christians who had, moreover, powerful friends abroad who demonstrated many times over their willingness to intervene on behalf of the Muslims' Christian subjects.

Jews, like the Christians, shared in the new economic prosperity that came to the Middle East in the wake of the Muslim conquest.[14] The Jews who lived in this network of communities across the face of the Islamic empire probably felt some kind of ethnic identity—culturally they were eventually Arabized, though Hebrew and Aramaic continued in use as learned and liturgical languages—but their more deeply felt bond was, as it had been for many centuries, a common observance of the Mosaic law and its talmudic corollaries, and a longing for Zion.[15] That bond was preserved and fostered by the rabbis. Efforts were made to standardize and simplify the text of the Bible for reading purposes.[16] More, the rabbis had been trained in a common legal tradition, and so accepted on behalf of themselves and their communities the religious and legal authority of the geonim.[17] For their part, the geonim intervened directly in the lives of the various communities by setting the liturgical lunar calendar and enunciating legal responsa for the resolution of disputes that could not be settled locally.[18]

## The Christian Church

The earliest Christian community was not unlike a Pharisaic habura or a Qumran yahad. Like the former, it had a formal table fellowship with a common meal (*agape*), though the Eucharistic communion was already at a considerable symbolic and liturgical remove from the Pharisaic habura. And like the Qumran yahad, it was a community united in eschatological expectation. The Christians held common prayer services on the model of a synagogue liturgy, and there was a familiar Jewish program of philanthropy to take care of widows and orphans. Jesus' immediate disciples stood at the head of the community, and at their head stood James, "the brother of the Lord."[19]

As is clear from the Acts of the Apostles, James did not act alone at Jerusalem, as a later bishop might; he was a first among peers. But it is equally clear that he was in a real sense the head of the congregation (*ekklesia*) there, and that after his violent death at the hands of a mob, he was succeeded in that office, at least until 135, by other of Jesus' relations, all of them practicing Jews of strict temple observance.[20] Elsewhere other Christian congregations came into being, often in connection with Jewish synagogue communities in the Diaspora, and there were appointed "elders" (*presbyteroi*) to govern them.

From the beginning, Jesus' followers had to face the question of their own Jewishness. The Hellenized and Pharisaic Jews made poor bedfellows and worse tablemates, inside or outside the Christian community, but Jesus' own exaltation of the act of faith in himself over a strict observance of the law raised even larger issues. Jesus, who did not observe a marked degree of ritual purity, might fit ill into a strict Christian habura, but Gentiles would scarcely fit at all. Some accommodation had to be worked out, at least for a time, but Paul for one, in his letters to the nascent Christian communities in Galatia and at Rome, refused to surrender the issue to pragmatic solutions.

Paul's attitude toward the Jewish law must be placed inside the context of his thinking about the Church. In Jesus' own words, a New Covenant had been sealed by his death and resurrection; a new Chosen People, a new Benei Israel, had been elected—a notion strongly underlined in the Letter to the Hebrews, which most of the ancient churches regarded as from Paul and included in the New Testament canon. The original Covenant had been accompanied by laws governing the behavior of God's people, laws regulating purity and sacrifice. The New Covenant had no need of such laws, in Paul's view. Jesus now dwelt in the body itself, transforming it from within. Each Christian was his own temple and his own priest: the new sacrifice was Eucharistic.

In his letters Paul attempted to give some guidance and moral instruction to the now de-Torahed Christian communities with which he was in contact. But this guidance was based on his own claims to be an Apostle; more generally the governance of individual congregations fell to the "elders" of that congregation, and to one of them who, like James at Jerusalem, was a collegiate first among equals. Already at the end of the first century, in the letters of Ignatius, for example, that *primus inter pares* was taking on a special status as "overseer" (*episkopos*) or bishop, who was coming to be recognized as the single "successor of the Apostles" and so the bearer and interpreter of the authentic Christian tradition.[21] But whereas the ordination (*semika*) of their Jewish counterparts appears to have been a simple act of delegation, the Christians' "laying on of hands" or ordination of the priestly presbyters, and par excellence of the bishops, was a charismatic act. Bishops were ordained by other bishops as part of the Apostolic succession; presbyters were ordained by the bishops of their own communities, whose delegates they were in the performance of liturgical functions.

With the spread of the new beliefs and the appearance of Christian communities both within and outside the Roman Empire, the individual parts of the Great Church began to arrange themselves, as neither Judaism nor Islam was to do, in an organic and hierarchical system. The local government of the bishop had sound precedent in the early practice of the Church, and the passage of the Christian message at first created no great discrepancies in the practice of the local churches that constituted the Great Church. But the simple relationship between the bishop and his community yielded to considerably more complex arrangements once Constantine had embraced the Great Church as his own.

The social, political, and economic consequences of the emperor's conversion constrained the local churches to fashion for themselves, and for the Great Church, an organizational structure congruent with their new responsibilities. In some instances, existing institutions were adapted, some of them going back to Apostolic times; in others, totally new offices were created. And in almost every instance the model followed by the Church was the parallel institution of the Roman Empire. The bishops within a single region began to conform to the hierarchical municipal pattern of that region: metropolis, cities, towns, and even villages had bishops at their head, but the bishop of the metropolis or provincial capital—he was later called an archbishop—had precedence and jurisdiction over the others.

Theoretically all bishops were equal in the light of the Apostolic succession, but some were clearly more equal than others in the light of Roman provincial organization. The arrangement did not yet do much violence to historical reality; the Church had in fact spread from Jerusalem through large metropolitan centers such as Alexandria, Antioch, and Rome. But Rome was the most equal of all. It had a true claim to the Apostolic succession in Peter and Paul, who early carried the Gospel there; it was, moreover, no mere provincial capital but the head of the empire. The evidence is unmistakable that the bishop of Rome was indeed accorded a kind of primacy of honor among his episcopal and archepiscopal peers.

The question of absolute primacy never arose in the early Church. The presence of many venerable and flourishing centers of Christianity, each ruled by a bishop who stood in a direct and equal line of descent from the Apostolic tradition, would have rendered such claims nonsense. Absolute primacy arose only when multiplicity had been reduced to polarity, when Rome and Constantine's new capital of Constantinople each stood alone at the head of a separate spiritual, cultural, and political tradition. Rome did intervene in the affairs of other churches from the beginning; no one protested, and there are even examples of the Roman church being appealed to in certain cases. Only in the fourth century did the bishops of Rome, who bore, like the bishop of Alexandria, the unofficial title of "pope,"[22] begin to insist on their de jure right of final jurisdiction based on Peter's position vis-à-vis the other Apostles.[23]

This particular line of argumentation found its definitive expression in the sermons of Leo, bishop of Rome between 440 and 461 c.e., who claimed, on his Petrine authority, universal jurisdiction. The Council of Chalcedon in 451, although accepting Leo's doctrinal formulation of a solution to the theological problem of the two natures of Christ, rejected the Petrine argument. Its twenty-eighth canon spelled out the message in unmistakable terms: the emperor and the Senate were now in Constantinople, which now had equal privileges with the Old Rome, and ranked second after it in protocol order. Rome, which supplied the theology of the council, did not put its name to Canon 28; the Eastern bishops did. Rome and its natural rival on the Bosphorus were only beginning their poisonous struggle. Their first formal rupture occurred as early as 484, and over the succeeding centuries the relationship between Latin pope and Greek patriarch went from bitterness to bitterness.

The Christian "tradition," as will be seen, was clear-cut in its ideological base but rather ill-defined in its content. New converts might be required to present it in the summary form of a "creed" at their baptism. Many of these latter were simple statements, no more complex than the Muslim profession of faith, but adequate to set the Christian off from pagan contemporaries. They by no means exhausted the Apostolic tradition, which was being energetically explored by Christians who no longer came from Jewish backgrounds, where behavior in accordance with prescribed norms was the most common measurement of community association, but from a Hellenized Gentile milieu with its own highly developed theology.

Views of the tradition were everywhere put forward, and judgment about the congruence of such views with the understood limits of that tradition was the bishops' responsibility. But what seemed within the limits of a commonly received tradition in one church did not always seem so in another community, and the question had to be taken up in a wider context. Bishops gathered in synods, much like the one held early in Jerusalem to settle the Gentile question. After the issue had been debated and resolved, the bishops' decisions were recorded in the official "acts" of these provincial or regional synods, and were followed by a set of anathemas imposing excommunication—normally exclusion from the sacramental life of the Church—on those who held to the contrary.

What was being constructed by these synods was a more and more detailed definition of the Apostolic tradition, which was accompanied by increasingly sophisticated creeds that were no longer simple baptismal formulas but could be applied as a test for orthodoxy and heresy.[24] The term of the process came with the summoning by the now Christian emperor Constantine of an ecumenical or Church-wide council of bishops at Nicea in 325 C.E. At it the bishops of the Great Church were asked to deal with a theological issue that affected the entire community of Christians. The Ecumenical Council of Nicea produced a creed that addressed not merely the general outlines of the Christian tradition but the specific theological issues that had prompted its convocation.[25]

Christianity had, then, two means of defining itself on an ongoing basis: the individual bishop's charismatic and Apostolic oversight of his own congregation, and a conciliar or synodal instrument that could speak authoritatively to more general questions through a form of consensus. The positive consequence of employing these instruments was dogma; the negative, heresy. Heresy did not begin with Nicea, of course. Jesus had foreseen it for his followers, and the pages of Paul's letters are filled with instructions and warnings against preachers of false gospels; Eusebius traced all heresy back to Simon Magus, a contemporary of Peter. What the early conciliar movement did was to institutionalize the episcopal magisterium and, by formally defining dogma, so institutionalize heresy.

In the Gospels Jesus is made to seem remote from the politics of his time, which we know were ferocious, and many of the circumstances of Jesus' life, particularly of his arrest and execution, suggest that his famous advice to "render to Caesar the things that are Caesar's and to God the things that are God's" was easier in the uttering than the doing. Christians were told by Paul, who had his own problems with Roman officialdom, to accept the current political and social order, which they seem by and large to have done. But the Romans did not much care for the new religious association and its members. Two things militated against the Christians. First, they were perceived as a group apart, mysterious and even clandestine in their rituals and practices. Second, it became increasingly clear to the Romans, as it was to the two parties concerned, that Christians were not Jews. Jews were not assuredly beloved by the Romans, who decried their "superstition," but for all their odd fractiousness, the Jews enjoyed exemptions and protections under Roman law,[26] whereas the Christians, cast or fled from the synagogue, did not.

The first to press the matter was the emperor Domitian (r. 81–96), who embarked on a broad persecution of the Christians.[27] The grounds were not so much for their beliefs, since beliefs were not much of a concern to the Romans, as for their refusal to accord the emperor divine honors by sacrifice, an act that any Roman would regard, correctly, as a pledge of political loyalty, and a Christian, equally correctly, as an act of idolatrous worship. There were arrests and some executions, and the storm passed. Other storms occurred intermittently throughout the second century under other circumstances and against a variety of Christian targets—the hierarchy, the clergy, laymen, property—but the pogroms had little apparent effect. The number of Christians slowly grew, in high places—some of the very highest—as well as in low. Finally, in 303 the emperor Diocletian unleashed the last and greatest attempt at eradicating the new faith. He declared that all churches should be destroyed and all Christians forced to sacrifice under pain of death.

Constantine, converted in 312 by a vision of the cross on the eve of a battle with a rival—"In this sign you will conquer"— became the first Christian emperor and set the Church, and the

Roman Empire, on a new course.[28] The persecutions were suspended, as they likely would have been in any event since they accomplished little. Indeed, they may have had exactly the opposite effect to that intended; far from suppressing Christianity, "the blood of the martyrs was the seed of the Church," as the Christian Tertullian put it. More consequentially, perhaps, the now devoted if not yet devout Constantine put the empire's enormous resources at the disposal of his Church. This was not unusual: the Romans had always invested large public sums in temples and priesthoods. Thus Christianity passed within 350 years from an ignored Eastern cult, to a prescribed clandestine religion, to a public and favored one until in 381, under one of Constantine's Christian successors, it became the official religion of the Roman Empire. There had been one such before—the cult of the Invincible Sun in the late third century—but this was to be a cult that brooked no rivals. The corollary soon followed: all forms of paganism were criminalized, banned, proscribed.[29]

Constantine took the Church by his firm imperial hand, and the younger, less mature institution accepted the embrace, though neither quite understood its implications. Constantine and his successors legislated for the Church—by the fourth century the emperor was the sole source of law—not always directly, to be sure, but to the extent that the Church's officials and properties were protected by law. The Church's enemies, the pagans without and the heretics within, were pursued and prosecuted. Constantine also undertook, at imperial expense, a vast building project in Palestine: the identification and enshrinement of Jesus' birthplace in Bethlehem and the site of his death and burial in Jerusalem. Thus began Palestine's conversion into a Christian Holy Land.[30] In 325, as we have seen, Constantine summoned to Nicea near his capital all the bishops of what would be, by the time they left Nicea, the Great Church. By this act of summoning the Church's leaders and then confirming their decrees, Constantine had effectively created a Church united in doctrine and quite as universal—the preferred term was the Greek-derived "catholic"—as the *imperium romanum* itself.

The Church for its part could intervene in the affairs of state on the same high level. Religious figures had been influential with emperors before Constantine, but once the emperor became Christian, he was subject not only to the spiritual authority of the bishop of Constantinople or Rome, but to the divinely sanctioned laws of the Church as well. The Christianization of the empire, for all the loyalty the Christians demonstrated for both the prince and the principate, was the single most effective curb on the growing absolutism of the Roman emperor. Emperors were branded as heretics, excommunicated, and successfully opposed on occasion by both the episcopate and that other source of power in the Church, the monastic establishment.[31]

## The Islamic Umma and the Abode of Islam

Christianity had three centuries to brace for the shock of finding itself the part proprietor of a Christian Roman Empire. Islam was from its inception both a religious and a political association; Muhammad was his own Constantine. In 622 he accepted an invitation to leave his native Mecca, where he was the charismatic leader of a small conventicle of believers, and emigrate to Medina as the ruler of a faction-ridden community of Arabs and Jews. This was a crucial period in Muhammad's life, and the years following his "migration" were spent in trying to forge some kind of community (*umma*) in accordance with his religious principles and the political realities of the situation. The first umma at Medina was not yet a fully Islamic association—both Jews and pagan Arabs were included—but as Muhammad's political fortunes began to prosper, religious considerations came to the fore. The Jewish tribes of Medina were purged from the coalition, and the pagans were dragged willy-nilly into it; the umma became a community of believers who accepted the dominion of Allah and both the prophethood and the leadership of Muhammad.

These were not artificial associations. Muhammad's role as a prophet within a community that he himself had summoned into being necessarily included the functions of legislator, executive, and military commander of the umma. God's revelations continued to spill from his lips. Now they were not only threats and warnings to nonbelievers, but more often legislative enactments regulating community life, particularly the relations of one Muslim with another.

Muhammad no more appointed a successor than Jesus had. In the case of Christianity, immediate eschatological expectations made that seem a natural course of events, but there is no trace of such expectations in Islam, and the umma undertook to guarantee its own political survival by choosing someone to lead its members. They reverted to a type of tribal selection, and the choice of the senior Muslims was designated "successor (*khalifa*; Eng., "caliph") of the envoy of God." He was no such thing, of course— the prophetic line was ended by Muhammad's own declaration— but from the manner in which the earliest caliphs acted we can get some very imprecise idea of what were thought to be the powers of that office.[32]

The caliph was, in fact, chief executive of the umma. He appointed and removed political subordinates. He decided military strategy and was commander (*amir*) of the armies of Islam. He was the chief judge and chief fiscal officer of the new regime. Most of the caliph's military, judicial, and fiscal responsibilities were soon delegated to others, however; the community was actually a number of armies on the march far from the centers of power, and though decisions might be made in the name of the caliph, they were increasingly made by others.

The caliph and his delegates might decide, but they could not or did not legislate. They now had the closed and completed Quran, and they could not add to that text which, like Jewish law, addressed itself in great detail to matters of personal status, but was mute on the political governance of what was rapidly becoming an immense empire. The caliph and his delegates resorted instead to a great many devices to shape their purpose; tribal practices, local customs, pragmatic necessities, and, to some extent, whatever precedents the practice of the Prophet suggested to them. Though the office was undoubtedly religious, there are only the slenderest suggestions that the caliph regarded himself or was regarded by others as the possessor of special spiritual powers. He was the head of the umma, and although the umma was based entirely on a shared acceptance of Islam, the caliph was not a religious leader but the leader of a religion.

It was the caliphs, the earliest ones at any rate, who had to face a problem that Muhammad himself had forestalled only with great difficulty during his lifetime. There was a tension in the community from the beginning between the notion of Islam as a universal religion that claimed the allegiance of all humanity, and that of the Arabs as a final version of the "Chosen People." The latter phrase is Judaism's own, of course, and speaks to God's election of Israel as a fellow in his covenant. Muhammad's own perspective was perhaps somewhat different. He knew, from his own understanding of history, that previous revelations had constituted their recipients a community, an umma. It had been true of the Jews and the Christians and now, in the final act of the drama of revelation, it would be so with the Arabs.

If this revelation of a "clear Arabic Quran" through an Arab prophet to Arabs of western Arabia was calculated to create a sense of unity among those peoples, the project cannot be judged entirely a success. Muhammad had problems with tribal rivalries in his own day, between the mighty and the low in the complex hierarchy of tribes and clans that dominated not only his native Mecca but most of the peninsula's Bedouin population. Boasting and vilification were common pre-Islamic instruments for establishing and maintaining that order, and though Muhammad decreed that the only aristocracy in Islam was that constituted by piety and merit, the tribal divisions of Arab society long outlived his efforts to suppress them in the name of either a single Arab umma or a universal religion for all believers.

With the death of the Prophet, the umma seemed on the point of disintegration. Only through the strenuous military efforts of his first successor, Abu Bakr (r. 632–634), was Islam reimposed on the tribes across Arabia who had read the Prophet's death as the death knell of Islam and declared their secession from the community. What followed was more subtle and perhaps more insidious in the long run. The enormous wealth that came to the community as booty and tribute was distributed according to a system devised by the second caliph, Umar (r. 634–644). It recognized and rewarded the merit of early conversion and a concomitant willingness to bear arms against the enemies of Islam, but in institutionalizing this system of rewards and pensions, Umar restored the distribution rights to tribal chieftains, permitted this to be done along tribal lines, and allowed it to be effected in the new Islamic garrison towns whose social organization was precisely tribal.

The consequences of these purely administrative decisions were twofold, and each was far-reaching in its social impact. They preserved and perhaps reinforced the old pre-Islamic tribal rivalries, which continued to disturb the equilibrium of the Islamic body politic for at least a century afterward; and they conspired to create a distinction between Arab and non-Arab within the bosom of Islam. That distinction always existed, of course, save in that pre-Babel world when all humankind was one (Quran 10:19, 2:213), but it had a particular significance in an essentially tribal society where identity and its consequent social and political protections were claimed on the basis of birth. There are ways of associating with tribal societies even if one is not born into them, but one of the most common—fictive adoption and its resultant patron-client relationship—provides the client with status of a decidedly inferior quality. What the *cliens* was to vestigial Roman tribalism, the *mawla* was to Arab tribal societies: a freed slave, protected but dependent. The concept was convenient enough to extend to the non-Arabs who converted to an Islamic society that had institutionalized itself into an Arab tribal one. It is not certain that Muhammad intended an egalitarian community. What actually emerged was a society where both tribal and ethnic rivalries died a lingering death.

The caliphate, though an obvious pragmatic success, did not exhaust the possibilities of leadership in early Islam. There was among some Muslims the concept of the head of the community as a prayer leader (*imam*) or an eschatological chief or Mahdi, literally "Guided One." The latter has been invoked from time to time in Islamic history as a challenge to the caliph or a magnet around which to energize Muslim political action, but its successes have been short-lived, and the figure of the Mahdi has receded, like that of the Messiah in rabbinic Judaism, into an indefinite future.

The ideal of an Imam has had a very different history. In the nonsacramental and nonpriestly system that is Islam, leadership in prayer must soon have become what it was in synagogue Judaism, a kind of honor that could be bestowed on any Muslim. Not so, said others: the imamate implied moral rectitude, and the Imam par excellence, the head of the entire community, must be the most moral of Muslims. This view had a brief vogue as the thrusting point of the sectarian community called Kharijites or "Seceders." They held that salvation consisted in membership in this new "communion of saints" whose members were distinguishable only by their virtue, not by their clan or tribal associations.

What the Kharijites had "seceded" from was the nascent group that would be known as the "partisans of Ali" (*Shiat Ali*), and who were rallying round Muhammad's nephew and son-in-law, Ali, who was the fourth caliph of Islam (r. 656–661). Though their ideology took some time to evolve, in its finished version, the Shiite vision of Islam regarded the imamate as a spiritual and religious office whereby a special charisma was transmitted through designated descendants of Ali down to the point in the ninth century when the historical Imam vanished, only to return in his eschatological role as Mahdi.[33]

These struggles about the nature of the Islamic community and its leadership are complicated by the fact that they chiefly appear in heresiographies as theological sects, whereas in fact they were deeply enmeshed in the politics of their milieu. By the time they were described as religious heresies, most Muslims had settled into a view of themselves as "people of custom (*sunna*) and the community (*jamaa*)," frequently shortened to "Sunnis," a conservative self-designation that has been succinctly defined as "the majority of Muslims which accepts the authority of the whole first generation of Muslims and the validity of the historical community." Those who undermined that community unity were guilty of "innovation," Islam's closest approximation to the notion of heresy, because they appealed away from history, now canonized as custom or tradition (*sunna*), to special and particularist views.

The point at issue here is who shall rule the community. The Sunnis were willing to accept the verdict of history as reflected in the choices of that "whole first generation" of Muhammad's contemporaries and their immediate successors. The Shiites argued against history in asserting Ali's preeminence, but in so doing they were forced, to one degree or another, to attack the consensual wisdom of the Companions of the Prophet from whom all the Prophetic sunna ultimately derived. Disappointed by history, the Shiites turned where some Jewish groups may also have resorted, to a Gnostic wisdom, a kind of particularist and underground sunna transmitted, generation after generation, by infallible Imams of the Alid house or by their delegates. In fully developed Shiism, which later found its most lasting base by connecting itself with Persian nationalism, the entire range of Gnostic ideas is on display: the exaltation of wisdom (*hikma*) over science (*ilm*); a view of historical events as reflection of cosmic reality; and a concealed (*batin*) as opposed to an open (*zahir*) interpretation of Scripture.

It was simply a matter of time before Shiite Gnosticism found its siblings within Sufism and philosophy.

Though the question of the caliphate or imamate was critical in early Islam, and was often debated precisely as such, there was also the larger question of membership in the umma. One form of the issue was the distinction between *iman*, or faith, and *islam*, the act of submission to God. Both terms are used in the Quran, though Muhammad more often designated members of his community as "believers" or "the faithful" (*muminun*) than as "Muslims" (*muslimun*). As a matter of actual fact, however, membership in the community depended directly and exclusively, except in the case of the Kharijites, on making an initial profession of faith (*shahada*)—"There is no god but the God and Muhammad is his envoy"—and a consequent sharing of community prayer and contribution of the alms-tithe.

In this form the shahada is merely a verbal formulation and leaves open the question of intention and the relative importance to be placed on interior faith and external good works. Was the grave sinner still a Muslim? The Kharijites emphatically answered "no" but few agreed. Most Muslims accepted the definition of faith attributed to the early jurist Abu Hanifa (d. 767): "confessing with the tongue, believing with the mind, and knowing with the heart." This constituted one a believer and so subject to Muslim law.[34] All agreed, moreover, that the unforgivable sins of polytheism (*shirk*) and unbelief (*kufr*) excluded one from the community. As regards other grave sins such as murder and fornication, eternal punishment in the afterlife was probable but not inevitable. The sinner could only trust in God's mercy and the Prophet's intercession; for their part, the other Muslims here below must suspend judgment.

This agreeably tolerant attitude of suspending judgment on the moral conduct of one's neighbor had some extremely disagreeable political implications that were, in fact, the chief point in the discussion. Postponement of judgment effectively removed the religious and moral issue from the political life of the Islamic empire. Its acceptance marked another stage in the secularization of the caliphate, whose tenants could no longer be challenged on the grounds of their personal morality. The predestination argument led in the same direction—de facto must necessarily be de Deo. The predestination versus free will argument drifted off into the metaphysical thicket of atoms, accidents, and "acquisition," but the postponement thesis held because it represented some kind of ill-shaped Muslim consensus that custom and the community were more important than tossing dead sinners into hell and live ones out of office or out of the community.

If the differences among Muslims were interpreted generously, the distinction between submission (*islam*) and disbelief (*kufr*) was strenuously maintained. This was an absolute antagonism that cut across another distinction, that between the Abode of Islam (*Dar al-Islam*), the geographical area under Muslim political control, and the Abode of War (*Dar al-Harb*), where the umma did not prevail. Infidels could not be tolerated within the Dar al-Islam: they had either to accept Islam or to perish. Their presence outside the Abode of Islam created the moral imperative of holy war (*jihad*).[35]

The complex of concerns and conditions that have collected around the Muslim notion of holy war reduces itself to a discussion of the circumstances under which the community of Muslims is obligated—for this is, most decidedly, a religious obligation, and a group obligation—to use force against an enemy. In the quranic passages on jihad, there is clearly a wider meaning to the term than simply the use of force. The believers must energetically "strive"—the root is the same as that in *jihad*—"in the path of God" to resist sin, and that ethos of striving, this so-called "jihad of the heart" is built into the Muslim moral code. But the Quran also deals with the "jihad of the sword," and the use of force, or "killing," as the Quran puts it. The Meccan suras are circumspect on the subject, as might be expected, but at Medina permission to use force was gradually broadened until, it seemed, war could be waged against non-Muslims at almost any time or any place (Quran 9:5).

It was the thrust of these texts and of parallel Prophetic reports that prompted later jurists to divide the world into the Abode of Islam, where Islamic law and sovereignty prevailed, and the Abode of War, lands not yet subject to the moral and political authority of Islam. Some have thought that the Abode of Islam is in a permanent state of hostilities with the Abode of War, at least until the latter submits, and jihad is the instrument by which God's will is to be effected. This view was put forward by jurists at the full tide of Muslim expansion, but even so, the same jurists who commended it appear to have exercised caution on the matter of hostility with the unbelievers. Some demanded that a provocation be present; all agreed that the head of the umma had, in effect, formally to "declare" holy war and had broad discretionary powers in its execution. As time passed, the combination of juridically imposed conditions and political realities has diminished the effectiveness of jihad as an instrument of political policy.

Although the classical Islamic legal tradition prohibits all forms of political force, whether as tribal raids, blood feuds, or full-scale warfare, *except* on the religious grounds just sketched, modern Western ethical theories have sanctioned "just wars" on natural law grounds but never for religious reasons. Most religious communities, in contrast, have permitted and even encouraged taking up arms in the name of God. Yahweh was a warrior God, and the Bible is filled with conflicts that are manifestly "holy wars" by any definition of that term. With the progressive loss of Jewish sovereignty and so of the practical capacity to use force against their enemies, war eventually became for the Jews an anticipated eschatological event, and then, with the diminution of messianic enthusiasm, merely a school exercise for the rabbis, who laid down the rules of war in the eternal (and peaceful!) present of the Talmud.

The Christian Church as such is not a state and so cannot formally declare or conduct a war. But on many occasions it has permitted and even encouraged its members to use force in the name of religion. The best-known examples are the crusades, or "pilgrimages in arms," whose stated objective, at least initially, was wresting the Holy Land, particularly the holy places in Jerusalem, from the grasp of the infidel Muslims. The enterprise was formally promulgated by Pope Urban II at Clermont in France in 1095 and the Church's richest spiritual and economic rewards were promised those of the faithful who voluntarily—and formally—vowed to "take up the cross." Later, as the project of permanently holding Jerusalem against the Muslims seemed increasingly illusory, the grounds were broadened. It was Pope Innocent IV (r. 1243–1254) who defined the new position on the legitimate use of force. The pope, as the vicar of Christ on earth, had the authority to order even non-Christian sovereigns (read Muslims) to admit preachers of the Gospels into their lands, and, if they refused, to authorize Christian princes to use force to effect their entry.[36]

As the Abode of Islam spread rapidly across the Middle East, westward along the southern rim of the Mediterranean basin and east as far as Sinkiang, it encompassed within it large numbers of "People of the Book"—Jews, Christians, and, latterly, Zoroastrians—whose legal status and social condition was governed by contract, the *dhimma*. In 627 Muhammad and his raiders approached the oasis of Khaybar north of Medina. When he had overcome polytheists, the Prophet offered them no quarter: either they became Muslims or they perished, peremptorily. The dwellers in Khaybar were, however, Jews, many of them in fact refugees from Medina, and Muhammad offered them another alternative. If they submitted without resistance and agreed to pay tribute to the Muslim community, they might remain in possession of their goods and continue to live as Jews. Later and elsewhere Christians capitulated to Muslim arms and were offered the same terms in the name of a shared possession of the "Book," that, a genuine revelation.

The principle of the dhimma—sometimes called the Pact of Umar after the version the second caliph supposedly offered the inhabitants of Jerusalem in 638—became embedded in Islamic law where it remains to this day, and the terms were gradually filled out in somewhat fuller detail. The *dhimmis*, as they were called, though free to worship in their own manner, might not proselytize, build new houses of worship, make public display of their religion, rule over Muslims, or own Muslim slaves, and they had to wear distinctive clothing. History shows that the Muslims had little to fear from the Jews and Christians under their sovereignty—most had become Muslims, perhaps as early as 950—but the Muslims continued to be uneasy on the subject, and in certain times and certain places the dhimma was enforced with great exactitude, even, and often, violated by persecution.[37]

The paradox of a ruler who possessed no direct religious powers governing a community whose common bond was the acceptance of Islam found its palliative in the growth of a body of Islamic law that, from the ninth century onward, the caliphs had to accept as normative. The law was administered, as Muslim affairs had been from the beginning, by a judge or *qadi* who was a caliphal appointee, and so an agent of government. The actual control of the law, its codification and subsequent modification, was in the hands of a body of jurisprudents known collectively as "the learned" or *ulama*.

The ulama were at first unofficial and unorganized students of the traditions of the Prophet, but with the institution and spread of law schools (*madrasas*), each supported by a permanent and inalienable endowment (*waqf*), the ulama acquired a remarkable power and cohesiveness. The jurisprudents had their differences, of course, on both detail and theory, which in time resolved themselves into four major "schools" of legal interpretation in Sunni Islam. But in the end they agreed to differ, and, more importantly, to accept each other's orthodoxy.

It is tempting to see in the ulama the rabbis of Islam. In a sense the comparison is just. Both groups constituted a relatively well defined class that enjoyed the power and prestige of a religious elite, and both received a standardized education in jurisprudence in an institutionalized setting. Neither were legislators in the strict sense, but both rabbis and ulama were at the same time the conservative guardians and the cautiously innovative exegetes of a long and complex legal tradition. Yet there were important differences. The rabbis were assigned a political role among their fellow Jews, first by the Romans and Sasanians and then by their Muslim masters. The Jews were granted a degree of community autonomy in the millet system under which they lived in the Roman and Sasanian empires as well as in the Abode of Islam, and the rabbis served, by delegation and with the acceptance of their coreligionists, as the administrators of that restricted autonomy. They not only maintained a legal tradition; they also administered it, as judges and surrogates of a higher judicial authority, that of the patriarch, the exilarch, or the geonim.

The ulama, in contrast, were only one element among the classes and elites contesting for power in the Abode of Islam. Before Ottoman times they neither possessed nor delegated any political authority, and they eschewed the administration of the Islamic law, a task that fell to the government-appointed and supported qadi. Their power lay elsewhere, in the prestige they enjoyed as the custodians of the obviously Islamic component in what was professedly an Islamic society; in their independence of the state, which they could castigate or applaud as circumstances dictated; and in the network of marriages by which they could forge ties with other powerful classes like the large land-owners and the wholesale merchants. Unlike their episcopal counterparts, the ulama did not hold the keys of the kingdom in their hands; they could neither bind nor loose nor force a caliph to his knees or out of the Church. But they possessed a genuine political power. Like their Jesuit contemporaries in Europe, they educated an Islamic intelligentsia in their school system: after the eleventh century higher education across the face of Islam was uniquely ulama-inspired and directed in madrasas where they shaped Islamic consciences and indeed Islam itself through the instrument of the Islamic law, the *sharia*.[38]

# CHAPTER FOUR

# The Law

## Torah, Mitzvot, Halakot

The tradition of a society governed by law is very old in the Middle East, and where societies were governed by sovereigns whose powers were intimately bound up with divine descent, designation, or approbation, the distinction between secular and religious law is not easily or even profitably made. The Israelites were no exception in this regard, and even the oldest parts of the Bible contain legal codes not very dissimilar from those we find among the Babylonians and Canaanites.[1] Then, with the return from the Exile, there is silence. The text of the Torah was complete, and there would be no more than the 613 absolute scriptural ordinances (*mitzvot*) that the rabbis later totted up in the Bible.[2] What we have in place of the direct written testimony of the earlier period is circumstantial evidence for continued legal activity among the Jews. There is the presence of a class of scribes (*soferim*) devoted to the study of Scripture and part of whose activity must surely have been legal in nature—that is, devoted to the discovery of "derived" legal statutes (*halaka* pl. *halakot*) that are only implicit in the Scripture.[3] The priests were the chief wardens and interpreters of the Mosaic law, but from Maccabean times onward, the party known as the Pharisees, whose chief preoccupation was also the Mosaic law, were on the scene.

In attempting to understand the Jewish legal tradition between the Exile and the beginnings of the Talmud, one might turn in two other directions: to Philo and to whatever legal evidence can be elicited from the Dead Sea scrolls.[4] Philo, the Hellenized Jewish intellectual of Alexandria, was not much interested in legal enactments as such, and yet he was engaged in commenting, from his own Hellenized philosophical point of view, on the legal books of the Bible, and so it is possible to understand something at least of his view of the positive precepts of the law—those concerning the Sabbath, for example. Philo, it has been maintained, followed Palestinian practice, or, with equal emphasis, was chiefly influenced by Greco-Egyptian legal custom. The truth may lie somewhere between the two theses, though what "Palestinian practice" was in Philo's day is not easy to discern.

The Dead Sea scrolls have provided a new and unexpected glimpse into the evolution of Jewish law. Though the community was admittedly sectarian, we must recall that there was probably no truly "normative" Judaism in the centuries just before and after the beginning of the Christian era, and that the Qumran Covenanters, and so their view of halaka, may fruitfully be compared with other contemporary Jewish views of the law and its derived positive prescriptions.

Two facts emerge at once: the Qumran community, like most other Jewish groups, derived its laws from an exegesis (*midrash*) of Scripture, and had no recourse to a theory of an oral law like that (later?) proposed by the rabbis. Indeed, the Essenes at Qumran did not hesitate to write down and publicly promulgate in the form of lists or orders their own exegetically derived halakot. When it came to exegesis, they did, however, draw an interesting distinction. All law was contained in Scripture, including the Prophets, and although some precepts flow from a plain understanding of the text, other "hidden" precepts can be derived only by the special understanding possessed by the "Sons of Zadok."

The hidden precepts of the Essenes are not the legal siblings of the rabbis' oral law, since this latter included halakot not explicitly derived from the written Torah, an alien notion at Qumran. The scrolls' hidden precepts stand rather closer to a Gnostic understanding of Scripture that distinguished, in all its manifestations, between a plain and a hidden sense of revelation, the latter the privileged terrain of the adepts of the community. The question of the oral law apart, the community at Qumran shows little that is surprising or anomalous in the evolution of Jewish law.

Post-Exilic Judaism is absolutely consistent in deriving its positive law directly from Scripture, narrowly from the Torah and somewhat more widely, on occasion, from the Prophets as well. Essenes, Pharisees and Hellenizers, rabbis and Karaites all turned to God's revealed Word for instruction on the good to be done and the evil to be avoided. There were differences, of course, on how literal or broad the scrutiny (*midrash*) of Scripture, which was the fount and origin of the law, should be. The fundamental disagreement arose over whether there was any other source from which religious law might be derived. The Sadducees, Essenes, and Karaites denied that there was such; the Pharisees, followed by the rabbis and the main body of medieval Judaism, affirmed the existence of a tradition from the Fathers that was an equally authoritative matrix of halakot.

## The Oral Law

The genesis and evolution of this tradition from the Fathers is overgrown, like much else in the study of revelational religions, with claims of absolute antiquity: "from the Fathers" meant at base from Moses and so from God.[5] All the historian can do is note that the claim for such was first explicitly advanced by the Pharisees, as both Josephus and the Gospels bear witness, and denied explicitly by the Sadducees and implicitly by the Essenes. It has long been assumed that the Pharisees' tradition from the Fathers was in fact the unwritten Torah frequently alluded to in the Talmud.

We cannot tell exactly when the notion of an authoritative oral tradition arose among the Jews. All religious communities seem to claim to have such, and almost from the beginning, but these same communities have to ascribe a greater antiquity to their "tradition" than the documentary evidence justifies. The Pharisees affirmed it in the last century before the Christian era and the contemporary Sadducees denied its binding authority, but not until the basic documents of "rabbinic Judaism" began to emerge in the era after 200 c.e. are we given a "foundation story" that explains and justifies the existence and authority of what is in effect a second Torah. Moses, we are told in the Mishna treatise "Pirqe Aboth," was given two Torahs on Sinai, one to be written down—our

Bible—and another that was not to be committed to writing and that was said to contain everything the community would need for its information and guidance. From Moses this oral Torah was transmitted to Joshua, thence to a series of more or less anonymous figures down to the first identifiable individuals, who date from Second Temple times.[6] This oral Torah was written down and stands behind the Mishna of the rabbi called Judah the Prince.

## Mishna and Talmud

So goes the received version of the story of the oral Torah, and though it grounds and validates the rabbinically derived halakot, it is difficult to square it with the Mishna that is now before us and that is never referred to as a written document by the subsequent sages who commented on it. It is perhaps more accurate to suppose that from the time of Rabbi Akiba (d. ca. 135 C.E.) onward there were in circulation written halakot, and that when these had been collected and arranged, they were committed to memory by a professional reciter, a *tanna*; and that once the whole had been memorized and recited, it was regarded as "published," that is, it possessed a canonical authority. Subsequent additions were made down to the time of Rabbi Judah, who made a new and, as it turned out, definitive edition of the Mishna. It is a guess, no more.[7]

As we possess it, Judah's Mishna is divided into six "orders" (*sedarim*) that are devoted to a discussion of the most minute details of the laws governing: (1) agricultural produce and the shares of it owed to the priests and Levites ("Seeds"); (2) the prescribed holy days ("Festivals"); (3) women ("Women"); (4) property, damages, penalties ("Damages"); (5) temple paraphernalia ("Holy Things"); and (6) ritual purity and impurity ("Purities").[8] To the secular eye, the Mishna is an extraordinarily detailed casebook compiled by lawyers for their own use and instruction. It deals chiefly with ceremonial practice, much of it already irrelevant to Jewish life in the new Diaspora, and has little to say on matters of ethics, theology, or devotion, with which Jews of that and later ages also concerned themselves. But it surely did not appear irrelevant to its editors, who preserved its contents as a testament to a tradition that they regarded, in the best Pharisaic manner, as the heart and essence of Judaism. The Covenant was the law, and the Mishna was the pledge of fidelity to both by a new generation of Jews.[9]

As has already been remarked, the Hebrew Mishna received two separate sets of Aramaic commentary ( *gemara*) in the generations following Rabbi Judah, one at the hands of the newly emergent rabbinic circles in Babylonia, and another at the hands of the Palestinian rabbis. The sages who labored over the gemara were known, in contradistinction to the earlier "reciters" (*tannaim*), as "speakers" (*amoraim*), and their number stretches from the successors of Rabbi Judah in the early third century to the last distinguished members of the declining academies at the close of the fifth century.[10] The body of halakot, whether derived by the exegesis of Scripture or by recourse to the oral tradition, was now complete, and the function of the amoraim was essentially to explicate, reconcile, and expound the inner logic of the halakot enunciated by their tannaitic predecessors.

The Mishna with its respective gemarot took final form as the two Talmuds, the Babylonian and the Palestinian, of which the former gained preeminent authority.[11] Though neither was intended to be, nor in fact became, the final word on Jewish law, the respect given to both Talmuds stemmed from the fact that they were the products of a scholarly and legal consensus at a time when the "academy," a rather overformal term for circles of teachers and their students, and the religious court (*bet din*) shaped and guided Jewish life without peers or rivals.[12] But no matter how great its authority, neither Talmud was a legal code; it was rather a shorthand transcription of discussions concerning legal questions that occupied lawyers from the second to the fifth century of the Christian era.

## Code and Commentary

The disengagement of the halakot, positive legal precepts with binding authority, from the surrounding mass of discussion, debate, and speculation occurred during the Islamic period of Jewish history and continued among scholars who lived in the rapidly expanding Jewish community outside the Abode of Islam, and at a time when the former paramount authority of the Middle Eastern rabbinic circles was flowing to new centers and new scholars.[13] Only two examples need be cited here. The *Mishneh Torah* of Moses Maimonides, which was written in Cairo and completed in 1190 C.E., though not the first such, is a genuine code produced by a scholar who belonged to a larger intellectual tradition than that of the Talmud.[14] Maimonides was a philosopher and theologian of the first order who was schooled in both Greek rationalism and the by then sophisticated legal traditions of Islam. His *Mishneh Torah* reflects both those strains in its introductory discourse on the modes of knowledge and the foundations of Judaism, its logical arrangement of the halakot, and its exclusion of what Maimonides judged to be irrelevant or nonlegal material.

Maimonides' view of the law was to a large degree determined by his political theory, much of which derived from the Muslim philosopher al-Farabi (d. 950), and through him from Plato.[15] For Maimonides no less than for al-Farabi, the prophet was both philosopher and lawgiver. By his surpassing intelligence, he had attained to—or been granted (there are important nuances here)—eternal truths, and by the power of his imaginative faculty he converted them into law. Law, then—revealed law—had the twofold aspect of regulating human life and society, just as human law did, and embodying the same truths that the philosopher struggled to achieve.

The Torah, in Maimonides' view, has this same double purpose: to order society and to bring humans to an understanding of the highest truths; in sum, an ethical and religious purpose. To concentrate exclusively on the first, as many of the talmudic scholars did, was simply to enter the grounds of the royal palace without going inside. To understand the second and more profound intent of the Torah, one must penetrate deeper into the mysteries of revelation through the use of allegorical exegesis, and this is in fact one of the purposes of his systematic treatise called *Guide of the Perplexed*.[16] Elsewhere Maimonides was far more direct, and presented in dogmatic form the articles of faith necessary for salvation, and so formulated the nearest thing Judaism had to a formal creed.

Maimonides provided guidance on the ethical intent of the Torah as well, guidance that must have sounded alien indeed in a *bet ha-midrash*. In a remarkable passage in the *Guide* (3.32), he compared God's indirect yet purposeful working through natural causes with his similar activity among humankind. Moses was given the law to modify pagan custom for the better, and so provide a bridge from idolatry to a belief in the unique God. The law appears, then—and most clearly in its cultic and sacrificial aspects—to be a transitional and ameliorative instrument rather than final and perfect, at least when viewed from a historical perspective.

This was not a widely shared view, but even among the traditionalists the Talmud was not looked on as a legal system that had been frozen in permanent stasis. A generation before Maimonides a French scholar, Rabbi Solomon ben Isaac (d. 1105), now generally known as Rashi, had written an immensely learned and exhaustive commentary on the Talmud that cast new light on its meaning and interpretation.[17] Other scholars continued to render legal responsa to Jewish communities all over the European continent and the Islamic empire.[18] Maimonides had ignored much of this new legal material in his somewhat idealized version of the law, but other, later attempts at codification were more responsive to the changing circumstances of Jewish life.[19] One such code eventually gained a position of almost absolute authority, the *Shulkhan Aruk* or *Set Table* of Joseph Caro (d. 1575). But no authority was absolute in the face of the Torah and the Talmud, and the *Shulkhan Aruk* underwent its own revisions, though chiefly in the form of deferential glosses and commentaries.[20]

## A Law for Christians

To return to the first century, the Gospels present Jesus in a world in which the Pharisees' preoccupation with the halakot is very much in the foreground. Jesus appears to have been "observant" as that term was generally understood in his day—he kept the Sabbath, for example, and participated in the Passover liturgy—but he clearly did not share the Pharisees' views on how close that observance should be: whether one might violate the letter of the Sabbath rest to perform an act of compassion, for instance, or whether ritual purity was a higher value than winning souls.[21] These were debatable questions, surely, in any era, but on other occasions Jesus appeared to suggest that it was not an argument about legal theory but rather his own messianic presence that rendered the ceremonial halakot moot, a theme that was richly developed by Paul.[22]

Not all of Jesus' Jewish followers construed the advent of the messianic age as abrogating either the mitzvot or the halakot—witness James and the observant Christian-Jewish circles in Jerusalem—but Paul did. He argued fiercely, if occasionally with some personal ambivalence, that the establishment of a New Covenant meant that the Mosaic law both as a general concept and in its specific precepts was no longer binding on the Christian who had found manumission from sin not in observance but in redemption. Jesus' death, Paul declared, bought freedom from sin and from its necessary corollary, the law. But in those selfsame letters Paul laid down his own Christian halakot for the regulation of a Christian life, and the elders and overseers of the early Christian community showed the same dual concern for faith and morals. Faith there must be, but faith alone would not suffice. The Christians, no less than the Pharisees, had to hold themselves apart from the practices of the pagan world that surrounded them, and precepts were set forth to regulate their conduct.[23]

## Canon Law

Much can be gathered from the preaching and catechetical teaching of the early Christian Fathers and from the anonymous "Apostolic constitutions" of 150 to 400 c.e. But there were, in addition, the disciplinary canons enacted by the provincial synods and ecumenical councils of bishops of the fourth and fifth centuries. This legal material continued to accumulate with each new council, but not until Emperor Justinian (r. 527–565) offered his own codification of Roman law in his Corpus Juris did the Church attempt to put its own juridical house in order. The Antiochene lawyer John, later the patriarch of Constantinople (r. 565–577), drew up his *Collection of Ecclesiastical Canons*, the antecedent of all later codes of canon law, which arranged the conciliar enactments by subject matter rather than chronologically by council. As a further innovation, he introduced into his collection certain patristic regulations, canons drawn up by Saint Basil, for example. Somewhat later John brought together those civil laws of Justinian that pertained to religious matters.

Justinian's translation of religious questions into civil law was in no way extraordinary. The process had begun as early as Constantine, who legislated on the Sunday rest, celibacy, and divorce. Far from usurping the Church's judicial prerogatives, Justinian's legislative work openly and officially recognized the parity of civil and canon law in a Christian Roman empire: whatever the ecclesiastical canons forbid, the civil statutes also forbid. The Church was accepted as a legislative partner of the state, just as earlier bishops had been granted the right to hear civil appeals. Indeed, by the time of Justinian, the Christian bishop had became a major administrative official, and was frequently used as a check on the unscrupulousness of secular functionaries at all levels of provincial administration.

The canons collected under Justinian were merely the first step in a long process that soon began to include another source in Church law. Very early on the bishop of Rome had begun issuing his own statutes in the form of written responses to inquiries or requests from other bishops. These papal responsa were called decretals—the earliest dates from 385 c.e.—and as the pope's authority increased, they too began to be regarded, along with the conciliar decrees, as a source of Church law. Thus there grew up in Western Christendom a body of statute law that constituted the basis for a legal tradition: books of collected canons and decretals, schools in which to teach them, and lawyers produced by those schools to explicate and enlarge them. By far the most important collection of canons was the *Decretum*—its formal title was *The Concordance of Discordant Canons*—edited and carefully arranged by the canon lawyer Gratian sometime around 1140.[24] There were later additions since the popes continued to issue decretals, commonly called "bulls" with reference to the papal seal (*bulla*) that authenticated them, but Gratian's book continued to serve as the basic text for the Church's growing corps of canon lawyers.[25]

## Quranic Statute

To pass even from Justinian to Muhammad, who was born only a few years after the death of that emperor, is to move from the province of a millennial tradition of Roman law codes and all the apparatus of a sophisticated legal scholasticism to the shadowy domains of unwritten tribal custom and of a society in slow and uncertain transition from nomadic to sedentary life. The Quran, particularly in its later suras, prescribes normative enactments, as Muhammad struggled to reform, in the light of a new Islamic consciousness, the customary practices (*sunna*) of his fellow Arabs. To the rabbinic scholar, Muhammad's enactments might appear to be taqqanot, the creation of new institutions to improve the conditions of social, economic, and religious life. But they were, in the eyes of the Prophet and his fellow Muslims, genuine mitzvot, absolute scriptural injunctions.[26]

However the historian might view it, the Quran presented itself as a divine revelation with a direct and explicit connection to those earlier and authentic revelations given to the Jews and the Christians, the *Tawrat* and *Injil* as Muhammad called them. Like those earlier Scriptures—Muhammad may have been uncertain about the contents of the Gospels—the Quran was intended to spell out what *islam*, "submission to the will of God," signified in terms of concrete human acts. Some small part of the quranic injunction is devoted to what might broadly be called ceremonial or liturgical acts: prayer, fasting, and so forth. But most specific acts prescribed or forbidden have to do with personal status, such as the treatment of heirs, women, slaves, and orphans; with the reformation of morals, criminal procedures, and the observance of binding contracts. Muhammad could address these issues as they arose in his small community of believers. We may suppose that he rendered at least some other prescriptions that are not recorded in the Quran and, almost certainly, that Muhammad acted as sole judge and arbitrator for the Muslims.

## Sharia, the Muslim Way

Implicit in all Muhammad did and preached is the notion that there is an Islamic "way" (*sharia*), which resembled the Jewish and the Christian "way" in that it came from God, and which stood in sharp opposition to both the religious paganism and the degenerate tribal custom of the contemporary Arabs. But the Islamic way was no more explicit or formal than the random precepts of the

Quran that defined it, and at Muhammad's death in 632, God's revelation was ended and the Quran forever a closed Book. At that very moment, however, the Muslim community, which was endowed with only the most rudimentary religious and secular institutions, was poised on the threshold of an immense military and political expansion that would swiftly carry it from Spain to the Indus.

We possess only the vaguest idea of how the Muslims conducted their legal affairs in the first century after the death of the Prophet. The caliph was recognized as the chief judge (*qadi*) of the community, as Muhammad had been, and he delegated this judicial power to others in the provinces of the new Islamic empire. But how the qadis rendered their judgments to other Muslims— Muslim justice applied only to Muslims; Jews and Christians continued under their own juridical traditions—we can only surmise, though it was probably on the basis of local custom, caliphal instruction, their own understanding of the Quran, and perhaps an embryonic sense of an Islamic "tradition."[27]

Some found such pragmatic and even secular arrangements in God's own community unsettling. Out of that dissatisfaction, which was reinforced by political, financial, and tribal disenchantment with the current dynasty of Muslim rulers, arose in certain traditionist circles the first debates over what it meant to be a Muslim and to pursue an Islamic "way" in all its ethical and legal implications. The results are sketchy, but we can observe that to validate their conclusions those early pioneers in Muslim jurisprudence (*fiqh*) appealed not only to the Quran, as might be expected in a revealed religion, but increasingly to the practice (sunna) of the Prophet. This latter was by no means the only or even the chief method used to fashion the norms of Muslim conduct at that point; legal scholars could still resort, in certain cases, to local custom or, like the rabbis, exercise their own legal discretion.

## Prophetic Tradition

One jurist (*faqih*) would not have it so. The Egyptian Shafii (d. 820) argued in his important and influential *Essay* for the absolute priority in Islam of the custom of the Prophet over that of Muhammad's contemporaries and followers, no matter how well-intentioned or pious.[28] Further, he maintained, with great consequence, that the Prophet's sunna was authentically contained in the great body of reports (hadith) transmitted by those who had lived and worked with him.[29] And what of the Quran, God's own Word? Shafii had already confronted the issue: the Quran never contradicts the traditions, but the traditions from the Prophet explain the Quran. No sunna ever contradicts the Quran; rather they specify its meaning.[30]

Shafii had not only canonized the position of tradition in Islam; he had specified and attempted to defend the medium of its transmission, to wit, the body of hadith already circulating in pious and legal circles in his own day. Shafii knew perfectly well that many of those hadith contradicted others reported by the very same authority, and that others were simply contrary to reason or common sense. There were various ways of reconciling some traditions and rationalizing others, but the method that eventually came to be favored by those who accepted Shafii's premise, as all came eventually to do, was to scrutinize the *isnad* or chain of transmitters of the tradition in question.[31]

All isnads went back to the testimony of the generation of Muhammad's contemporaries, who were later canonized as the Companions of the Prophet."[32] Were they and the others in the chain reliable reporters? The question sounds like a historiographical one, and to some extent it was: were X and Y in the same place at the same time, to enable them to pass on the story? But when Muslims spoke of reliability, they meant moral probity, a quality that was eventually stipulated for the entire first generation of Muslims. The Companions of the Prophet may have enjoyed an ex post facto infallibility in the eyes of later generations of Muslim lawyers (*fuqaha*), but they were in fact and in theory mere eyewitness reporters of the words and deeds of the Prophet: there was no Pentecost and no laying on of hands at this critical point in the Islamic tradition. Nor was there any parallel to the unwritten Torah; Muhammad was simply and not unreasonably understood by Shafii and succeeding generations as the best interpreter of the Quran, and the conclusion flowed easily that the Prophet's interpretation of the Quran was best displayed in his own words and acts.

Jesus is described by the author of Hebrews as "in all things like us, sin alone excepted." Jesus was an exemplary model for

Christians, but neither of his primary images—that of *Christos Pantokrator*, Christ Regnant, in the Eastern Church or of Jesus Crucified in the Western—suggested emulation.[33] The Church found its moral heroes elsewhere, in the martyrs who "witnessed" their faith by dying for it or later the "confessors" who bore witness to it by their blameless lives. Muhammad was more genuinely "in all things like us"; there was no mirror-image Godhead to either outshine or overshadow the Prophet's humanity. Though the person and personality of Muhammad lie well concealed behind the Quran, which was delivered by him but is only very occasionally about him, there is no such reticence about the Prophet outside the Book. An enormous body of Prophetic reports were in early circulation in Muslim circles and they professed to give the Prophet's moral instruction on every conceivable subject. Moreover, they provided moral vignettes of Muhammad as statesman, military leader, political sage, husband, and father, at meals, at prayer, or on campaign. Tradition provides, then, a fully fleshed-out if at times self-contradictory portrait of the Prophet and it has served from the time of its construction in the eighth century down to the present as the template and measure of the ideal Muslim.[34]

## The Problem of the Hadith

The historical problem is that not everyone accepted, acted on, or even knew about the premise proposed by Shafii, and many of the oldest hadith concerning the Prophet have what were, by later standards, extremely untidy isnads. The fact that the later isnads are far more complete than the earlier ones has raised a great deal of modern skepticism on the historicity of most of the hadith, many of which are, in addition, tendentious and reflect issues and controversies that arose long after the Prophet.[35]

The Muslims were aware of at least some of these problems and long ago collected, examined, and attempted to verify the vast body of traditions that purportedly came down from the Prophet. And since it was a question of normative halakic hadith, not the haggadic or historical variety, it was chiefly lawyers who were engaged in this critical enterprise. It is their judgment that is reflected in the selection and arrangement of "sound" hadith in the great canonical collections of the late ninth century.[36]

The early legal theorists in Islam had grounded the case for their own view of the law on a consensus (*ijma*) of the scholars of their own somewhat casually defined "school." Shafii was uneasy with that notion of consensus and preferred, if there was no explicit hadith on a given subject, to appeal to the agreement of the entire Muslim community—its acceptance of a practice such as circumcision or of an institution such as the caliphate, for instance. To bolster his own wavering confidence in the legal applicability of consensus, Shafii not unnaturally cited a hadith to the effect that the umma would never agree in error.[37]

In the traditional Islamic view, then, the Quran was Scripture, whereas the sunna of the Prophet and, by extension, the consensus of the umma that was presumably reflected in the same sunna, was tradition, neither in the sense of customary law nor in the charismatic sense understood in the Christians' Apostolic tradition, but somewhat in the manner of the Mishna. The Mishna possesses some very imperfect isnads, few of which go back before Hillel and none before the Maccabees. For the earlier period one must always be content with "Moses received the Torah—always glossed to include the unwritten Torah—from Sinai and handed it on to Joshua, Joshua to the Elders, the Elders to the Prophets," and so on.[38] Constantine's biographer Eusebius is rather more detailed in drawing up in his *Ecclesiastical History* the lines of the Apostolic succession in the various episcopal sees of the Great Church, but bishops were not much given to reciting isnads of their predecessors back to the "Companions of Jesus" before pronouncing on faith and morals. Episcopal consecration sealed what was an internalized tradition; Islamic tradition, in contrast, was reported, often copied down by the recipient, and certified by the tradent in the manner of a contract.

Since the jurisprudents of Islam were essentially rabbis, not bishops speaking comfortably ex cathedra, they had early begun to employ various forms of legal reasoning that have been the staples of lawyers always and everywhere. In Islamic law, this use of legal reasoning is called *ijtihad* or "personal effort,"[39] and its most common formal manifestation is the argument from "analogy" (*qiyas*): A is explicitly forbidden, and since B is like A (aye, there's the rub!),[40] B is also forbidden. "Analogy" was acceptable to Shafii, as it was to most subsequent jurists, but uneasily and only if (1) it was used to erect "hedges for the law," to use the talmudic phrase, to protect observance and not to extend exceptions into general rules; (2) it start from the literal and not the allegorical understanding of the text; and finally, (3) it be regarded as the fourth and weakest of the "roots of the law" after the Quran, the custom of the Prophet, and the consensus of the umma.

## Consensus and the Law

Consensus is an often overlooked key to the sharia.[41] It arose of necessity from a system based on a revelation that was closed by the single definitive event of the Prophet's death rather than by a prolonged process of agreement as occurred in Judaism and Christianity. More, the Quran was pronounced in a narrow and underdeveloped society but had shortly to be applied in a cosmopolitan empire. The discrepancy was met in part by the rapid proliferation of hadith, but as a legal instrument the hadith soon collapsed under their own weight. For ninth-century Muslims there were too many of them to be true, just as for the modern non-Muslim they are too good to be true.

Quran-based reasoning had its own difficulties. Scriptural argument is always selective in the sense that for Jews, Christians, and Muslims alike all parts of the revelation—every book, chapter, verse, and, according to some, even the individual letters and the spaces between them—have significance so that the citation of any one of them is, in theory, decisive. The quranic *ipse dixit* is enough to settle a moral matter and the same attribute seems eventually to have prevailed in the case of the hadith. Such an attitude of "all's fair in Quran and hadith" leads inevitably to moral probabilism, namely, that any Quran- or hadith-supported position is a permissible one, and however attractive that position might be to radical or amateur moralists, it did not much recommend itself to Muslim jurists.[42] How, then, in the absence of a determining moral authority, was the Muslim to choose among the varying "probable" opinions founded on Quran or hadith, or, more discomfortingly, among the opinions of jurists who attempted to work out answers to moral questions by their own personal effort? The answer lay in consensus, the agreement of the Muslim community.

The agreement of the community of Muslims has its own seeds of anxiety, of course—in its suggestion, for example, that moral truth was what most Muslims thought it was rather than what God had decreed it was. A solution was quickly forthcoming in the already noted Prophetic saying that inevitably appeared in all discussions of the subject: "My community will never agree in error." Another approach to the matter was addressed in another widely circulated hadith. "You are better judges than I in temporal matters," the Prophet is reported to have said in addressing future generations, "and I am a better judge than you in what concerns religion." In matters of faith, then, the Quran and hadith rule alone; in matters of morality, community consensus will provide a reliable guide.

## The Lawyers and the Law

The early evolution of Islamic law took place in widely scattered centers across the Abode of Islam, and not even Shafii's attempts at imposing a kind of order on its development eradicated or even inhibited the continued growth of different schools of legal interpretation, each of them recognized as orthodox and legitimate by the others. Thus the Shafiite, Malikite, Hanafite, and Hanbalite schools founded by and named after early masters of Islamic jurisprudence flourished and continued to flourish among Muslims.[43] They differ on specific points of theory and practice, but their differences are not very substantial, nor do their practices much differ from the positive precepts of Shiite law, though this latter has a considerably divergent view of what lawyers call "the roots of jurisprudence."[44] The four major Sunni schools recognized, with varying degrees of enthusiasm, the Quran, the sunna of the Prophet (as expressed in the hadith), the consensus of the community, and a measure of personal interpretation (ijtihad) as the basis of the sharia. The Shiites, in contrast, relied heavily on the infallible teachings of the Imams and rejected the consensus of the community out of hand.

After Shafii and as a result of the debate over the validity of independent reasoning, the freedom granted to earlier jurists to elicit legal conclusions from even the most traditional material was severely circumscribed, and by about 900 C.E. a new consensus was developing, that the "gate of ijtihad" had closed.[45] The phrase has an ominous ring, but it should be understood in a sense comparable to that of the closure of the Talmud, as a herald for the advent of scholasticism, when scholars had to couch their legal speculations in the form of commentary and explication on an established body of masters, in this case the developed doctrine of the canonical schools.

The analogy with the Talmud should not be pressed too closely. In a sense the sharia or Islamic law was fundamentally in place by the beginning of the tenth century, just as the Mishna was complete in the third, and the two Talmuds by the sixth. But all these latter were formal texts, whereas the sharia continued to exist, even after the tenth century, in the form of a somewhat inchoate, if consensually agreed on, mass of propositions whose exact formulation had only as much authority as the jurisprudent from whose pen it came.

## *Adjustments*

A more serious consequence of the closing of the gate of ijtihad was to confirm the tendency in Islamic law—a tendency already present in talmudic speculation—to create a body of idealized law whose legitimate sources were so carefully and artificially defined that it became all but impervious to local custom and the changing circumstances of life under Islam. But even here Islamic jurisprudence no less than Jewish legal practice had at hand sophisticated resources. Though the qadi in his court had to judge cases on the letter of the sharia, the individual Muslim could resort to more informal types of arbitration, or could appeal away from the qadi's court to the jurisdiction known as *mazalim*.[46] The mazalim was a type of court of complaints that had its justification in the discretionary powers of the ruler and that could address grievances or inequities ignored by the sharia. Again, individual cases could be submitted to legal specialists known as *muftis* who, like their Jewish counterparts, could render a fatwa or responsum.[47] The muftis could neither judge nor legislate, and their fatwas had no binding force in the qadis' courts. But the appeal of the fatwa literature is that it reflects on how actual and specific cases were addressed by Muslim lawyers, and so supplies a corrective to the idealizing qualities of many sharia treatises.

The clash of the ideal and the real against the background of the sharia has led some scholars to look on the sharia as an impressive but unrealizable ideal that most Muslims ignored in practice. This judgment may, however, be as idealized as it claims the sharia to have been, and a closer inspection of at least some areas of legal practice has revealed a somewhat more complex reality. Commercial law in particular was a marvelously intricate exercise in enlarging the sharia categories dealing with commerce to permit the inclusion of a large body of customary law.[48] The sharia denied, for example, the validity of written documents in cases at law, but permitted their extensive and obviously indispensable use in dealing with commercial contracts.[49] And it was here too, in commercial law, that the lavish use of "devices" (*hiyal*), the legal fictions familiar from Roman and Jewish law, enabled Muslim merchants to bring their customary practice in line with the letter of the sharia.[50]

The needs of the state were less easily satisfied than those of the merchant by the resources of Islamic law. There had been no Jewish state since the dissolution of the Hasmonean monarchy early in the first century c.e., and so the Jews of the talmudic period had no need of either a secular law code or a constitutional theory. There were, however, Christian states—the Byzantine Empire was the first—and an Islamic empire that eventually dissolved into Islamic states. They differed in that the Christian states had an antecedent tradition of Roman law, and the later Roman emperors, both before and after they became Christian, had among their principal powers that of legislating. Thus civil and canon law could and did exist side by side, each influencing the other, but possessing separate and autonomous jurisdictions nonetheless.

Islam had no such tradition: the caliph was the chief judge of Islam, but he was never a legislator. The caliph, it was understood, did possess certain discretionary powers, if not to legislate then at least to ensure the general social and political circumstances under which the idealized Muslim life envisioned by the sharia might unfold.[51] These generalized powers were later called "policy" (*siyasa*). Though there was no lack of theory on the subject, siyasa had no real claim to autonomy, and there was no vehicle for either its expression or its promulgation until the later Middle Ages, when both the Mamluk rulers of Egypt and the Ottoman sultans began to legislate in a relatively open fashion.[52]

# CHAPTER FIVE

# Scripture and Tradition

## Midrash

Before the Talmud and hadith, there were the Torah and Quran, and those who affirmed that the latter were indeed sacred Scripture were committed to an understanding of what was meant and what was intended by the words of God in them.[1] There is no getting at the beginning of that process; we possess only sophisticated finished works of commentary on Scripture. But the existence of a class of professional scribes or bookmen (soferim) in the Jewish community after the Exile suggests that already the task of expounding the Jewish Scriptures for learned and laity alike was well under way. The work itself and some of the works that embody it are called midrash, and midrash is the single most characteristic act of post-Exilic Judaism.[2] The root from which the word derives means simply to "study" or "expound," but when it was connected with Scripture, it took on for many Jews the quality of a liturgical act.

From the available evidence we can conclude that in the decades following the return from exile two processes were occurring. In their own study centers, the soferim were extracting, comparing, and combining legal precepts (halakot) derived from Scripture, a work that came to term in the Mishna;[3] and in more general religious contexts, perhaps the forerunners of the later synagogues, these same and other scriptural texts were adduced and expanded, in the manner of a homily (*haggada*), for purposes of moral formation, edification, and piety.

We have already spoken of halakic midrash, the rabbinic process of extracting implicit statutes—as opposed to the explicit mitzvot—from the text, or even, just as frequently, from the *sense* of Scripture. Here we will examine the narrower sense in which midrash is, generally understood—that is, haggadic or homiletic midrash. Even though the two genres are distinguished here and elsewhere as a matter of course, there is no essential conflict between halakic and haggadic midrash. They differ widely in style, but their fundamental agreement rests on what has been called Jewish "monobiblism," the presence of a single, authoritative Scripture accepted by all interested parties. Whether explicitly referred to or not, the Bible underlies all Jewish midrash. There are, moreover, halakot in the homiletic midrashim and the haggadic method was often applied, as we shall see, to halakic material.

A further distinction must be drawn. Haggadic midrash, hereafter simply midrash, is a method that appears in many different contexts. Translations of the Bible are a prime locus for the exercise of the midrashic method, for example. The language of post-Exilic Judaism was changing from Hebrew to Aramaic in the immediate pre-Christian centuries.[4] Since large numbers of the laity could no longer understand Scripture in its original form, it was translated into the common Aramaic tongue of Palestine, just as it was turned into Greek at Alexandria for the Greek-speaking Jews living there and elsewhere in the Diaspora. The Alexandrian Greek translation, the Septuagint, whose origins are surrounded by stories calculated to guarantee its authenticity, was, for all its sometimes easy manner with the Hebrew text, still recognizably a translation.[5] The Aramaic treatments, called *targums*, were paraphrases rather than translations and often approached commentaries in their haggadic manner.[6] Their principal use was for oral liturgical recitation in the synagogue service.

## From Midrash to Midrashim

The targums are obviously midrashic but not yet midrashim in the formal, literary sense. The earliest preserved examples of the latter are the sectarian commentaries called *pesharim* from Qumran and the works of the rabbis, both tannaim and amoraim, of the talmudic era.[7] The latter fall into two general categories. The first or expositional midrash is a commentary proper that puts the midrashic method at the service of halakic concerns. It treats the Scripture in the order of its verses, each verse expounded by an appropriate tale or parable. The purely homiletic midrashim differ in two ways. First, they treat Scripture according to its liturgical divisions, that is, the Torah pericopes read daily in the synagogue over a cycle of three years or the "section" (*pesiqta*) reserved for Sabbaths and special festivals. Second, the homiletic exegete began each of the divisions of his work by citing a verse drawn from the Writings to which was added one or more explanations from different sources. The last of these was designed to lead into the homily proper, which generally confined its attention to one significant verse of the original pericope.

The earliest rabbinic midrashim, as has been remarked, had as their object the extraction of halakic material from Scripture by an application of the midrash method. They are, moreover, treasure-houses of Jewish biblical legend, and their composition stretches well into the Islamic era.[8] There are in fact stories similar to the rabbinic midrashim in both content and homiletic style in the Quran and many more in the "Tales of the Prophets" that began to circulate in Islam with the conversion of increasing numbers of Jews and Christians. It is not always clear who borrowed from whom in any given instance.[9]

## The How and the Why of Explaining Scripture

The development of midrash is not unlike the history of logic. There is a kind of logic in almost all forms of human thought, but it was only after arriving at a certain degree of self-consciousness about the process that the "rules" governing such thought were first formulated. Aristotle did not invent logic; he simple abstracted and formalized an operation many could perform but few could describe. The early soferim too may have been practicing midrash without knowing it, or at least formalizing the process, though their growing self-consciousness is clearly reflected in the encomium of the sofer and his work in the second-century B.C.E. *Wisdom of Jesus ben Sira* (39:1–8). Tradition, however, grants Jesus' contemporary Hillel the glory of being the Aristotle of Jewish midrash. Some of Hillel's rules for elucidating the meaning of a text were by then commonplace in the Greek and Roman rhetorical and philosophical schools—so commonplace, perhaps, that there was no need to "borrow" them in any formal sense of that word.[10]

If we turn from the methods of Jewish exegesis to trying to understand its motives and intent, we are confronted with a far more complex problem. A distinction is occasionally drawn between "pure" exegesis, which attempts to understand the meaning of a text, and "applied" exegesis, which has as its intent the eliciting of a scriptural answer to what was essentially a nonscriptural question.[11] The first type of midrash arises out of the obscurities, lacunae, and self-contradictions of Scripture itself, or the impossibility of accepting what the plain sense (*peshat*) says. There are words in the Bible whose meaning was obscure at best. Stories sometimes lacked important details, and biblical mitzvot do not always spell out the terms or conditions of their applicability.[12] Further, the Bible is a composite book, and its various enactments were not always harmonized by the original editors; the task fell to the exegetes. Finally, some of the accounts in the Bible—instances of polygamy and incest, for example—had to be explained and mitigated for a generation that found them somewhat less than edifying.[13]

It was a Pharisee, it should be noted, who codified the rules of exegesis, perhaps, as has been argued, because the Pharisees could not claim the priestly authority of the Sadducees and their scribes in the interpretation of Scripture, and so if they wished to depart from the literal sense, as the Sadducees refused to do, they had to justify their midrash carefully on technical grounds. But the Pharisees were not the only ones to "apply" Scripture to their own point of view. The community at Qumran did the same, and so did the followers of Jesus.[14] Pharisaic midrash, and the rabbinic midrash that grew out of it, had as its chief aim the extraction of a deeper understanding (and a wider application) of the legal and ethical principles inherent in Scripture. The Essenes and Christians had other interests: to read in the Scriptures the foreshadowing of future events, the future that was now present or still to come in the messianic age or the End Time.

## *Allegorical Exegesis*

The exegetical technique of both the Essenes and the Christians involves a kind of allegorizing in that it takes as its premise the principle that although Scripture is talking about one thing (the present), it is really referring to something else (the future). But the method of allegory found its broadest extension in Philo of Alexandria (ca. 20 B.C.E.–45 C.E.), whose understanding of "the other" was the whole body of contemporary Greek philosophy.[15] Philo understood well enough the value of the peshat, and could also compose moral midrash in the best Palestinian style. But his chief contribution to scriptural exegesis was his application of the peculiar Greek sense of *allegoria* (other-referent) and *hyponoia* (under-thought) to the Bible.[16] The Greeks, particularly the Stoics and Neoplatonists, allegorized Homer and the poets for much the same reason that Jewish exegetes "interpreted" patriarchal polygamy and incest: the stories were morally offensive and yet occurred in a context of divine inspiration. Philo did not allegorize on quite the same moral grounds, but rather because of his conviction that Scripture and philosophy were speaking of the same truths, though in different forms of discourse.[17] The Scriptures themselves invited allegorization, somewhat the way the poets did, by presenting things in a manner that made the literal interpretation offensive or unintelligible.

It was Paul who made allegoria a staple of the Christians' reading of Scripture.[18] In his Letter to the Galatians (4:21–27) he boldly pronounced the story of Abraham, Sarah, and Hagar an "allegory" and proceeded to unpack its true spiritual meaning. And it was he too who pioneered the notion that the Scriptures—for Paul and the other early Christians that meant only the Jewish Bible—foreshadowed the events of the coming Christian dispensation. Adam was the analogical "type" or model of the future (and now present) Messiah in that the sin of the first prefigured the redemptive death of the second Adam (Rom. 5:14), whereas the Israelites' experiences in Sinai occurred "typically" to warn the Christians of the results of resisting God—the same use to which the Quran puts the Bible. Succeeding generations of Christians were extremely fond of this foreshadowing or typological exegesis and so quite unintentionally ensured that the "Old Testament" of the Jews would always be linked to the "New" of the Christians, the prefiguring to the prefigured.

When we turn from Paul to the Gospels, we find ourselves in a not terribly different world. Here too the Bible (and the Apocrypha) are scrutinized for their foreshadowing of Jesus as the Messiah. None of this is particularly novel in the context of Jewish midrash—in Luke 4:16–30 Jesus is shown doing much the same thing in a Galilean synagogue service—and it was obviously a persuasive way of arguing Jesus' claims on a Jewish audience. The early Jewish Christians went a step further; one of their number, Symmachus, prepared a new Greek translation of the Bible. It no longer survives, but from Eusebius's remarks, it was almost certainly a targum that argued as well as translated. A very early example of Christian exegesis that comes directly out of a context of Jewish midrash, and perhaps written by a converted Jew, is the Letter of Barnabas, which allegorizes the Bible, particularly its dietary laws, in a quite remarkable fashion.[19]

## From the Gentiles to the Fathers

Over time the Christians lost their audience of Jews or Jewish converts to whom Barnabas addressed his letter, as a result they turned away from the methods of rabbinic midrash to the allegoria of Philo, which would be more congenial to the Hellenized, once Gentile, Christian. The Christian Fathers knew Philo's allegorical method very well. Whether or not they read Philo himself, they received ample instruction on allegorical interpretation from two who had: the early-third-century Alexandrian Christians Clement and Origen. All of these scholars—Philo, Clement, Origen, and their Greek and Latin successors—tried their hand at formalizing allegoria by subdividing it.[20] There was general agreement that both a literal and a "spiritual" sense of Scripture existed. A common division of the latter was into a moral sense not very different from rabbinic haggadic midrash and a Philonian allegoria that penetrated into the deeper, that is, philosophical truths embodied in the sacred book.

Though the Christian Fathers paid lip service to the literal sense of Scripture, they did not expend a great deal of exegetical energy on explaining it. This was not unnatural, perhaps, in the case of the Jewish Bible, whose mitzvot they had quite explicitly rejected. One who did take it seriously and who, as a Christian, was led to conclude that the Jewish Bible was not Scripture at all was the second-century Christian Marcion. Where Barnabas managed to embrace the Jewish Bible by allegorizing it almost beyond recognition, Marcion simply rejected it as unusable, unfitting, and unlikely the Word of God—not the God worshiped by the Christians, at any rate. Marcion was rejected by the Church in turn: he was excommunicated at Rome in 144 c.e. The Church kept the Jewish Scripture, though most of the Christian Fathers followed the example of Paul and the Gospels, offering a typological rather than a literal interpretation of what they called "The Old Testament,"[21] or else they followed where Philo had led, converting a "Mosaic philosophy" into a Platonic one.

In the end, the most influential early Christian interpreters of Scripture—Clement (ca. 156–215) and Origen (ca. 185–254) in the Greek East, Augustine (354–436) and Gregory the Great (540–604) in the Latin West—all recognized that various figurative or allegorical readings might complement, or even override, the literal sense of Scripture, and each had attempted to reduce them to some kind of order.[22] Origen thought there might be three levels of understanding Scripture: the literal, the moral, and the spiritual sense. Augustine argued for four: "what things are related as having been done," that is, the literal or historical sense of the text; "what things are foretold," the now familiar prophetic or typological sense; "what eternal things are intended there," a spiritual reading of the text; and "what we are intended to do," Scripture as moral guidance.

Augustine's fourfold scriptural understanding became popular throughout the Latin West, though without unanimous agreement on precisely what the divisions were. In subsequent discussions there was little disagreement about the literal sense of Scripture: the historical truth of the Bible and, to an even greater extent, the New Testament Gospels had to be taken seriously, while the moral sense remained the staple of both preaching and contemplation. Typology became less important in time since there was no longer any need to argue the case of Jesus as Messiah to Christians who now accepted the New Testament alone as irrefutable evidence for Christ as Savior. The spiritual sense also became the reading of choice for both the mystics and the theologians of the Church, as it did for their Jewish counterparts, all of whom found there divine truths hidden from the ordinary believer.

## Scripture and Tradition

Scriptural exegesis was no mere school exercise. The New Testament text became the battleground for the fierce debates over the nature of Jesus, God and man, that were waged in the fifth century and exegesis was the weapon that all the combatants wielded with both skill and conviction.[23] The scriptural witness, often couched in familiar, popular, and even homely language, had to be converted into the abstract and learned currency of theology, the language of choice of the Church's intelligentsia. Scripture, as it turned out, was merely the starting point. The steering mechanism was exegesis, and behind the exegesis, the helmsman at the rudder, stood another elemental principle: tradition.[24]

Judaism, Christianity, and Islam each possessed a Scripture that was, by universal consent, a closed Book. But God's silence was a relative thing, and his providential direction of the community could be detected and "read" in other ways. Early within the development of Christianity, for example, one is aware of a subtle balance operating between appeals to Scripture and tradition. It was not a novel enterprise. By Jesus' time the notion of an oral tradition separate from but obviously connected to the written Scriptures was already familiar, if not universally accepted, in Jewish circles. Jesus and the Pharisees debated the authority of the oral tradition more than once, and though he does not appear to have denied the premise, Jesus, his contemporaries remarked, "taught on his own authority," not on that of some other sage. He substituted his authority for the tradition of the Fathers. Thus Jesus was proposing himself as the source of a new tradition handed on to his followers and confirmed by the Holy Spirit on the day of Pentecost.

The Christian view that there was a tradition distinct from the Scriptures may have begun with the early understanding of Scripture as synonymous with the Bible—serious exegetical attention did not begin to be paid to the Gospels until the end of the second century—whereas the "tradition" was constituted of the teachings and redemptive death of Jesus, both of which Jesus himself had placed in their true "scriptural" context.[25] Thus, even when parts of Jesus' teachings and actions had been committed to writing in the Gospels, and so began to constitute a new, specifically Christian Scripture, the distinction between Scripture in the biblical sense and tradition in the Christian sense continued to be felt in the Christian community.[26]

## Bishops and the Rule of Faith

If the Christian "handing down" (*paradosis*) came from Jesus, its witnesses and transmitters were the Apostles. The written Gospels go back to them and so does that other, unwritten part of the tradition that in the second century came to be called "the rule of faith" or "the rule of truth," and that, in the words of Irenaeus, was "received from the Apostles and guarded in the Church by the succession of presbyters." Here the Apostolic tradition, which included the correct interpretation of Scripture as well as certain prescribed forms of behavior, is explicitly tied to the bishops' being the direct spiritual descendants of the Apostles. This notion was formalized about 175 C.E. and was held by the entire Church.[27]

The bishops spoke, then, with the authority of the Apostolic tradition behind them. At times their voices were single but authoritative, that of an Ignatius, an Irenaeus, a Basil, or a Chrysostom, but there was also a broad stream of consensual tradition that manifested itself by the bishops sitting in synods or, from the fourth century, in the ecumenical councils of the Great Church. They might refer to Scripture, but Scripture was not their justification any more than it was for the rabbis in the Mishna.[28] But unlike their rabbinical counterparts, the bishops' synodal pronouncements were cast in the form of dogma—"It has been decided"—the voice was that of the Apostolic tradition and so of Jesus himself. Once expressed, it suffered no appeal.

The "teachings of the Fathers" was an important ingredient in the formulation of Christian doctrine and of canon law, but its influence is no less visible in the interpretation of Scripture.[29] In all three religious communities, Jewish, Christian, and Muslim, tradition controlled the interpretation of Scripture in the first instance by its definition of the canon of sacred writings, by its choice of proof texts, and by its authoritative understanding of the meaning of those texts. Attacks on tradition and its guardians were made by appealing back to a literalist reading of Scripture and an assertion of its absolute priority, as was done by the Sadducees and Karaites in Judaism and, somewhat differently, by the Hanbalis and Zahiris in Islam and the Protestant reformers of Christianity. Attacks might also be made by recourse to an alternate Gnostic form of tradition, one more akin to a private revelation, which permitted a more allegorical and spiritual reading of the sacred book and so freed the adept from the law of the traditionalists. This was the approach of the Jewish Kabbalists, Christian Gnostics, and the Islamic Shiite and "Esotericist" groups.

## Quranic Exegesis

Since the Quran was not a historically conditioned revelation but rather reflects an eternal heavenly archetype, the "Mother of the Book" (Quran 13:39; etc.), composed of the same Arabic words, the Muslim approach to its exegesis was initially quite different from that pursued by the Jews and Christians, though the Quran did not easily suffer either translation or paraphrase.[30] On the Christian premise, Jesus was his own revelation. He could teach its significance with authority and pass on that teaching to his disciples in a formal and imperative fashion. Muhammad, in contrast, was the conduit of God's revelation, much as Moses was, and during his own lifetime there was no question that he and only he was the authoritative interpreter of that revelation for the Muslim community. His verbal explanations of the Quran formed part of the later collected body of hadith already noted.

We may posit, then, a body of oral tradition in early Islam, some of it historical narrative, later incorporated into the Lives of the Prophet; some of it halakic, the discrete pieces eventually shaped into Islamic law; and some, finally, exegetical in character.[31] These overneat categories were by no means observed by Muslim authors themselves. Since they, like us, were using quranic texts to illuminate the life of Muhammad and vice versa, long exegetical passages occur in early biographies of the Prophet, whereas professed works of exegesis (tafsir) devoted considerable attention to describing the historical circumstances surrounding the revelation of individual suras or even verses of the Quran.

According to one tradition, there was an early prohibition against interpreting the Quran.[32] It does not seem to have been much observed, however.[33] The earliest identifiable types of quranic exegesis were very similar to the familiar forms of Jewish haggadic midrash, and showed some of the same motives: to fill in gaps in quranic narratives, and to construct a genuine Islamic piety.[34] Most of the narratives in question were biblical and, according to the Muslim tradition itself, details for their haggadic elaboration were supplied by new converts with a particular knowledge of the Jewish tradition, both biblical and midrashic.

Fashioning an Islamic piety through homiletic means is not the same as deriving a body of legal enactments—*hukm*/pl. *ahkam*, in this context the semantic equivalent of the Hebrew *halakot*—out of Muslim Scripture. It is not certain precisely when the Muslim exegetes turned to the common Jewish practice of what was called halakic exegesis,[35] but in order to achieve this they had first to establish the so-called occasions of revelation, the contextual setting of each revelation.[36]

## *The Quranic Commentary*

A common form of Muslim commentary on the Quran is the explication of the text itself, a procedure that presumes the existence of an authoritative canonical text. The language of the Quran was, of course, Arabic, a "clear Arabic speech," in the Scripture's own words (Quran 16:103, 26:195). If quranic Arabic was "clear" to Muhammad's audience at Mecca and Medina, as it surely must have been to some degree, it is not so to modern scholars, and there has been considerable controversy over whether the diction of the Quran was a local dialect, perhaps that of the Quraysh of Mecca, which is the traditional view, or a kind of ecumenical art-speech common to Bedouin oral bards.[37] Nor was it entirely "clear" to a later generation of Muslims, many of whom did not have Arabic as their native tongue, and who turned in a somewhat unexpected direction for help in the explication of the text—to the works of the otherwise reprehensible pre-Islamic poets. This turning promoted a parallel activity in the collection and editing of that poetry.

Many of these developments in Islamic exegesis are traditionally attributed to Muhammad's much younger cousin Ibn Abbas

(d. 687), but like many other such attributions in early Islamic history, its object may have been to confer antiquity on something that occurred a century or more later.[38] What we know for certain is that most of the earliest Islamic exegesis was assimilated into the *Collection of Explanations for the Exegesis of the Quran*, called simply *The Exegesis* (*al-Tafsir*), of al-Tabari (d. 923), which from that day to this has held pride of place in the Muslim interpretation of the Quran.[39] *The Exegesis* proceeds majestically through the Quran sura by sura, combining legal, historical, and philological comment of great density, and it supports each judgment by a chain of authorities going back to Muhammad's own contemporaries, the famous Companions of the Prophet.

Since he occasionally addressed himself to the question, it appears from al-Tabari's commentary that in his day there was already understood to be another distinction in exegetical approach that cut across the categories just discussed: that between *tafsir* or "plain" exegesis, and *tawil*, which is often broadly understood as allegorical exegesis. The distinction may go back to the Quran itself (3:7), which seems to suggest that there are two kinds of verses in Scripture, those whose meaning is clear and those that require some kind of explanation, which the Quran itself calls tawil.[40] The explanation may originally have been no more than the application of personal reasoning (*ijtihad*) or research (*nazar*) to the text, as opposed to the acceptance on authority of the plain meaning— a distinction current, and debated, in legal circles. On that understanding, the difference between tafsir and tawil was not between exoteric and esoteric passages but rather between clear and ambiguous ones. Where tawil took on its allegorical association was its use in "applied exegesis," that is, the use of exegetical principles to elicit from Scripture dogmatic and mystical understandings of which both Muhammad and the Quran were perhaps totally innocent.

## *Challenging the Tradition*

Most of the commentators and commentaries discussed to this point operated within a tradition that regarded the body of hadith as the primary exegetical instrument for understanding the Quran, particularly on legal matters, much in the way the Talmud served that end vis-à-vis the Torah in Judaism. But the tradition did not go unchallenged. In both religious contexts there were challenges from "spiritualists" who claimed a deeper understanding of the Book, and hence a freedom from the body of positive prescriptions that the sages had exegetically extracted from it by resort to "tradition." The Essenes and the Christians confronted the Pharisees with just such a special understanding in their day, as later the Kabbalists did the rabbis. In Islam, Sufi and Shiite alike could counterpose the spiritual tradition passed on by their spiritual fathers and infallible Imams to the tradition-derived halakot of the jurisprudents.

But the challenge could be mounted in another way. Josephus's brief remarks about the Sadducees characterize them as a group that rejected any law not explicitly contained in the Torah. This was a direct denial of the Pharisees' tradition of the Fathers: the Torah alone was revelation, and it should be interpreted in a direct, literal fashion; all else is at best speculation and at worst innovation. We hear this charge once again in Judaism, there urged by a group called the Karaites against Babylonian rabbis of the eighth century. As we have already seen, it was also a fundamental charge of the Reformers against the Roman Church's interpretation of Scripture.

The Karaites were literally "readers" who confined their reading to Scripture and attempted to live according to its explicit precepts and those alone.[41] We do not know how the Karaites managed this in a society already remote from the mores and manner of life of the patriarchal age. Literalism brought freedom from the rabbinic halakot, it is true, yet many of these latter were not the "burden" sometimes suggested by Christian sources but effectively brought the biblical mitzvot into line with local custom and evolving circumstances, much as the hadith did in Islam. The Karaites' attraction was the threat they posed to the power of the rabbinate.[42] But it is doubtful whether the millennium-old Torah could indeed serve in its literal sense as a normative code for an eighth-century Jewish community, and the version of a Torah society put forward by the Karaite leader Anan ben David may have foundered on its own literalism.

A later generation of Karaites under Benjamin al-Nihawandi and Daniel al-Qumisi took a different path; they granted Jews the privilege of being their own rabbis, of constructing their own

Talmud out of a commonly held Torah. It was, once again, an attractive possibility, and Karaism spread far from its Babylonian place of origin to Jewish communities all over the Abode of Islam and beyond. The intellectual leadership turned away from the mitzvot in what at first seems like an unexpected direction, to philosophical speculation and the allegorical interpretation of Scripture. They may have been following an Islamic lead. As the early Muslim theologians known as Mutazilites had shown, Scripture could be controlled as effectively by rational inquiry as by an appeal to tradition.

In Islam we find distinct parallels to the Karaite position in the Kharijites, whose sense of Islamic community has already been discussed. The Kharijites attempted to establish a Muslim community and a Muslim way of life based on the Quran without benefit of "interpreting" the plain meaning of the text, and again like the early Karaites, took a severe stance toward associating with those who did not share their outlook. The Kharijites were putting forward their views late in the seventh century, well before the imposing body of hadith and its derived prescriptions were in place, and so they were likely reacting to what they construed as worldly and non-Islamic behavior rather than to an oppressive tradition.

## Tradition in Islam

Tradition was and is a powerful force in Islam. Though the evidence is not plentiful, it can hardly be doubted that the tribal life of the pre-Islamic Arabs, and that of their seventh-century brethren in the somewhat more urban milieus of Mecca and Medina, were governed by sunna, custom either decreed or instituted by an individual that later became the common practice of the tribe. There are instances of the Prophet himself regarding his own acts as setting a precedent for the umma, but the firmest evidence for the existence of the idea that the custom of the Prophet was somehow normative in Islam is its inclusion in the oath sworn by the third caliph, Uthman, at his accession in 644.[43]

Shafii neither invented nor popularized hadith as a form of popular piety; he was discussing the priority of certain legal principles. The broader reach of hadith may be observed in the "traditionists" (ahl al-hadith), a large and amorphous category of Muslims who,

like the Kharijites, longed for a Quran-oriented society, now supplemented by that idealized version of the earlier generation of
Muslims that found its definitive portrait in the hadith. They venerated the Quran next to God himself, and inclined toward a rev-
erentially strict interpretation of its text.

Opposition to the traditionists came from Islam's nascent theologians, the *ahl al-kalam* or "partisans of dialectic," particularly
from the group known as the Mutazilites. Whether the Mutazilites
rejected hadith or, as seems more likely, took a more hypercritical
view of it than was common in most Muslim circles is not known.
They preferred to rely on the Quran, which they did not hesitate
to interpret metaphorically in order to avoid the gross anthropomorphisms of the simple-minded pietists. But their dispute with
the traditionists went deeper than this. The latter's veneration for
the *ipsissima verba* of the Quran and the Mutazilite insistence on
using dialectical methods of analysis came to term in the profound
debate on whether the Quran was created, as the Mutazilites and
tradition asserted, or whether it was eternal, coeval and coequal
with God.[44]

## Tradition and Reason in Islamic Exegesis

For the Mutazilites, an uncreated and eternal Quran was a theological affront to a unique God as well as a manacle that chained
human reason and conscience to a text, however revered the latter
might be. In traditionist eyes the uncreated Quran was a mysterious embodiment of the sacred, an almost sacramental link between a transcendent God and his earthly creation. In a verbal
struggle in which all the weapons belonged to the dialecticians, it
is difficult to piece together the nuances of the traditionist position, but out of the ahl al-hadith came two Islamic "schools,"
those of Ahmad ibn Hanbal (d. 855) and Dawud ibn Kalaf (d. 884),
from which a coherent position can be derived. Both insisted on
the evident (*zahir*; Dawud's followers were called Zahiris) sense of
both the Quran and the hadith—on pious, conservative grounds,
to be sure, but almost as surely as a reaction to Mutazilite exegesis
based on analogy and what they called "investigation" (*nazar*).

As we shall see in our discussion of theology, exegesis lay at the
heart of the debate over the conflicting claims of faith and reason

in the domain of revealed religion. The rationalizing theologians wrested some of the rights of exegesis away from the lawyers because they were more skillful in allegorical exegesis. Traditionists were tied by their own legal premises to the literal interpretation of Scripture, a connection that committed them in nonhalakic passages to certain gross anthropomorphisms that the dialecticians could devour with arguments. More, the theologians permitted themselves a far wider exegetical range, and could apply both learning and imagination to the text of Scripture, whereas the traditionists were largely limited to arguments derived from rhetoric and philology. The attractiveness of theological tafsir is demonstrated by the position won by the Mutazilite Zamakhshari's quranic commentary among all segments of the Islamic community, and by the fact that Philo's discredited allegorical exegesis found a new audience once Jewish theologians under Islam rediscovered philosophy.

## Jewish Exegesis, Arab Style

As we have already seen, rabbis cultivated both the legal and the homiletic types of exegesis of the Bible, but then, in the tenth century, under the unmistakable influence of their Muslim environment in the Middle East, Jews began to pursue a new approach to reading Scripture. Its first proponent was Saadya ibn Yusuf (882–942), the Egyptian-born scholar who became gaon of the Iraqi rabbinic circles, which by then had moved from provincial Sura to metropolitan Baghdad, the seat of the caliphate. Saadya produced a first Arabic translation of the Bible for the now Arabic-speaking Jews of Mesopotamia. But equally importantly, his translation was accompanied by an extensive commentary on the text, and the latter set biblical exegesis on a new path.[45]

The rabbis who engaged in midrash had never to that point much concerned themselves with context. Their attention was fixed almost exclusively on the text itself or, more accurately, its words: what they were thought to have said (or not said) and, perhaps more importantly, what they intended. Muslim commentators on the Quran looked at their Book differently, however. They read it as a literary product, not of Muhammad, of course, but of

God himself, yet as literature nonetheless. Thus the Quran was open to, and indeed required, the same kind of literary and rhetorical analysis as the Arabs' rich (and profane) poetic tradition.[46] And again, and quite counterintuitively, the Muslim commentators read the Quran, with its almost defiant lack of historical context, as a historical document. They searched out the very concrete occasions of revelation in the life of Muhammad and attempted to fit them to verses of the Quran.

With Saadya, rabbis began to do the same with the Bible, employing the method that became known as peshat, sometimes called the "plain" or "literal" reading of Scripture but actually a profoundly contextual address of the text. The rabbis may have had the advantage over their Muslim models. The latter generally had only Arabic at their exegetical disposal, whereas Jewish scholars had not only Hebrew, biblical and rabbinic, but Aramaic and, of course, their now native Arabic, a language that had by then developed into a supple and elegant literary tool capable of expressing everything from the commonplace to the most demanding technical matters. The Jews absorbed the Arabic literary tradition and put it to good use, not only in the interpretation of Scripture, where the peshat or contextual method became widespread among the Sefardim, the Jews in Muslim lands, but, most startling of all, in the resurrection of Hebrew as a literary medium for the production, in Spain, of an extraordinary body of quite secular poetry.[47]

The Frenchman Rashi perhaps illustrates the full flowering of the rabbinic midrash method.[48] But the Spaniard Abraham ibn Ezra (1089–1164) carried the contextual method with its concomitant language skills from the Muslim world, where it was practiced by Sefardic exegetes, to the Jewish commentators of Christian Europe who knew little or nothing of the Arabic literary tradition. Born in Spain, Ibn Ezra traveled widely across the Abode of Islam, but the conversion of his son to Islam in 1140 pushed, or forced, him into Christian exile, where he traveled in Italy, France, and even, on occasion, England. Like Saadya, Ibn Ezra was a polymath and a cultural historian. His Hebrew writings, in particular a Hebrew grammar and a history of Hebrew linguistic studies, offered Jewish scholars of western Europe a convincing and attractive introduction, in Hebrew raiment, to the poetics and philology of Muslim Arab Spain. Ibn Ezra's multiple commentaries on Scripture are often boldly innovative and often on the same text from differing perspectives, and they were all highly influential on the scriptural perspectives of Christian Europe's rabbinic elite.[49]

CHAPTER SIX

# The Worship of God

Most religious communities have mandated or commended various forms of worship to their adherents, that is, the acknowledgment, in some formal way, of the existence and power of God. Its chief forms are prayer, or direct address of God, generally using God's own words, to wit, Scripture, and ritual, the performance of certain acts thought to be acceptable or pleasing to God. The word "liturgical" adds to both prayer and ritual the notion that either or both are formal, public, and, often, social.

## The Torah Explains Worship

Though the Torah has remarkably little to say about prayer, it is highly detailed and prescriptive on the subject of ritual, principally in the form of sacrifice (offerings of animals, grains, wine) to be offered at specific times, in specific places, by specific personnel. The Bible projects these prescriptions back to the Israelites' days in the wilderness of Sinai, where the rituals unfolded in a sacred precinct within the Israelites' mobile camp. They received their classic form, however, in Solomon's temple in Jerusalem, particularly after 621 B.C.E., when King Josiah centralized all Israelite sacrifice, which was still being offered in other cult centers in Eretz Israel, in the temple in Jerusalem.[1] Even after the temple was destroyed by the Babylonians, the Jews returning from Exile restored both the building and its rituals, and sacrifices continued to be offered in the House of the Lord on Jerusalem's eastern hill until its final destruction by the Romans in 70 C.E.

The Pentateuch spells out the modalities of sacrifice in great detail, whether by and for the community or for individuals, but always in the temple and all in a purified state—priest, offerer, and sacrificial object. Community sacrifices were offered daily, at each new moon—the Jews follow a lunar calendar—and on the three great pilgrimage festivals of "Booths" (*Sukkoth*) in the fall, and "Passover" (*Pesach*) and "Weeks" (*Shavuoth*) in the spring.[2] The most solemn time of the liturgical year was the penitential period that opened with New Year's Day (*Rosh ha-shana*) and closed by the Day of Atonement (*Yom Kippur*), when a great atonement liturgy was conducted in the temple.[3]

These almost constant sacrifices were exclusively conducted from the beginning by the hereditary caste of males established at God's command.[4] These priests (kohenim), the descendants of Moses' brother Aaron, took up their posts in the temple's inner courts in assigned rounds under the direction of a high priest. They received, prepared, and sacrificed the offerings from the other Israelites. Some of the offerings were entirely consumed by fire, a "holocaust" in Greek; others were only partially consumed with the rest reserved for the priests. It could hardly have been otherwise since everything offered in the temple was rendered taboo and removed from common use. The priests themselves as well as their families had to observe a higher degree of ritual purity than the other Israelites. Priests continued to serve in the temple and in general to act as religious guides for the community until the temple's destruction in 70, when their leadership role, though not their liturgical functions—held in abeyance until the temple was rebuilt in the messianic era—passed to the rabbis.[5]

In post-Exilic times, all the great liturgical feasts, with the possible exception of Rosh ha-shana, were intimately linked with the Jerusalem temple, and with its destruction in 70, they had to be transferred to either the home or the synagogue. The origins of this latter institution are still the subject of debate. Some argue that it arose as a community center during the Babylonian Exile, when Jews were cut off from the Jerusalem cult center. Others see it as a Pharisee-inspired institution with a totally different intent. Whatever the case, the synagogue had evolved, perhaps even before the destruction of the temple, from a simple house of assembly (*bet ha-knesset*) into a genuine house of prayer (*bet ha-tefilla*). It became the focus of Jewish liturgical life after 70, and by the fourth Christian century had developed not only a fixed liturgy but a distinctive architectural form.[6]

## Jewish Worship after the Destruction: The Synagogue

Jewish sacrificial cult ended with the destruction of the temple, and thereafter its place was taken by services that offered prayers of praise and expiation rather than live sacrifices for those same ends. But Judaism was far more than the offering of prayers or even a certain type of ethical behavior. What Moses had been given at Sinai, the written law of the Torah and the oral tradition finally embodied in the Talmud, were not simply the terms of a covenant to be observed by every Jew but the stuff of a special liturgical vocation. The bet ha-midrash, where the Talmud was studied with such loving care, was as much a place of worship as the synagogal bet ha-tefilla, and the study of Torah and Talmud was a moral imperative as efficacious as prayer.

The public synagogue service took place on the Sabbath, a weekly day of rejoicing and restraint from work, and on other holy days of celebration, atonement, or recollection. It began with recitations from the Scriptures. First were serial passages from the Torah distributed across either a three-year cycle current in Palestine from the second to the fifth century C.E., or a single-year cycle that was in use in Babylonia at about the same time and that eventually came to prevail in most Jewish communities.[7] The recitation of the weekly Torah passage, which was accompanied verse by verse by the Aramaic translation (targum), was followed by the *haftara*, an appropriately chosen passage of about ten verses drawn from the Prophets and again accompanied by a targum. After the chanting of a psalm, the preacher began the homiletic part of the liturgy. He first cited an "opening verse" (*petiha*) of his own selection from the Prophets or the Writings, and then proceeded to weave all the readings into a coherent exegetical and ethical whole.

We can reconstruct this ceremony because early preserved homiletic commentaries on Scripture follow this format and presumably reflect synagogue practice. Private prayer, normally three times daily, and the domestic liturgy of Judaism, which has no real parallel in either Christianity or Islam, have left far fewer traces of their evolution.[8] Even though they are largely composed of scriptural passages, and some, like the Shema and the benedictions of the Amida, were already being recited in some form during the Mishnaic period and perhaps even earlier, the formalization of the Jewish liturgy—even allowing for regional and sectarian differences—was the work of medieval scholars in Europe and the Abode of Islam.[9]

## *Jesus and the Worship of the First Christians*

Jesus, we can be certain, participated in the Jerusalem temple liturgies as well as in synagogue services in Galilee. But his lasting liturgical legacy is the so-called Last Supper, a meal that Jesus celebrated with the Twelve on the night of Passover, the day before he died. As described in the Gospels and Paul, it has many similarities to a Passover meal (many disparities as well), and that was how the early Christians chose to see it. Its reenactment—the Eucharist, as it was called from the Greek *eucharizein*, to give thanks—became the chief form of Christian liturgical worship. As the prototype is described to us, Jesus took bread—unleavened bread, *matzoh*, if it was indeed a Passover meal—gave thanks, broke the bread, and gave it to those present with the words "Take. This is my body." Likewise, with a cup of wine, he said, "This is my blood of the New Covenant which has been shed for many." Paul, whose testimony on the event is the earliest, added, "Do this in memory of me."[10]

Jesus lived in late Second Temple times and had no visible quarrel with temple sacrifices. It is difficult to say whether he had that temple in mind in the scene of the Last Supper. Elsewhere in the Gospels, however, Jesus himself is explicitly identified as the "lamb of God," the prescribed sacrificial animal for Passover, and the Passover associations are made quite explicit in Paul: "Christ our Passover lamb has been sacrificed" (1 Cor. 5:7). If Jesus was the Passover sacrifice for Paul and others of that generation, he became both the sacrifice and the sacrificing high priest for the author of the New Testament's Letter to the Hebrews. This image of

Jesus as both the sacrificial victim and, at the same time, the priest of sacrifice endured in Christianity. So too the liturgical reenactment of the Eucharistic meal was universally construed, at least down to the Reformation, as a sacrifice, the "sacrifice of the Mass" in Latin Christianity, with the Church's sacerdotal minister standing in for Jesus and the elements of the bread and wine on the table-altar transformed into the sacrificial body and blood.[11]

## The Eucharistic Liturgy

As the Christians became more self-aware and began to develop their own particular liturgy, it is natural to think that they behaved like the Jews they were and built on Jewish liturgical practices familiar to them.[12] The earliest Christians seem in fact to have had a prayer meeting (*synaxis*) constructed on the model of the emerging synagogue service and a separate Eucharistic celebration with Passover sacrificial associations. Eventually the two were fused in the Eucharistic liturgy, whose elements are still fairly evident. The first was the so-called Mass of the Catechumens, that is, the part of the liturgy still open to those under instruction (*katechesis*) for baptism.[13] Here the synagogue antecedents are obvious: scriptural readings (Old Testament/Paul/Gospels, usually on an interlocking theme), followed by a homily based on these readings and concluded with a common prayer.[14] At the completion of the prayer, all but the baptized were dismissed and the Eucharist proper began: the offering of the bread and wine, their consecration by Jesus' own formula at the Last Supper, and, through it, their transformation into the body and blood of Christ, which was then distributed and consumed by the congregation.[15]

The Eucharist and other forms of Christian worship became more elaborate and standardized with the passage of time.[16] As Christianity moved out of its original Jewish environment into the Hellenic and Gentile world there was doubtless an interpenetration of spirit and vocabulary with pagan rituals, particularly with those of the so-called mystery religions in their apogee in the third century. At first the Christian rites were celebrated, like some contemporary synagogue services, in private homes, which could also serve as an assembly center, a bet ha-knesset—in Greek, *ekklesia*—for the community. In times of persecution, the Christians quite literally went underground, into the burial caverns called catacombs, for their rituals. When the persecutions ended, the Christians constructed special prayer halls, some local and modest, some imperially lavish. They took over a common type of Roman building, the imperial audience hall called a basilica, and used it for their increasingly elaborate liturgies.[17]

## Christian Liturgy: Theme and Variations

The exact form of the Christian liturgy varied from place to place. Most of the available material for the reconstruction of the early Christian Eucharistic liturgy, like the Didache of the late first or early second century and the Apostolic Constitution of about 380 C.E., refer to a type of service in use in the urban centers of Syria to about 400 C.E.[18] Another different form was current in Egypt about the same time. Both of these were in Greek, but the Eucharist was early celebrated in Christian Aramaic—the dialect called Syriac—at Edessa, and it is still in use in Eastern churches today under the rubric of "the Liturgy of Mari and Addai." In Rome and the African provinces of the empire, services were in Latin, and again, the form of the Roman "mass," as the Eucharistic liturgy was called, differed in details from contemporary Eastern versions of the same service.[19] What followed in the East testifies, as certainly as the evolution of the hierarchical structure, to the growing centralization of the Great Church and the consequent standardization of its practices. A "liturgy of Saint James," which may have had its beginnings in Jerusalem, and a parallel service attributed to Saint Mark began to drive out all the local liturgies in the patriarchal sees of Antioch and Alexandria, respectively. And with the growth in political power and prestige of Constantinople, its liturgical practice, the so-called "Saint Basil," not only dominated in the churches of Anatolia but, as nationalism and separatism grew in Syria and Egypt, gained an official cachet as the liturgy of the Eastern Orthodox Church.[20]

Within these types there were, of course, all manner of variations, but certain elements remained constant.[21] The division into two parts has already been mentioned. The first, the synaxis, was preceded by the "little entrance" of the celebrants into the sanctuary area, and was composed of scriptural readings interspersed with psalms and concluded by the dismissal of the catechumens. At this point began the Eucharist proper. After the "great entrance" were various prayers of greeting and commemoration, the recitation of a creed (*symbolon*), and the kiss of peace. The diptychs, lists of the living and the dead in communion with a particular church, were read and a number of offertory prayers recited. The priestly celebrant than began the most sacred part of the liturgy, the *anaphora*, which he initiated by exhorting the faithful to lift up their minds to God. A hymn to the angels followed, then a remembrance (*anamnesis*) of Jesus' passion, and an invocation (*epiklesis*) directed to the Holy Spirit to descend on the bread and wine that had been placed on the altar. There was a final blessing, and the anaphora ended with the Lord's Prayer. What remained was the breaking of the bread, now transformed into the body of Christ, and the sharing of the wine/blood with the faithful.

## Bishops and Priests

At some very early point that cannot be exactly determined, someone was presiding over the Eucharist, or "celebrating" it, as was later said. As Paul's letters show, the earliest Christian communities, still overwhelmingly Jewish, had various authority figures. We hear of "teachers," "prophets," "elders," and "overseers," all of whom received the gift of the Spirit, though there is no very clear indication how their functions were exercised in the community. It may be assumed that all of them reflected current synagogue practice in the Diaspora. Fairly soon, however, it was the overseer (*episkopos*) who was playing the leadership role in each ekklesia or congregation. Already at the end of the first century the bishop was being referred to as a successor of the Apostles and so the primary bearer of the authentic Christian tradition. As such, the bishop was in unique possession of the *magisterium*, the teaching power in the Church.

The evolution of the "elders" (*presbyteroi*) seems to have been a separate but parallel development. As already noted, the New Testament Letter to the Hebrews announces Jesus as the new high priest inaugurating a new priesthood. But Jesus appointed no one to stand in for him at the Eucharistic ritual, whatever form it took at the beginning, neither his Apostles nor anyone else; nor, indeed, could he or did he "make" anyone a priest as the term was understood at that time and place. Nevertheless, in the earliest sources the bishop invariably presides at the Eucharist. Bishop and presbyter may in fact have been a single office that became separate and distinct over the second century as Christianity spread into more remote areas. The presbyter emerged as a distinct officer charged with performing some of the bishop's functions, notably presiding over the community Eucharist.

## Worship at Mecca

Jesus' religious environment is like a floodlit stage compared to the dark theater of pre-Islamic Mecca. Not only are the sources for the latter late and uncertain; Islam's militant monotheism all but obliterated the traces, both the rituals and the accompanying etiological myths, of Mecca's paganism. We know that the stone-built central shrine called the Kaaba was very old and that it was reckoned the "house" of Mecca's aniconic deity called simply "the god," in Arabic *al-ilah*, by elision *Allah*.[22] We also know that other gods and goddesses—the Quran calls the latter "the daughters of Allah"—were worshiped in the same sacred precinct (*haram*). Sacrifice was the chief form of ritual, but there were others, some of which were carried over into Islam, like the ritual jogging around the Kaaba and back and forth between two nearby hills. One form of prayer was the "acclamation," a shouted ejaculation of praise. The Quran was not impressed: it characterizes the Meccans' prayers and rituals as "clapping and whistling." And finally there is Muhammad's own practice: it seems highly likely that Muhammad's chanted "recitations" at the Kaaba, which is where they began, were a familiar form of religious expression in pagan Mecca.

Muhammad's insistent monotheism eventually drew his prayer (*salat*) away from the pagan versions, and possibly their styles as well. Sacrifice was banned—we know not how or when—even to Allah at the Kaaba, and in what may have been the most drastic move of all, the Quran prohibited intercalation (9:27), the periodic insertion of a month into a lunar calendar to keep step with the seasonal observances of the solar calendar. Unlike the Jews and Christians, the Muslims would have no seasonal feasts.[23] In other regards, however, the rhythms of time were observed. The Muslims were enjoined to pray five times a day at fixed solar times (and, like at least some of his pagan contemporaries, facing the Meccan Kaaba).[24] The ritual fast lasts the entire lunar month of Ramadan, from new moon to new moon, daily from sunrise to sunset.[25] The hajj or pilgrimage, another carryover from paganism, unfolds during six days of its own lunar month.

## Muslim Ritual: Prayer and Pilgrimage

The Muslim's prescribed daily prayers are a combination of short, semivocalized expression of divine praise, most of them quranic, and various postures almost certainly pre-Islamic in origin. They may be performed in private in any dignified setting, but the noon prayer on Friday has a special liturgical significance in that it is a prescribed congregational prayer, whose most particular feature is a sermon (khutba).[26] In Muhammad's day the congregation, which was in effect the umma, assembled in the courtyard of Muhammad's house in Medina and the Prophet himself delivered the sermon, a homiletic blend of moral exhortation and political militancy that has survived to this day. His house was reckoned the first mosque (masjid) in Islam—such public yet separate devotions would have been unthinkable in Mecca—though the more common term in Arabic, al-jami, is the exact analogue of both synagoge and ekklesia, "the assembly."[27]

The Medina mosque's successors in the rapidly expanding Abode of Islam differed only in sumptuousness and scale; indeed, the Prophet's mosque in Medina is now one of the most grandiose of all. All have an open court with a place for ablutions before the prayer hall. Within the latter the direction toward Mecca, the qibla, is marked by a niche on the front wall, the mihrab, a functionally simple marker that rapidly developed into a significant element of architectural decoration. Next to it stands the pulpit (minbar), which the preacher ascends to deliver the Friday sermon, seated. Outside is a minaret, a tower squat, slender, modest or monumental to taste, into which a "summoner" (muadhdhin > muezzin) mounts to call the faithful to prayer at the stipulated hours.

Daily prayer is, like the profession of faith, ritual fasting, and the annual alms-tithe, one of the Pillars of Islam, obligations incumbent on all Muslims, though women are rather readily exempted by reason of family obligations, fears regarding modesty, or the danger of ritual impurity. A fifth ritual pillar is the hajj, the pilgrimage to the holy places in the vicinity of Mecca that every capable Muslim is bound to make at least once in a lifetime.[28] This complex ritual, which must have been practiced long before the coming of Islam, is time- and place-tied and unfolds between the eighth and the thirteenth of the lunar Pilgrimage Month. As already remarked, the myths explaining the origins of complicated rituals like the hajj have either disappeared or been suppressed beyond retrieval. Islam, which appropriated the hajj (with adjustments), simply supplied its own.[29] Abraham and Ishmael had built the Kaaba, and Abraham, at God's command, had instituted the hajj, whose chief moments were tied to one or another incident in the Abraham cycle. These practices had somehow survived the paganism that had overwhelmed Mecca in the generations of Ishmael's offspring there. It awaited the arrival of a new prophet to revive the religion of Abraham and to restore to their pristine form the rituals of monotheism that the "friend of God" and his son had established on that holy ground.

## Muslim Feasts and Festivals

Daily prayer and pilgrimage by no means exhaust the liturgical and ritualistic side of Islam.[30] The Muslims, like the Christians, possess a liturgical calendar that marks the occurrence of certain days of festival (id) across the lunar year.[31] Two of them are observed by all Muslims.[32] The "sacrificial feast" (id al-adha) was and remains connected with the animal sacrifice that was an original, pre-Islamic part of the hajj ritual, but was "Abrahamized" by Islam and eventually extended by way of privilege to all Muslims, whether on pilgrimage or not. A second festival, "breaking of the fast" (id al-fitr), is celebrated on the first day of the month following the penitential season of Ramadan. Both require community prayer, whether they fall on Friday or not. Another nearly universal festival is the birthday of the Prophet (mawlid al-nabi), although it has been opposed at various times and places by Muslim purists who objected to such veneration of a mortal, or who were scandalized by some of the more extravagant Sufi manifestations that accompanied the celebration.

The birthday of the Prophet is not the only mawlid celebrated in Islam. The veneration of great men after their death is an ancient practice based on the belief that they continued to possess, in some manner, the political or religious power they had in life.[33] The tombs of Abraham and Sarah and other Jewish patriarchs are still venerated at Hebron, and at least some of the Muslim shrines in the Middle East commemorating biblical figures likely go back to a pre-Islamic and pre-Christian Jewish tradition, though we have no idea what rites might have been celebrated there.[34]

## The Cult of the Saints

For Christians, the first posthumous heroes were the martyrs who died for their faith in the Roman persecutions, much as the Maccabees were thought to have done by an earlier generation of Jews.[35] By the third century C.E. there were, in any event, memorial buildings over martyrs' graves outside the cities of the empire, and the anniversary of their martyrdom was being celebrated in both liturgical and literary form. In the new religious climate established by the conversion of Constantine, simple tombs were expanded into magnificent churches where the feast day of the saint could be celebrated before large crowds with liturgical pomp. It was Constantine too who converted Palestine into a Christian Holy Land by constructing notable churches over the sites associated with Jesus' life and death.[36]

The cult of saints, living or dead, was not an entirely natural development in Islam, which placed an almost infinite gulf between a transcendent Allah and his creation here below. It occurred nonetheless, and with some speed.[37] Note has already been taken of the opposition to the mawlid al-nabi. Muhammad, who never claimed to be anything other than mortal, and stoutly refused to produce supernatural signs to verify his claims as a prophet, was soon after his death credited with marvelous powers.[38] Those gifts and graces (*karamat*) bestowed by Allah on his Prophet were quickly extended to Allah's "friends," men and women, who thus became the objects of a special cult, even during their lifetimes, and whose tombs and shrines are centers of local and even pan-Islamic veneration.[39]

Islam possesses one prototypical martyr, Husayn, the son of the fourth caliph, Ali, and Muhammad's grandson. He and his companions were slaughtered in a political uprising at the town of Karbela in Iraq on the tenth day of the month Muharram in 680 c.e. Both the day and the place have taken on extraordinary significance for Muslims, particularly the Shiites. Not only has Karbela become a richly endowed shrine and pilgrimage city, but the celebration of Muharram has generated a vivid liturgical and dramatic reenactment (*taziya*) of the martyrdom of Husayn.[40]

Christianity early institutionalized the veneration of its holy individuals. The martyrs were the first to be so honored, as we have seen, but the same practices were soon extended to the "confessors," those holy men and women whose lifelong pursuit of virtue proclaimed their sanctity as eloquently as the blood of the martyrs did theirs. There appears to have been little opposition to the liturgical rites that grew up around the tombs of the Christian saints or their physical remains (*reliquiae* > relics). Nor is there any reason to think there should have been such in a community whose founder had already sanctified flesh by appropriating it to his own Godhead.

However it was defined and whatever it was called, the public and private veneration of the sainted dead worked its way deep into the devotional life of the Church, Eastern and Western, and as the number of the venerated increased, so too did their posthumous apparitions and the miracles attributed to them. The Roman Church sought, as in all else, to control the process. Sainthood came to mean that, whatever the level or extent of popular devotion, some authority had pronounced dogmatically on the authenticity of a given saint, and that authority came inevitably to mean the bishop of Rome. Papal vigilance seems scarcely to have slowed the growth in the cult of saints and their relics, the latter of which grew from a trickle to a tide from East to West in the wake of the Crusades. It took the Reformation to apply a brake to the process, and thereafter the Roman Church began to tighten its own procedures. The process became formal, evidentiary, stringent, and it was called canonization.

## *Some Comparisons*

Judaism and Islam produced their own ranks of both martyrs and confessors whom they honor but to whom they are reluctant to extend the veneration owed only to God. Jews and Muslims share the biblical jealousy of adoration, and the Christian theologian's willingness to distinguish, carefully in theory but somewhat less so in liturgical practice, between the adoration paid only to God and the veneration legitimately granted the saints has not convinced them otherwise. The doctrine of Jesus' death on the cross was truly a "scandal to the Jews," as Paul had foreseen (1 Cor. 1:23), and was equally so to the Muslims (Quran 4:157–159). The liturgical veneration of the saints, which flows as naturally as the sacramental system itself from that doctrine, was simply a lesser form of the same scandal.

Jewish liturgy is both symbolic and historical. It remembers events; it commemorates promises received and weeps for disappointed hopes. Like the Bible, it is both a record and a celebration. Muslims neither commemorate nor weep in their orisons; Islam's calendar is fixed in God's eternal present, and its liturgical mode on the great exaltation of God and, as its very name suggests, the humble submission of the believer. Christian liturgy, in contrast, is cosmic and yet professedly literal. "This is my body" seeks at the same time to draw God down from heaven and exalt matter to a supernatural plane in a manner alien to Muslim and Jew alike. Both of the latter know how to be literal—all prayer is literal—but do not endeavor either to ground God or to sanctify matter. God will intervene in history when and where he will; but he will not dwell among us.

# CHAPTER SEVEN

# Renunciation and Aspiration

The behavioral patterns of all three monotheistic communities rest on a profound perceived distinction between God, "who alone is holy," and the human condition and circumstances. The latter are often referred to in shorthand as "the world" or "this world." Though according to Genesis God looked on this world, which was, after all, his creation, and pronounced it "good" (Gen. 1:4, etc.), his creatures often took a more pessimistic view of their condition, as did God himself on occasion. God's disapproval expressed itself in taboo substances and forbidden acts, like the elaborate lists in the Pentateuch and the equally strong if less detailed prohibitions in the New Testament and the Quran. Humans for their part went even further and denied themselves objects and acts that were otherwise quite legitimate. God's prescriptions are called divine law; human self-denial constitutes part of what is known as asceticism.[1]

## Were There Jewish Ascetics?

The Israelites showed little inclination toward outdoing God and practicing voluntary self-denial, though fringe groups like the Rechabites and Nazirites chose what can fairly be described as an ascetic path to holiness.[2] Post-Exilic Judaism seems to live in a different world, however. Philo gives a circumstantial description of a group of Jewish ascetics who lived in monastic communities and devoted themselves to the study of Scripture.[3] We hardly know what to make of this story, since we have no other evidence of Philo's "Therapeutae," but early Christian authors such as Eusebius, who were well acquainted with Philo's work, cited the account with enthusiastic approval.

Although we cannot fathom the motives of the almost idyllic, quasi-academic asceticism of the Egyptian Therapeutae, we are better informed about Palestine. There, as we have seen, a number of groups were seized with the notion of the approaching End Time and adapted a lifestyle they felt would put them in a higher state of preparedness, a lifestyle that incorporated one or more ascetical elements. Such were the celibate Essenes at Qumran and the movement promoted by John the Baptist, clothed in animal skins and eating locusts and honey while he awaited the onset of the Kingdom (Matt. 3:1–4).

## Christian Asceticism

This is the religious environment from which the Jesus movement came forth, and if Jesus himself was neither an Essene nor an ascetic of the hard-edged Johannine type, there is a more than coincidental resemblance between Jesus and his followers and those other two groups. His followers included women, but Jesus himself appears to have been celibate, though no particular point is made of it. His inner circle, the Twelve, seem also to have cut themselves off from their families—of which some point *is* made—and to have taken up with their master an itinerant life of casual poverty. Jesus did not so much deny the flesh as ignore it. Others felt more strongly. Jesus' brother, James, who led the movement in Jerusalem at 30 c.e., was a severe ascetic, perhaps out of an overscrupulous sense of ritual purity, and Paul's own problems with the flesh blaze out from his letters. Hovering above them all was a sense of the impending End Time, the cataclysm and then the triumph of Jesus' Second Coming that would render this world less than relevant.

When and where an eschatological unworldliness yielded to a fully realized ascetical life as a more perfect path to holiness open to all Christians cannot be determined, though celibates and other ascetics show up early in the Christian tradition.[4] The classical prototype of such a life was Antony, an Alexandrian who died in 356 C.E. Though he was surely not the first to choose withdrawal from the world (*anachoresis*) as a way of life, his well-publicized career of prayer, fasting, and vigils alone in the murderous desert of eastern Egypt provided the model and incentive for future generations.[5]

## Sanctity in Common

Antony attempted to live his remarkable life in solitude, but soon his eremitical existence drew many others into the wastelands beyond the fertile if narrow reach of the Nile. Community (*koinobion*) life offered important psychological support for the like-minded souls who had entered on an enterprise of daunting difficulty. More importantly, it provided the ultimate corrective to an aspect of the human appetite that had previously lain concealed under that same moral exemplarism. The first solitaries (*monachoi*) quickly discerned that they had carried "the world" with them into the desert. It was located not in the distant Alexandria that Antony had so feared but in their own unruly limbs and heads. To combat it they produced the most astonishingly fierce forms of self-deprivation. Self-denial gave way to mortification and, as it has seemed to some, masochism pure and simple, all in a physical environment where mere survival required a prodigious effort.

Practitioners of these vigorous and often violent forms of self-abasement were sometimes called "athletes of God," a title even truer than intended since those dauntless ascetics in Egypt, Palestine, and Syria turned out to be highly competitive in their race toward perfection.[6] One-upmanship came to the desert, followed by the blazing insight that here lay a truly cardinal vice that had gone unnoted in the Christians' Torah: the will was being softly massaged even as the flesh was crying "no más." And equally quickly these clinicians of the soul found its antidote: obedience of the spirit. Obedience was the final and crowning piece in the great triptych of Christian monastic virtues. Poverty meant owning nothing and craving even less. Celibacy required a voluntary renunciation of even licit sexual activity, foreswearing, in effect, marriage. But the desire for goods and sexual pleasure were relatively easy to detect in comparison with the needs and demands of what would later be called the ego. The ascetics devised an institutional cure, however. Monks living in a community would be governed not by their own wills but by a rule, an imposed superego to which their own wills would be subject, and its human voice was that of one of their own, an elected or appointed superior whose (generally innocuous) commands would represent the will of God writ small, so to speak. The monastic rule and the monastic superior were the last and most potent instruments of self-abnegation created for ascetic community life, and obedience, of the letter and of the spirit, its most difficult demand.

## The Monastic Rule

One who had considerable experience of monasticism in most of its Middle Eastern varieties was Basil (d. 379), the wealthy nobleman who had himself become a monk and later the bishop of Caesarea in Cappadocia. He had visited monastic communities in Egypt, Palestine, and Syria about 358 c.e. and his own earlier experience of the disorganized and even anarchical monastic tradition in his native Cappadocia led him to draw up a set of rules for the governance of monastic life. These are extant in a longer and a shorter version, and they set out in some detail not only the ideals but the practices of the monk's life from standards of admission to the monastery to the manner of dress there.[7]

For Basil, community life was far preferable to the eremitical because of its greater social good. It was, in fact, Basil who established the social goals—with their economic and intellectual consequences—so evident in monastic life in the West,[8] where Benedict (d.ca. 550) took over much of Basil's thinking for his own *Rule* at Monte Cassino.[9] Basil believed in work, physical and intellectual, and the life of the monk was to be one of work and prayer. Daily morning and evening prayers were not uncommon in some of the larger Christian churches, but Basil set a standard of monastic prayer eight times a day, beginning at dawn and proceeding at about three-hour intervals through the day and the night as well, since the monks were obliged to rise at midnight and just before dawn to pray once again.

Basil put the monastery under the firm control of the superior (*hegoumenos*) or abbot, as he was called in the West, but the Great

Church went further in its own enactments. Monastic communities, it turned out, could be as troublesome to Church order as individual monks, and the theological disputes of the fifth and sixth centuries were often accompanied by monastic riots.[10] The Council of Chalcedon reacted in 451 c.e. by placing monastic communities under the jurisdiction of the bishops, and succeeding councils attempted, not always successfully, to strengthen the hierarchy's grip on the sometimes overenergetic athletes of God. When in the sixth century the imperial government began to intervene more directly in the affairs of canon law, the emperor too took up the cause of monastic regulation and reform.

## The Path Upward

Basil thought to guide monastic spirituality by regulating its discipline. The Eastern monks never quite accepted the premise of the *sacra regula* to the extent their Western counterparts did.[11] Their spiritual paths led in other directions, to the theologians whose chief concern was mysticism rather than asceticism. Even before Antony withdrew to the desert, theologians such as Origen, again following Philo and before him Plato and Aristotle, were fashioning a new ideal for the ascetic: that of the contemplative life. Whereas the earliest Christian ascetics, many of them illiterate, stressed a simple scriptural meditation, imitation of Christ, and the training of the will, such fourth-century masters of the spiritual life as Evagrius of Pontus (d. 399) in the East and John Cassian (d. 435) in the West changed their regard from the will to the intellect and its illumination. At the upper end of the ascetic's "spiritual ladder," whose lower rungs still consisted of pragmatic asceticism, stood the new ideal of unity with God, *theoria* or *theologia*, as it was called in the new Hellenic-inspired vocabulary.[12]

One of Evagrius's most prominent disciples was John Climacus (d.ca. 649), a monk of Sinai whose *Ladder of Divine Ascent* stands a world apart from Basil's community-oriented and highly regulated version of the monastic ideal.[13] John's monk strives, in the best Evagrian tradition, for the tranquility (*hesychia*) of body and mind that invites the divine grace to fill the soul with light from on high. Neither tranquility nor divine illumination was a novel idea in the fifth century, but both were becoming the centerpieces of monasticism in the East—in the writings of Symeon (d. 1022), the so-called New Theologian, for example. They erupted into controversy on Mount Athos, a veritable society of monasteries in northern Greece, where by the fourteenth century the achievement of hesychia was conditioned by an elaborate set of physical exercises that had less to do with traditional Christian asceticism than with a type of Byzantine yoga: contemplation of the navel, regulated breathing, and the repetitious intoning of the "Jesus prayer" formula.[14] The climax of this regimen was an infusion of the divine light, the same seen by Jesus' disciples on Mount Tabor (Mark 9:2–8; Matt. 17:1–8), and a union with the divine essence—in short, a kind of deification.[15]

## The Muslim Path

The portrait of Muhammad that has come down to us is filled with sometimes contradictory details. Indeed, many of the Prophetic reports seem to be fighting later wars, some praising asceticism, others deploring it; some making the Prophet parsimonious, others lavish. The Quran granted him a large share in the spoils of his increasingly successful raids (59:6) and it permitted him as many wives as he chose to have, "a privilege granted to no other believer" (35:50–52). But for all that, Muhammad does not appear as either self-aggrandizing or particularly concerned with personal wealth, either at Medina, when he possessed it, or at Mecca, when he did not. And he was clearly no ascetic. He seems neither excessive nor particularly abstemious in his behavior. "I am but a mortal like you," he is made to say in the Quran (18:110), and both the Quran and the sunna confirm that assertion. Nor did he preach to others any discernible degree of voluntary self-restraint or self-denial with respect to the legitimate pleasures of life.

What prompted the first Muslims to separate themselves from their fellows by the practice of asceticism (*zuhd*), that is, the pursuit of a lifestyle with a notable degree of voluntary self-denial, appears to have been a sense of contradiction between the astonishingly successful and extravagant ways of many Muslims and the general simplicity and otherworldliness of the quranic message. That disparity, already visible in Medina, did not seem to bother Muhammad himself, who professed neither regret nor nostalgia over his Meccan poverty, though the prosperity that he and his companions enjoyed at Medina was but a faint presentiment of the imperial splendor that was to follow. In any event, among the personalities known to us from the first Islamic century, some few individuals quietly and unostentatiously withdrew from contemporary society. A number of them bore the title of "Sufi."[16]

The ascetical pursuits of these Sufis, which tended to be more occasional and less wilderness-oriented than in Christianity, were divided by later theoreticians into a series of "stations" that roughly coincide with the Christians' via purgativa. They were the result of the Sufis' own exertions—scrutiny of conscience, self-restraint with respect to even legitimate pleasures, voluntary poverty—and once they were achieved, the Sufi traveling along the path of perfection passed from the stations to the "states," from the condition of the ascetic to that of the mystic.[17]

The spiritual terrain that led from asceticism into the very presence of God was as carefully mapped out by Sufi writers as the Christians' was by their moral theologians.[18] The landscape of the states, where God's grace rather than the individual's exertions led the Sufi's now purified soul toward a union with the divine, was well charted. The theory too is brightly lit and schematic, but the actual spiritual paths traveled by individual Sufis were darker, more painful, and at the same time more exotic than the handbooks would lead us to expect.[19] The closest we come to the sense of actual experience of God is in the great body of Sufi poetry, much of it in Persian, that has charmed, edified, and inspired many Muslims and perhaps startled and even shocked, by its anthropomorphisms and eroticism, almost as many more.

## The Spiritual Master

The novice Sufi was put into the hands of a spiritual master (*murshid, pir*), who was not only a skilled director of souls but a charismatic guide, like the East Christian *starets* and the Hasidic *tzaddiq*, a true "spiritual father" who himself possessed the gift of divine grace (*baraka*).[20] He introduced the novice into two of the most common practices of Sufism, the "recollection" (*dhikr*) and the "hearing" (*sama*). *Dhikr* has its spiritual, internal sense of recollecting God's blessings, but its more visible form in Sufism is the repetition of set formulas, notably the Muslim profession of faith or of the ninety-nine quranic names of Allah. The repetition was rhythmical and often accompanied, as was the "Jesus prayer" used to the same end in Christianity, by controlled breathing. The ecstatic state of annihilation (*fana*), which was for the Sufi a natural antecedent of union with the Divine, was often accompanied by an elaborate ritual of singing and dancing within which the dhikr might be commingled. This sama, as it was called, though highly characteristic of certain Sufi associations such as the whirling dervishes, was not everywhere approved or accepted, however.

The attraction of charismatic holy persons is universal, and in Islam it brought crowds of disciples to the feet of Sufi masters. The baraka passed from master to novice, and so was established an ongoing chain (*silsila*) of spiritually authenticated adepts whose external regime might be common knowledge but whose share in the mysteries of the divine union was at base ineffable. The mystic's gnosis was understood as a special knowledge (*marifa*) of the "higher realities," and though it might be communicated obliquely in the poetry of a Jalal al-Din Rumi or an Ibn al-Arabi, the central "reality" could not and should not be revealed to the uninitiated.

## The Sufi Orders

Like the parallel phenomena of religious orders in Christianity and Hasidic communities in Judaism, the starting point of the Sufi brotherhoods called—like Sufism itself—a "way" (*tariqa*) was the imitation of and instruction by a renowned holy man.[21] There was no question at first of rules or a formal way of life for the loosely associated members. By the thirteenth century, however, the system had been transformed and the elitist aspects of the movement yielded to a more general membership. It was then that the greatest and most prolific of the Sufi "orders" came into existence, each with many spiritual offspring of its own.[22] Teaching became systematized into a doctrine and a method, and the life of those living in the community was governed by a rule. Tariqas began to shape their own identification, which was validated by a chain of masters going back to the holy "founder" or better, its anchor, since it is transparently clear that none of those "friends of God" had intended founding anything. Finally, in the fifteenth century, under the Ottomans, Sufism became a fully articulated system of distinct and characteristic "religious orders," both popular and corporate in character, with an emphasis on both "membership" and the now full-blown cult of the saintly founder.

Sufi tariqas had an immense popular appeal in Islam, not least because they were a social and spiritual reaction to the increasingly clerical and legal character of what had come to be official Islam, dominated by a rabbinate with powerful economic, social, and political connections. Functionally, the Sufi orders filled many of the same roles as the Christian clergy generally in the medieval West. Like the diocesan or local clergy of the Western Church, the Sufi "brethren" (*ikhwan*) were drawn from and remained close to the local community and its people, and they offered, like their Western clerical counterparts, a variety of spiritual and corporeal services to their fellow Muslims. Their dhikrs in town and countryside provided an ongoing liturgy with an emotive, dramatic, and mystical content not present in the daily salat, which was, in essence, a private devotion. Finally, the tombs of holy Sufis became, as we have already seen, a rich source of blessings (*barakat*) and graces (*karamat*). What the dead saint delivered from beyond the tomb, so too could the living sheikh of the tariqa as the recipient of the founder's own charismatic karamat. Both were channels through which blessings and favors might flood to the ordinary Muslim and protectors against ills and tragedy. The Christian Church directed those blessings through the highly institutionalized and depersonalized sacramental system; Sufism accomplished the same end through its personalized and decentralized rituals celebrating the friends of God, both living and dead.

## Religious Orders, East and West

If they resembled the religious orders of the Christian West, the Sufi tariqas also differed in important regards. A Sufi tariqa was essentially a collection of local chapters bound together by their common devotion to a single saintly founder, from whom they derived both their legitimacy and their spiritual privileges. The

Western religious orders, monks, friars, and clerks regular, all formed societies that were closely regulated within the Church they served, and many of them were, no less than the Church itself, international in scope. The Western Christian orders were legitimized by formal papal approval of their rule and organization and they were regulated by the norms of canon law; they were controlled from Rome through a superior general who resided there and internally through visitations and general chapters. Islam had no supreme spiritual authority like the pope, nor did the tariqas have elected officials. The sheikh's authority was charismatic and permanent, not attributed and temporary, like that which prevailed in Christian monastic communities, and his jurisdiction was local. Muslim rulers, like the Ottoman sultans, who also claimed the title of caliph, attempted to control the tariqas by appointing a "sheikh of sheikhs" to serve as a liaison between them and the orders, but the efforts were only indifferently successful. The sheikhs and their followers in the tariqas were essentially a local phenomenon grounded in popular support, and though the government might squeeze the waqf endowments that supported them, it had no way to limit or undermine the tariqas' charismatic authority.

The Western Church could dispose its religious orders when and where seemed good: to proselytize the nonbelievers in newly opened lands, for example—as the Franciscans did in the New World and the Jesuits in the Far East—or to combat the Church's enemies at home—as the Dominicans did the Albigensians in the south of France and relapsed Jewish and Muslim converts in Spain, and as the Jesuits did Protestants in southern Germany. Indeed, the Jesuits, who took a particular fourth vow of obedience specifically to the pope, were founded precisely to provide the Holy See with a rapid response force. The Sufi orders, in contrast, though they generally recognized the political authorities under whom they lived, did not serve them, and their relations with Islam's other spiritual elite, the ulama, were often antagonistic. The ulama never explicitly condemned the Sufis' striving for a closer, more personal relationship with God—the Sufis' link with the Prophet was perhaps too strongly forged—but the more conservative among them were often outspoken in their condemnation of Sufi practices, the dhikrs that included music and dance, for example, and the Sufis' often extravagant veneration of the sainted dead.

## Gnosis and Gnosticism

Whereas the Sufi orders represent the popular side of mysticism in Islam, its more elitist and esoteric aspects are associated with that peculiar strain of religion, myth, and philosophy known as Gnosticism. If a religion is a complex of attitudes toward God, humans, and the world, then Gnosticism was indeed a religion. But it was a most peculiar form of religion, since it appears to have had no independent existence but rather to have survived as a parasitic ideology deep within the bodies of the more formal and institutionalized religions of Judaism, Christianity, and Islam. Gnostics and gnosis there indeed were; but Gnosticism is our construct.[23]

Rapidly defined, gnosis, a Greek word meaning knowledge or understanding, is, in our present context, the wisdom necessary for salvation. Unlike the understanding of the philosophers, which is rationally derived and openly taught, gnosis is grounded in revelation and transmitted through restricted channels from one initiate to another, chiefly through an esoteric understanding of religious texts already in the public domain. The content of the gnosis is in some ways familiar. There is a single transcendent and unknowable God who, together with his successive emanations, generally called Aeons, constitutes the spiritual universe, which the Gnostics called the *pleroma*, the "Plenitude" or "Perfection." But unlike the later forms of Platonic thought to which it is obviously akin, Gnosticism viewed the material cosmos, the "Emptiness" (*kenoma*), as it was known, not as a mere diminution of God's creative emanation but as the product of a totally different metaphysics and ethic: the kenoma was created and is ruled by an autonomous principle of evil, a Bad God.

The heart of the gnosis was a cosmic drama in which one of the spiritual beings of the pleroma fell from grace, and by its fall broadcast fragments of the divine essence into the darkling world below, sparks of the Divine Light that were thereafter immersed as soul in the bodies of humans. At some point a Redeemer ventured down into the kenoma to reveal to those who would hear the message of salvation, whence they had come and whither they were intended to return.

## *Hidden Origins*

No one is quite sure how the phenomenon began, whether among disappointed apocalyptic Jews, world-denying pagans, Iranian dualists, or some combination of all three. Until 1945, when the papyrus remains of a fourth-century Gnostic library were discovered at Nag Hammadi in Egypt, all the texts identified as "Gnostic" were, as a matter of fact, adduced as aberrations from true doctrine by the early Christian authors who cited them.[24] Indeed, there are provocatively Gnostic-type notions circulating in the earliest versions of Christianity.[25] Certain passages in the Gospels and Paul and even more explicitly in the Hellenically immersed Clement and Origen's understanding of what the Christian "tradition" was and how it was transmitted suggest a "hidden wisdom" in the Church that it was not available to all.

In the end, Gnosticism's rejection of the world and of history were of little interest to religions committed to the historical process and God's direct intervention in his creation. More attractive, however, was its seizure of the commonplace Greek idea of a literal and allegorical sense of Scripture, and its endowment of the latter with a salvational value. Gnosticism created a dual community of believers in its host bodies: exoterics who were condemned to the limited horizons of the literal truths of revelation, and esoterics who could penetrate surface banalities to the "realities" that lay beneath.

Even though Christianity presents us with the first concrete evidence of a system that came to be labeled as "Gnostic," it may not be the absolute source of the phenomenon. There are traces of that same way of regarding the cosmos and humans' role within it in an even earlier religious context—the same, in fact, that produced Christianity itself, namely, the body of anonymous apocalyptic and wisdom literature circulating in post-Exilic Jewish circles. The roots of Gnosticism may very well lie there, in the disappointed hopes of the same Jews who produced the Book of Enoch. The authors and their circles are so carefully concealed behind the fictive names and contexts that we have only the most general idea of the historical setting for the individuals or groups who were meditating on those ideas of a Heavenly Wisdom.

At Qumran we now have just such a context.[26] On the evidence, the Essenes who lived there show no signs of being mystics, and

the community of Qumran may not have been a Gnostic association at all. But its preserved literature, which includes several of
the Apocrypha, reveals that they entertained apocalyptic expectations, and that such expectations deeply colored their reading of
the canonical Scriptures and the Apocrypha. They were, moreover, the likely bearers of that apocalyptic tradition into the nascent Christian community. Qumran, Christianity, and Gnosticism
come together in another interesting context. The Christian
sources attribute the origins of Gnosticism to Simon Magus, the
Samaritan wonder-worker who was a contemporary of Peter. Simon's own teacher was Dositheus, who was connected with John
the Baptist, and who may have been an Essene.[27]

## Jewish Mysticism

If a path, however uncertain and ill-defined, leads from Second
Temple Jewish apocalypticism to Christian Gnosticism, the
connection between the mystical element implicit in that same
apocalypticism and the observance-focused Pharisaic and rabbinic strain in Judaism is almost totally invisible. But there is reason to think that the Pharisees—Josephus is our best example—
deliberately underplayed this side of Jewish piety, particularly for
the benefit of the Gentile Romans. We cannot, at any rate, get at
the absolute beginnings of Jewish mysticism since what pass as the
earliest mystical texts date from the ninth century. There are persuasive arguments, however, that the matters being discussed in
those texts should be located much earlier. We have, for example,
an account of Yohanan ben Zakkai (d.ca. 80 c.e.), a crucial figure
in the passage from Pharisaic to rabbinic Judaism, engaged in
matter-of-fact discussions of mystical and apocalyptic themes.[28]
Other clues also point to the rabbis of the post-70s era as the likely
starting point to speculation about more intimate contact with
God.[29]

On somewhat closer inspection these and similar themes appear on occasion elsewhere in the Talmud, and from them and
other, anonymous works written between 200 and 500 c.e., it is
possible to fashion a preliminary portrait of early rabbinic mysticism. The Talmud was, of course, a public text whose study
was generally commended. But as the Talmud itself points out,
meditation on the mysteries implicit in two of the most common

ground-texts of Jewish mystical speculation—the opening chapter of Genesis and that of Ezekiel, where God's throne-chariot is described—was not recommended for the body of Jewish believers.

Recommended or not, over the succeeding generations a great deal of careful thought would be given to both subjects, the cosmic vistas of Genesis and the heavenly chariot in the first chapter of Ezekiel. Indeed, the divine enthronement on that mystical chariot (*merkaba*) gave a name and a starting point to an entire strain of Jewish mysticism.[30] A second strain was called *heykalot* or "palace-temples" after the celestial stations on the mystics' heavenly journeys toward God.[31] Merkaba and heykalot are the twin poles around which early Jewish mysticism unfolds, all of it in an otherwise highly legalistic-observant rabbinic culture from the second to the tenth century in the Middle East, when they were supplanted by the system known as Kabbala then emerging in France and Germany.[32]

Since much of this early speculation is anonymous, it is extremely difficult to date, but two such anonymous works, the *Measure of the Body* (*Shiur Qomah*) and the *Book of Creation* (*Sefer Yetzirah*), may go back to talmudic times.[33] The first is a mystic's meditation on the "body of God," its shape and dimensions, and is a typical Gnostic exercise of turning literalism in on itself to reveal deeper realities. The second is more philosophical in nature, and clearly shows Greek ideas working on Jewish mystical speculation about the origins and form of the universe. The occult meaning of names and numbers is explored; the hierarchy of divine emanations (*sefirot*) is laid out in detail.

## Kabbala

The development of this esoteric and mystical form of Judaism, which evolved simultaneously, if far less publicly, with the halakic work of the rabbis, eventually came to be called Kabbala (*qabbala*), literally "that which is handed down." The Mishna too had once been "handed down," but the distinction is the same as that which can be seen between Greek philosophy and the occult sciences; between Christian theology and Gnosticism; between the teachings of the Islamic lawyers and those of the Sufis. One kind of knowledge is public, literal, and discursive; the other is esoteric, allegorical, and mystical. It is the difference between theology and theosophy; between law and allegory; between intellect and intuition.

The Kabbalistic tradition has had a long and distinguished history in Judaism.[34] That it was deeply esoteric is manifest at every turn, and nowhere more clearly than in what became one of its classic texts, the *Zohar*, which was written—or better, composed—by Moses of León in Spain between 1270 and 1300 C.E.[35] The bulk of the *Zohar* is given over to a Kabbalistic midrash on the Torah, divided, in the classic fashion of the rabbinic midrashim, according to the liturgical recitation cycle of the law. This arcane and convoluted understanding of the "reality" behind plain texts and the material world now appears hopelessly difficult, as it was probably intended to be from the outset. But deep within it lay the mystic's urge to approach God in a paradoxically more direct way, an urge too powerful to remain concealed within the folds of esotericism. In Islam mysticism became popularized in the Sufi orders; in Christianity by such clerics as Ignatius of Loyola and Francis de Sales, who in the late sixteenth century brought the monks' spiritual exercises to the secular clergy and the laity alike; and in Judaism by the Hasidic movement, which in the eighteenth century divested Kabbalism of some of its more esoteric and inaccessible features to render it a kind of popular revelation.[36]

## The Illumined Mystic

Note has already been taken of the Gnostic current in Islamic Sufism and its eventual wedding with a parallel strain in Shiism. Though this union was officially consummated in the creation of the Safavid state in the sixteenth century, the liaison was being prepared much earlier. It is not certain when the affinities between Shiism and Sufism first developed, but they were already present when Shiism elaborated its theory of the Imam as a charismatic figure who possessed an authoritative spiritual knowledge and imparted it to adepts. The distance between the Shiite Imam and the Sufi saint, particularly the archetypical saint, the "pole" (*qutb*) around whom the saints of each generation revolved, was not great. From the twelfth century onward the distance grew even smaller with the evolution of what has been called "theosophical Sufism," "Sophiology," or "Illuminationism." Wisdom (*hikma*), as it turned out, was quite simply gnosis.

The chief agent of this turning of both philosophy and mysticism in the direction of theosophy was the philosopher Ibn Sina (d. 1038), or Avicenna as he is more generally known in the West. His contribution to the development and refinement of Islamic philosophy in its then current blend of Plato and Aristotle was enormous, but there are hints throughout his work that Avicenna had, behind and beyond his public and scholastic treatments of philosophical themes, a more esoteric "oriental philosophy" whose contents could only be hinted at.[37] The obliqueness of Avicenna's own allusions make its identification somewhat problematic, but a great many Muslims who came after him understood Avicenna's esoteric philosophy as some form of mysticism, and identified its author as a Sufi.[38]

Whether or not he was a Sufi in any formal sense, Avicenna laid heavy emphasis on some form of divine illumination (*ishraq*) as the means whereby the philosopher received the knowledge that was the object of his quest. Avicenna's "illumination," like that of Evagrius of Pontus, probably owed a great deal more to Neoplatonism than his many commentators and imitators were prepared to admit. It was, at any rate, an individual effort and an individual achievement, this pursuit of union with God, and there is nothing in Avicenna of the passage of a spiritual baraka from master to novice, no charismatic "chain" by which to mount on high.

One of Ibn Sina's most influential interpreters read him somewhat differently, however. Suhrawardi (d. 1191) took up and completed the Avicennan "visionary recitals" and interpreted the philosopher's illuminationist philosophy as a genuine renaissance of Persian wisdom.[39] For those ancient sages of Iran, the First Being was Xvarneh, "the light of glory" of Zoroastrianism, and that opened for Suhrawardi the opportunity of converting what had been for Ibn Sina and al-Ghazali an epistemological metaphor into a true metaphysic: existence and light are identical; the Necessary Being is Absolute Light. The "light" is Iranian, perhaps, but the notion of an "absolute" derived directly from the Greek tradition that underlay the thought of so many Muslim thinkers.

Though the Sunni lawyer and theologian was probably a less congenial figure to him than the Shiite philosopher, Suhrawardi learned as much from al-Ghazali as he did from Avicenna. Al-Ghazali (d. 1111) had already anticipated, as we shall see, a new task for that perennial handmaiden—philosophy—and Suhrawardi developed it with enthusiasm. Speculative knowledge, the wisdom that comes from research and investigation, was simply a preparation for the "wisdom that savors," the experimental knowledge of God. Philosophy thus received its justification and at the same time was assigned an appropriate place as a preparation for the final stages of the search for the Absolute. Suhrawardi likewise followed al-Ghazali in his elaboration of the rich possibilities of allegorical exegesis in the service of mysticism.

Suhrawardi's work, with its assertion of Persia's place in the history of wisdom, its attractive metaphysic of light, its developed theory of allegorical exegesis, and its valorization of experience over theoretical knowledge, provided a program for both the philosophers and the mystics of Iran, and a convenient bridge on which they might thereafter meet. That the meetings were frequent and rewarding is attested by the twin traditions of mystical poetry in Persian and the ill-charted but impressive course of theosophical and philosophical speculation during the reign of the Safavids in Iran.[40]

## Doctor Maximus

The doctor maximus of Islamic mysticism is beyond doubt the Spaniard Muhyi al-Din ibn al-Arabi, or simply Ibn Arabi (d. 1240).[41] His mystical experiences are described in engaging and often startling detail—he unabashedly tells about his conversations with God and a variety of Sufi saints, near and far, dead and alive—in the enormous body of his writing.[42] These personal anecdotes are embedded in an extraordinary confection of metaphysics and epistemology that constitutes his "system," unfolded piecemeal and randomly in his work. The details are both familiar and impenetrable. The familiar flow from the combination of Neoplatonic metaphysics and Gnostic theosophy that is the common possession of Islamic mysticism from Ibn Sina onward. Impenetrable is his manipulation of those concepts within his own unsystematic system, spiced with his fondness for paradox, his loving embrace of contradiction, and, at base, the originality of his spiritual vision.[43]

Ibn Arabi's quest for God plunges directly into the heart of the great cross-cutting issues of monotheism: God's similarity or dissimilarity to us, his own creation, and how God can be one and at the same time patently multiple in his manifestations. Ibn Arabi embraced both ends of the paradoxes. The mystic should be "the one with two eyes," who acknowledges God's transcendence and at the same time savors and builds on what Ibn Arabi called God's "with-ness" with respect to ourselves. In Ibn Arabi's version of creation, God "unfolds" himself in time and space out of a longing to contemplate himself in the mirror of the cosmos: *tajalli*, "self-disclosure" and *kashf*, "unveiling" are two of the most pervasive concepts in Ibn Arabi's understanding of God. Thus for Ibn Arabi our world is nothing other than the self-manifestation or reflection of God; the cosmos is the same as God, differing only in its degree of perfection and by its admixture of nonbeing. It seemed to follow, then, that God and the world, the Creator and Creation, are one and the same. This is the basis of the notorious doctrine dubbed the "Oneness of Being," the ontological pantheism that became the focus of the later traditionalist attacks on Ibn Arabi.

Sufism took eagerly to Ibn Arabi's verion of a pantheistic universe and its supporting apparatus of Gnostic esoterics, and such traditionalists as Ibn Taymiyya (d. 1328) were equally quick to discover the dangers of the Sufi metaphysic and its freewheeling exegesis to what had by then been shaped into a consensual version of Sunni Islam. But the Sufis were by no means the only proponents of Gnosticism in the Abode of Islam. There are Gnostic premises at the base of most of the occult sciences that flourished in the ancient and medieval world—alchemy for one.[44] The ease with which so many of them passed from one to the other of the very different religious climates of ancient Greco-Roman paganism, Middle Eastern Islam, and both Eastern and Western Christianity and Judaism underscores both the appeal and adaptability of Gnosticism. And in Islam Gnosticism demonstrated that it could adapt itself as readily to political as to scientific ends.

## Radical Theosophy: The Ismailis

The Ismailis were a subdivision of the Shiite movement who, unlike the main body of the Shiah in the Middle Ages, had a political program for overthrowing the Sunni caliph and replacing him with a revolutionary Mahdi-Imam.[45] They were not successful, but they had access to and put to effective use the entire Gnostic apparatus of cosmic history, in which the Shiite Imams became the Gnostic Aeons; a secret revelation of the "realities" that lay hidden in the concealed rather than the evident sense of Scripture; an

Imam-guide who possessed an infallible and authoritative magisterium (*talim*); and an initiated elite that formed, in the Ismaili case, the core of an elaborate political underground.[46] At their headquarters in Cairo, a city that the Ismaili Fatimids founded in 969, agents were instructed in the Ismaili gnosis and program and were sent forth with the "call" of the Mahdi-Imam to cells and cadres that had been set up in the caliphal lands in Iraq and Iran.

Sunni and Ismaili Islam shared a common foundation of reliance on authority and tradition. For the Sunni, that tradition was embodied in the elaborate structure of Muslim law which in turn rested on hadith reports. These went back to the Prophet's own words and deeds, and so constituted a second revelation with an authority equal to the Quran's own. The Quran and the sunna of the Prophet prescribed a certain order in the religious sphere, but that order was impossible to achieve without the establishment of a parallel political order that could guarantee the performance of religious duties by securing for each believer his or her life and property, and was capable at the same time of maintaining the unity of the community in the face of civil disorders. From this was derived the political authority (*siyasa*) of the caliph and his delegates.

For the Ismailis, the Imam was not a political corollary of a religious system but an integral part of the religious system itself. In a famous Shiite hadith, Muhammad, on return from his "ascension" to the highest heavens where the truths of creation were revealed to him, cast his mantle over his daughter Fatima and his grandsons Hasan and Husayn and so signified the transmission of those same truths to his Fatimid-Alid descendants. Thus it was the Imam alone who held, at least in theory—every Sufi and philosopher from the twelfth century onward claimed the same privilege—the key to tawil, the allegorical exegesis of Scripture that penetrated the surface meaning to the truths beneath.

## The Deliverer from Error: al-Ghazali

The intellectual defense of Sunnism against this claim was undertaken by the Baghdad lawyer and theologian al-Ghazali in a series of tracts that mounted a frontal attack on what he called "the Esotericists."[47] But the issue appears in all its complexity in a more personal statement, his *Deliverer from Error*, a work that describes his own investigation of the competing claims on the faith of the Muslim.[48] Faith tied to simple acceptance on the authority of others was insufficient for al-Ghazali; it could be shaken by the conflicting claims put forward by different parties and sects within Islam and by the equally strong adherence to their own faith by the Christians and Jews. Unless he was prepared to lapse into an agnostic skepticism, as al-Ghazali was not, there had to be some other way to certitude for the seeker after truth. Four possibilities presented themselves: the way of speculative theology, *kalam*, which professed to support its religious beliefs with rational argument; the way of the philosophers, who laid claim to true scientific demonstration; the Ismaili way, which promised religious certitude by reliance on the teaching of an infallible Imam; and finally the way of the Sufis or mystics, who offered intuitive understanding and a certitude born of standing in the presence of God.

Al-Ghazali found his anchor for his certitude in mysticism. It was, as remarked earlier, a "way" (tariqa) that could be entered from its scholastic, intellectualized side or by approaching it through experience. Al-Ghazali, with deep intellectual commitments and training—"knowledge was easier for me than activity"—entered by the first path: he read the classical theoretical treatises and the lives of the Sufi saints. It was a mistake, as he soon learned. It is better to experience intoxication than to know how to define drunkenness.[49] Al-Ghazali in fact began straightway to define it. The Sufi way begins with the via purgativa of asceticism and leads to an annihilation of self (*fana*). Higher states follow, visions of the angels and the spirits of the prophets. Finally, the desired experience of God is achieved by some, whether it be called "infusion," "connection," or "identity" (*ittihad*). There al-Ghazali broke off and retreated. It was all wrong. The apprehension of God is an incommunicable experience, and one can learn more by associating with Sufis than by explaining their activities.

Al-Ghazali's spiritual autobiography might appear to be a series of radical turnings, of entrances and hasty withdrawals. The withdrawals are more apparent than real, however. He accepted and never surrendered the case for an intellectually strengthened theology. He admitted the philosophers' claims to possess in the logical method an instrument for gaining certitude. He conceded that for most Muslims a simple acceptance on faith was an inevitable and not entirely unworthy course. And he argued strenuously yet prudently that there was a legitimate and important place in Islamic life for the experimental knowledge of God claimed by the mystics. All of these themes are woven together in his great summa for Sunni Islam, the *Revivification of the Sciences of Religion.*[50] The entire work has to do with what al-Ghazali called "the science of the Hereafter." It is in fact a remarkable attempt at interiorizing Muslim life. It deals with both knowledge and action, with external acts, the duties of the Muslim, and the internal dispositions that were too often ignored by Islam's lawyers and that al-Ghazali here proposed to reintegrate into everyday Muslim life. Islam could be, al-Ghazali showed, intellectually rigorous, spiritually dynamic, and firmly grounded in an unshakable faith.

The *Revivification*, which may be the most influential book ever written by a Muslim, had its desired effect. Muslim theology did become more rigorous by prudently expropriating the methodology of the philosophers, without accepting all their conclusions. Mystical union with God and the Sufi way that led to it won a degree of cautious acceptance. Al-Ghazali's language on mysticism in the *Revivification* is a carefully moderated version of "sober intoxication." When speaking more personally he could and did go further. His *Niche of Lights* is a meditation on the famous "Light verse" in the Quran (24:35), which served for Muslim mystics the same provocative function as the opening chapter in Ezekiel and the Gospels' Transfiguration episode did for Jews and Christians.[51]

The doctors of Islam embraced the *Revivification*; the mystics meditated the *Niche of Lights* and found there all the themes that were converging in the Sufi consensus: the identification of God's essence with a Light whose ontological radiance was creation and whose cognitive function was to illumine the intellects of the saints and prophets; the distinction between the plain and the concealed sense of Scripture, and the need of allegorical exegesis to elicit the latter;[52] the elitism that distinguished the mystic from all others in Islam and the esotericism that made revelation of the "realities" to the nonadepts a dangerous and highly inadvisable enterprise.[53] Suhrawardi and Ibn Arabi are already present in embryo in the *Niche of Lights*.

Al-Ghazali made Islam safe for Sufism, but he did not disarm the Ismailis, whose ideological and military assault on Baghdad continued for more than two centuries, though not always with the same methods. In the twelfth century, the Ismaili apparatus in

Iraq and Iran broke loose from Egyptian political control and pursued its own revolutionary course. It decentralized the insurrection by seizing isolated strong points and took up the demoralizing weapon of assassination against Sunni political and religious figures. Sunni opposition hardened against these so-called Esotericists, and the Ismailis were forced to play their final trump, the announcement of the End Time, the Spiritual Resurrection (*qiyama*).

The Ismaili Resurrection was not a variant of the Jewish or Christian apocalypse. It was the glorious termination of the cosmic cycle of history. The millennia-long series of prophets and Imams, of public revelations and private understandings was at an end: the Age of Perfection had dawned. There is something faintly Pauline in the Ismaili declaration of the end of Islam and the abrogation of the Islamic law. But whereas Paul could substitute a New Covenant for the Old and hail the New Law of Jesus indwelling in the members of the *ekklesia*, the Ismaili theology of the Resurrection did not give its adherents a reenergized sense of mission, but represented an admission that Sunni Islam was beyond its reach. Paul might surrender the Jews, but for the Ismailis there was no Gentile mission. Paradise was limited to the narrow confines of their mountain fortresses, where the Mongols found and destroyed them.

# CHAPTER EIGHT

# Thinking and Talking about God

Theology, discourse about God according to the principles of reason, was the formulation of the Greeks, a people without benefit of revelation. But not from the beginning. It is unnecessary here to discuss the origins of Greek religion except to note that by the time they began to produce a literary record, the Hellenes were already expressing at least some of their religious sentiments in the form of myth, complex narratives about a whole family of anthropomorphized gods and goddesses.

## Mythos and Logos

Myth is a special form of discourse divorced from time and only circumstantially connected with place. Like art, it presents itself rather than explaining or arguing. But for all its aesthetic splendors, a later generation of Hellenes grew unhappy with the mythological account of the gods. Both the mythical form of discourse and the value system inherent in the myths themselves were being challenged in an evolving Greek society by new ethical attitudes, particularly by a different kind of human understanding that found its external and formal expression in the form of discourse called *logos*.[1]

Logos is essentially a mode of understanding that pursues natural causes and a mode of discourse that can give an account of that pursuit; that argues and demonstrates rather than simply narrates; and that is subject to verification by criteria external to itself.

The categories of truth and falsehood, which are totally irrelevant to myth, are part of that verification apparatus. Logos is, in short, what we call science and what the Greeks more broadly termed philosophy.

By the generation of Socrates and Plato, logos was being applied in every corner of the known universe as well as to the domain of human activity. In the next generation Aristotle both formalized the method of logos in a series of works on logic (the science of logos), and distinguished and organized the already vast body of knowledge that had been won by philosophy. It was not Plato and Aristotle who introduced God or the gods, once only the subject of myth and the object of ceremonial worship, to the scrutiny of logos; nor, once introduced, did the supernatural surrender its other domains in the minds and the hearts of the Hellenes.[2] But Plato and Aristotle joined God and reason in a manner that profoundly influenced Western thinking about God, and that both stimulated and disturbed the chosen guardians of the divine Self-portrait, the Jews, Christians, and Muslims.

Greek philosophy, or rather its branch called "logos about the divine" (*theologia*), did not begin by presuming God's existence, though every Greek accepted the fact of that existence. Its task was rather to demonstrate the existence and nature of the divine. Few had any doubts this could be done, and the Greek theologians laid out with their usual elegant ease the various arguments, later so familiar, from the design and order of the universe, the consensus of humankind, and the necessity of a first cause in the "great chain of being" as it descends and a final cause to which it returns.

All of these arguments simply demonstrated, in a more or less rigorous form, what the Greeks, Romans, and others already knew. Where the new science departed more radically from commonly held opinions was in the portrait of that being or beings whom the Greeks called "the Immortals." The method of logos soon stripped from the divine two of its most obvious and universally recognized attributes, plurality and anthropomorphism. Theology, with its hierarchical view of reality, struck at the heart of ancient polytheism and denied as well that God could be anything but pure spirit, beyond flesh and bones, surely; beyond human affects such as love and hate; beyond thought, perhaps; and even, it was maintained, beyond being itself.

The theologians' vision of God as a single, transcendent, and spiritual cause was not yet monotheism. Although it removed the Supreme Being from direct contact with the material universe, it posited a great many intermediary beings below the remote transcendence of God, some of them intelligences without matter, and others who dwelled in the planets. These too were divine, God's own eternal emanations, which descended by degrees to the intelligences shared by humankind.

The theologians were not unmindful of the shambles they had made of popular religious attitudes and beliefs. Some professed not to care, but others such as the Stoics attempted to salvage the traditional myths by allegorizing them: Homer too was a theologian, it was held, but his manner of describing the nature of the gods was determined by the nature of his audience, whereas the speculative theologians could present the same truths in the unvarnished scientific language of philosophy. Even the mystery religions with their transparently primitive rituals could be explained in rationalistic terms for the newly sophisticated intelligentsia.

The Greek thinkers' desire to save Homer and the poets was not born of a conviction that they somehow represented a divine revelation, but was maintained because Homer was well understood to carry the traditions of the entire Hellenic cultural past. Revelation in the Judeo-Islamic style was an alien notion to the Greeks. If the gods spoke to mortals, as they assuredly did in dreams and through oracles, it was to warn or counsel some fairly circumscribed act, not to proffer covenants or salvation. If there was to be salvation, it would be through humans' use of their own intellectual faculties to discover what the good life was and the skillful and prudent way to achieve it.

## The Pioneer: Philo

Theology was one of the manifestations of Hellenism that came to the Middle East in the wake of Alexander the Great's conquests in the fourth century B.C.E. It took root in the schools of higher learning that grew up in newly founded cities like Alexandria and Antioch, and in more popular form spread among the Hellenic and Hellenized intelligentsia that was a by-product of Greco-Roman urbanism in the area.[3] Note has already been taken of the encounter of Hellenism and Judaism in both Palestine and the Diaspora. Greek ethical ideals, for example, are already apparent in the third century in the biblical Qohelet—Ecclesiastes in the Septuagint— and in the second-century B.C.E. *Wisdom of Jesus ben Sira.*[4] Jewish resistance to the new learning and style is charted in the various books of Maccabees.

Whatever one finds in such works falls, like the works themselves, into the category of semipopular attitudes intended for a general, literate audience. For evidence of more formal philosophical and theological speculation among the Jews one must turn from Palestine to the diaspora community in Egypt. The first Jew we know professed interest in Greek theology was a certain Aristobulus, who was from a high-priestly family and worked in Alexandria in the second century B.C.E.[5] The scattered fragments of his works, which were written in Greek, show a typical theologian at work, though for the first time on Jewish scriptural material. At once we are counseled against being trapped into a literal interpretation of the Torah, which in Aristobulus's own day had been translated into Greek. A literal approach to the text shows nothing particularly unusual about the Torah, but an allegorical understanding reveals Moses as a true prophet who shared the philosophers' gift of wisdom, though Moses' account is, for all its metaphorical expression, superior to the Greek version of wisdom by reason of its obvious antiquity.

The themes touched on by Aristobulus—the identity of Greek and Jewish wisdom, for example, which is revealed by the prudent application of allegorical exegesis—were not only taken up by his fellow Alexandrian Philo, but are surrounded by such a considerable body of philosophical theory that it is possible to locate the later theologian rather precisely in the eclectic blend of Stoicism and Platonism current in the Roman world of his day.[6] Philo's allegorical exegesis is in the true Stoic manner, but some of his refinements of Platonic and Stoic metaphysics are far more remarkable.[7] The God of the philosophers was too transcendent and too remote to have a direct hand in either the creation or the governance of the world, and so Philo had recourse to an intermediary, or rather a series of intermediaries. God for Philo, as he had been for Aristotle, was self-thinking thought, and it is God's ideas (*eide*) that are the spiritual archetypes of creation. The first external manifestation of these is the Logos, both Word and Idea, whom Philo personified as "the second God." The Logos serves as both the heavenly spiritual archetype of human intelligence and the instrument whereby all the other "ideas" (*logoi*) are disseminated in matter. They not only bring the material universe into existence but they govern it according to God's providential plan as well.

Greek theologians had for some time been experimenting with the notion of a Logos or Word as God's first emanation and the instrument of creation, and their influence is perhaps visible in earlier Jewish authors' treatment of "Wisdom" as a personified entity somehow distinct from God and even as an agent in Creation. If Philo's language on the Logos is somewhat bold, it is certainly not to be construed as a retreat from monotheism. On the contrary, it was designed to protect God's transcendence and at the same time establish a link between this now philosophically remote Creator and his distant and somewhat degenerate creation.[8]

Philo is the first we know—Greek, Roman, or Jew—to advance the notion that the Platonic *eide*, those spiritual and eternal archetypes of reality, are actually the thoughts of God, a remarkably fruitful idea for those Jewish, Christian, and Islamic theologians who could thus restrain themselves from following the Greeks farther down the same path and deny even thought to God.[9] And though Philo's doctrine of Logos as God's instrument in creation had no great future in Judaism, it had an immediate and obvious appeal to Christian thinkers.

Earlier theologians had to take into account that poets and others had had their say on the subject of God, and had attempted to reconcile "poetical" and "speculative" theology by allegorical exegesis. Philo's task was somewhat different. He accepted the fact of a historical revelation to Moses on Sinai without hesitation or reserve, just as he accepted the truths contained in that revelation. He also accepted the truth of philosophy, and saw no contradiction between the two, at least in principle. There were, in fact, differences—the Greeks generally believed, for example, in a universe that was created but eternal and in a providence that was general but did not descend to particulars—and where they existed, Philo came down firmly on the side of the scriptural witness. Some of the apparent differences between Scripture and philosophy could be resolved by applying rationalizing exegesis to the former, but where Philo deemed reconciliation impossible, he followed Moses, not Plato.

Philo's language was Greek, and his version of Scripture was the Greek Septuagint translated in Alexandria in the mid–third century B.C.E. By this apparently simple act of translation, Scripture was clothed in Greek raiment with its own set of connotations, some of them already philosophical. But it was the theologian Philo who took the decisive step in converting scriptural notions into philosophical ones by his method of allegorical exegesis, thereby opening the Septuagint to discussion in a manner denied to the legal exegetes. What remained to his successors in Judaism, Christianity, and Islam was to measure the new currency against the old, reason against revelation, a necessary but necessarily impossible task.

## The Logos and the Christ

Philo's work was greeted with no visible enthusiasm in Palestinian circles. To the Pharisees and other non-Hellenized Jews it was probably inaccessible in any event, and although the voice of the Palestinian "Hellenists" of the day can be heard on political questions, it is inaudible on religious matters. But Philo's works must have been read in the Diaspora—Paul for one appears to have been aware of them—and they found, as has been said, their most appreciative audience among the Hellenized converts to Christianity, first the Jews and then the Gentiles. The Logos of the opening of John's Gospel probably owes nothing to Philo, but it was obviously capable of Philonian interpretation, which was freely applied at Philo's own city of Alexandria less than two centuries later by the Christian Hellenists Clement and Origen.

Theology did not come into Christianity through Philo alone. Already in Paul and the Gospel of John there are theological notions, that is, ideas expressed in the abstract conceptual terminology typical of theological rather than scriptural discourse, with the latter's preference for the concrete on one hand and the metaphorical and parabolic expression on the other. Paul and John were no doubt exposed to theological ideas that they accepted and used. There was already a plentiful supply of such in Jewish apocryphal literature, which portrayed the divine Wisdom and the Messiah as spiritual realities that existed from the moment of Creation. Paul took up and combined both notions in his description of Jesus as the preexistent Logos.[10]

Neither Paul nor John argued theologically, however; they simply asserted by virtue of their own authority as Apostles. Logical demonstration and proof were the hallmarks of the philosophical method, as every Jewish and Christian thinker who came into contact with philosophy at this time was aware. Apostolic authority did not much appeal to Gentiles as an alternative to proof, and so something the Gentiles could and did understand began to be substituted; public miracle was the scriptural equivalent of demonstrative proof.[11] But these same thinkers were equally aware of the attractive dangers of speculative theology, and although some, like Philo and Justin, thought the wisdom of the Greeks and the wisdom of God could be reconciled, Paul was the first but by no means the last to set the two at odds as natural antagonists.

One example of how a Christian became a theologian is provided by the career of Justin, who was born of Hellenized pagan parents in Samaria and was martyred for his Christianity about 165 C.E. His *Dialogue with Trypho*, probably the "Rabbi Tarphon" mentioned in the Mishna, gives some account of the spiritual odyssey that led Justin to Christianity.[12] A need for religious satisfaction drove him first to philosophy; "conversion" to philosophy was not uncommon at this period—later Greek philosophy with its strong emphasis on ethical regimens and its noticeable interest in piety was assuming for many the role of a religion[13]—but after he had investigated the major schools he finally found spiritual peace in Christianity. Conversion to Christianity did not mean, however, either the rejection of philosophy or its total acceptance. Christianity was the true "philosophy," and the anticipation of many of its tenets—the immortality of the soul remained a perennial example in this type of literature—was a clear demonstration that Jesus, the eternal Logos, had been at work in the world from the beginning. "In the beginning was the Word. . . ." The argument worked equally well against Judaism: not only Socrates but Abraham himself was a Christian before Christ.

If Justin represents a modest accommodation of philosophical and theological discourse with Christian revelation, the first wholesale and radical attempts in that direction took place in Alexandria in the same century, at the hands of such Gnostics as Basilides and Valentinus. The Christian Fathers who took up its refutation were convinced that the seed of Gnostic error lay in Greek philosophy. We cannot easily judge for ourselves, since most of the Christian Gnostic treatises that came to light at Nag Hammadi in Egypt in 1945 are "scriptural" rather than philosophic in form, that is, they are principally apocryphal Gospels, apocalypses, and wisdom literature.[14] Irenaeus and Hippolytus are certainly correct to the extent that the Alexandrian Gnostic writings are filled with Greek philosophical concepts and terminology. But there is as little genuine demonstration in them as in Paul, and it seems far more likely that Christian Gnosticism is essentially a mythic system, a cosmic drama in which the chief actors have been clothed in the abstract costumes of Greek philosophy.[15]

Whatever the modern historians might say, the Fathers made their own judgment: Gnosticism was another example of the perversions of the Greeks, and its spread among the intelligentsia simply underlined the basic opposition between pagan and Christian wisdom. The firmest statement of that opposition was expressed by a Latin Christian, Tertullian (d. ca. 240), who rhetorically exclaimed, "What has Athens to do with Jerusalem? What agreement between the Academy and the Church?" Tertullian had witnessed the effects of Gnosticism, and had like others traced its errors to Greek philosophy. It served to confirm his conviction that faith and faith alone was sufficient for the Christian, since the entire truth had been revealed. More, Tertullian was willing not merely to accept but even to boast of the differences: the Christian believes in the paradoxes of Christianity precisely because they are absurd.[16]

## Clement and Origen

Tertullian, who had considerably greater confidence in human reason when it manifested itself in the form of Roman law rather than Greek philosophy, may reflect a basic cultural difference between the Latin and Greek forms of Christianity. Clement of Alexandria, who lived about the same time, came from a totally different environment and showed none of Tertullian's disdain for philosophy, and uttered no apostrophes against "wretched Aristotle." For Clement the works of human reason served the same purpose for the Gentiles as the law did for the Jews: they were an "evangelical preparation," as the historian Eusebius later called it. Greek wisdom was true wisdom in that it was the product of an intelligence that humans share with God, or of a special kind of natural revelation that the Logos gave to the Gentiles. Clement, who knew Philo's work exceedingly well, was aware of one of the latter's arguments justifying recourse to philosophy, that the Greek thinkers had read the Scriptures and expropriated many of its doctrines, and did not hesitate to invoke it for his own case.

Most of Clement's thinking about theology is found strewn across a work he called *Stromata* or *Carpets*.[17] It is not an unnatural distribution, perhaps, since from Philo onward the compatibility of speculative theology and divine revelation was principally demonstrated in the exegesis of Scripture and the sequence of the sacred writings that provided the form within which both Jewish and Christian theologians worked. No Christian had undertaken that exegesis on the same scale and with the same penetration as Philo until Origen, Clement's successor in the nascent Christian school in Alexandria. Origen could do the same kind of philosophical analysis of Scripture as his Jewish antecedent, but as a Christian he added typology, the foreshadowing of events in the New Testament by the Old, a method already popularized by the Gospels themselves. Origen was, in addition, a considerable textual scholar.[18]

On the Philo model, every Christian theologian had necessarily to be an exegete. But Origen was more. He was the first Christian to put his hand to systematic theology by arranging his material in the logical order of an academic school treatise—he may have attended the Platonic Academy in Alexandria—rather than in that dictated by the order of Scripture. The result was *On First Principles*, a detailed statement of the truths of Christianity derived from Scripture but stated and argued in theological form.[19] Thus, in speaking of the Father, Jesus the Logos, and the Holy Spirit, Origen described each as a separate "essence" or "substance" (*ousia*) and "individual" (*hypostasis, hypokeimenon*), and he characterized the Trinitarian unity as "consubstantial" (*homoousios*).[20]

## Theology and Creeds

Christianity had perhaps little choice but to embrace the Hellenic theology: its early intellectuals had all been educated in that system. Thus, if they were going to explain Christian doctrine to themselves and others in what was to them and their audience a familiar and convincing manner, they had first to convert scriptural mythos (as the Hellenized Paul had already begun to do) into the currency of Hellenic-style logos. "Son of God," for example, was the Gospels' biological metaphor to explain Jesus' relationship to Yahweh. The philosopher-theologians of the fourth century were not averse to metaphors, but in this case they preferred to substitute the terms of current scientific discourse, generation and substance, and to explore their relationship by invoking concepts like modality, subordination, and eternity. An attempt to think and talk about Jesus after this manner led the Alexandrian cleric Arius (d. ca. 336) to propose that Jesus, as "Son," had necessarily to be subordinate to his "Father," who was by definition eternal and unbegotten, whereas for Jesus, "there was a time when he was not."[21] Logically this made sense, perhaps, but when this teaching became widespread, the bishops convened in council at Nicea in 325 C.E. declared it heretical and issued their own dogma, couched in the very same theological terms, affirming that Jesus was "begotten, not made" of the Father and was, as Origen had said, consubstantial (*homoousios*) with him, the latter a term of art in logos but exceedingly remote from Scripture.

There was more. The Greek definition of the Trinity as "three individuals (*hypostases*) in one being (*ousia*)" became in Latin "three persons in one substance," the very translation causing an additional problem. The bishops continued to support their positions by citing Scripture, but invariably dogma was set forth in the language of theology. Not surprisingly, though there were important canon lawyers, the theologians among the clergy (a double filter) constituted Christianity's elite for much of its history.

At Nicea the bishops pronounced dogmatically on the relationship of the Father and the Son, but the work of translating scriptural ways of talking and thinking into the scientific (i.e., theological) idiom of the times had scarcely begun.[22] The issue of Jesus himself remained. Christology was a matter of decoding titles in the New Testament, but in the decades that followed Nicea, Christian intellectuals attempted to understand the Jewish messiah who was their God in theologically coherent terms. The Scripture might simply assert that he was both man and Son of God, but fourth- and fifth-century theologians had to reconcile those assertions in terms of contemporary philosophical discourse: how could the single personality of Jesus encompass both a human and a divine nature, as that latter term was understood? Culture, tradition, and theological ingenuity supplied varied answers. Some emphasized Jesus' humanity: he was a man whom God had glorified to divine status. This view may have developed out of an original Jewish-Christian position that saw Jesus' messiahship as acquired or bestowed, likely at his resurrection. Others, under a demonstrably more Hellenic influence, regarded Jesus as eternally and dominantly divine, the Godhead clothed in flesh, so to speak. The first position came to be known as Nestorianism, and perhaps reflected an older, Jewish way of looking at Jesus; the second was termed Monophysitism, and was clearly more congenial to some of the Hellenically minded theologians.

The ecumenical council convened at Chalcedon in 451 C.E. condemned both and asserted against all logic, but unmistakably *with* Scripture, that Jesus was "complete in Godhead and complete in manhood, truly God and truly man." Moreover, each nature, the human and the divine, could use the faculties of the other. As the thesis of redemption had already implied, God had to have died on the cross; by its dogmatic definition, the Council of Chalcedon affirmed that this had indeed occurred. Hellenic philosophy had as one of its objectives "to save the *phainomena*," or, as we might put it, "to explain the evidence" by a reasonable hypothesis. Sacred theology's intent, as demonstrated clearly at Chalcedon, was "to save the *theologoumena*," the beliefs of the faith.[23]

## The Muslims Encounter Aristotle

The scientific mode of inquiry, that is, an investigation or explanation of phenomena on rationally and dialectically defensible principles, came in contact with revealed monotheistic religions on several different occasions, but nowhere so painfully or productively as in their contact with Hellenism. In some instances the monotheists learned Greek, as Jews did in the Diaspora in the second and first centuries B.C.E. and the Christians two or three centuries later, and so became Hellenes in the narrower linguistic sense. Elsewhere, however, Hellenism's cultural goods had to be translated, into Syriac, for example, for the benefit of the only fitfully Hellenized Christians of inner Syria and Mesopotamia;

into Arabic for Muslims and Jews of the ninth- to the eleventh-century Abode of Islam; and finally, into Latin for Christians of eleventh- and twelfth-century Europe who had all but forgotten their Hellenic heritage.[24]

Muslims probably first came into contact with theology not in its Greek form but in its Christian adaptation, which has already been characterized as sacred theology, that is, Hellenic rationalism in the sometimes awkward service of scriptural faith. The setting was probably the debates and polemics that occurred when Muslims moved into what were still overwhelmingly Christian milieus in the Middle East. The evergreen monotheist problems of free will and predestination, which the Quran had raised anew—and not resolved—seem to have been high on the list of debate topics between Christians and Muslims, and likely the Trinity, which the Quran itself had questioned.[25] The debate must have been rather one-sided, at least until the Muslims began to equip themselves with the dialectical weapons of their religious adversaries.

Sometime late in the eighth century, Muslim intellectuals, principally in the new cosmopolitan capital of Baghdad, had put at their disposal the very foundation works of intellectual Hellenism: summaries and adaptations of Plato's dialogues and full translations of practically all of Aristotle's works (together with various later Greek commentaries on them), as well as the geometry of Euclid, the astronomical geography and alchemy of Ptolemy of Alexandria, and the medical works of Galen, among others. This was technology transfer on a massive scale, this passage of the intellectual goods of one culture into the quite different idiom of another. The bridge-builders of this transfer were the highly cultured Syrian Christians of Iraq, most of whom had left the ecumenical fold in the wake of the Council of Chalcedon and consequently had little esteem for the "imperial" (Melkite) church of Byzantium. It was their language, Syriac Aramaic, that served as the intermediary stage between Aristotle's Greek and the Muslims' Arabic.[26]

The translation movement from Greek into Arabic lasted no more than two hundred-odd years—it was all but over by 1000 C.E.—and its effects, along with a parallel absorption of Indian and Persian material via Iran, were profound. It gave new and highly creative energy to Muslims' interest in medicine, pharmacology, mathematics, physics, optics, astronomy, astrology, and alchemy. Both of the latter were exact and highly esteemed sciences in antiquity and the medieval era, though viewed with disapproval by the religious authorities: astrology because it was too fatalistic, alchemy because it was too creative. But this Hellenic inheritance also confronted and challenged the very principles of Islam, as it already had those of Judaism and Christianity, and there its effects were considerably more problematic.

## Learning to Speak Dialectically

Among their opponents, the early Muslim lawyers were accustomed to distinguish between the "partisans of hadith" and the "partisans of kalam" as two opposed positions whose adherents were unwilling to be drawn into the Shafiite consensus.[27] The first, the "traditionists," refused to sanction local legal usages, what we might call customary law, and preferred to rely as closely as possible on the Quran and the Prophetic reports whose history we have already inspected. The second rejected the hadith reports in favor of using their own powers of research (*nazar*) and applying a certain degree of personal judgment (*ijtihad*) on the revealed Quran. This dispute occurred in a legal context, and though the traditionists continued to make their principal case within the domain of jurisprudence, the partisans of kalam found other, more congenial terrain for their preoccupations. They acquired another name as well, that of Mutazilites.[28]

In Arabic *kalam* means literally "speech," but we know too much about the Muslim history and development of the word to regard it simply as that, or even as an elliptic Arabic translation of the Greek *theologia*, "speech about God."[29] At first kalam may have appeared as such inasmuch as it seemed to oppose investigation (*nazar*) to an unquestioning acceptance on the authority of another, what is called in Arabic *taqlid* or "acceptance." When, however, a genuine philosophical tradition appeared in Islam in the wake of the Greek translations, and generations of Muslims and Jews had an opportunity of observing the difference between it and what they called kalam, the true nature of the latter became manifest.[30] *Kalam* is probably best translated, then, as "dialectical theology" in that it took as its starting point not the first principles of reason, but commonly held opinions. Nor did it proceed in the strict syllogistic method prescribed by Aristotle in his *Analytics*: rather it invoked the shorthand, persuasive arguments described in the *Topics* as "rhetorical" or "dialectical."[31]

In the eyes of Islam's philosophers, kalam was at best a defensive and apologetic weapon, and at worst a misleading replica of true philosophical discourse, a tin man without a heart. But it was in fact some kind of theology in that it attempted to explain and argue its positions on God and the universe instead of simply asserting them. Muslim lawyers had been using that type of ijtihad in their legal reasoning, but where the Mutazilites broke new ground was in applying analogy and the like to nonlegal and even nonquranic topics such as substance and accident, cause and effect, matter and spirit.

This is familiar ground for us, who have observed the progress of Greek philosophical concepts and reasoning into the vitals of Jewish and Christian religious discourse, but it was exceedingly alien to the partisans of hadith, who knew nothing of such notions and found them threatening to Islam's scriptural heritage. The Mutazilites were not Greek rationalists, of course; they began with the givens of the Quran. But they extended those givens well beyond both the problematic and the conceptual currency of the Quran and into a view of the physical world that they felt accorded well with their view of God's omnipotence, and into a distinction between God's essence and his attributes that they felt safeguarded the spirituality and simplicity of the Godhead.[32]

If the concepts of the Mutazilites appear familiar, we are at a loss to explain how these transparently Greek notions got into heads in eighth-century Basra and Baghdad. These "kalamists" (*mutakallimun*) were not Greek intellectuals converted to a new faith, but Arabs who antedated most of what we know of the translation movement in Islam. We do know that the same caliph who sponsored and supported the beginnings of the translation movement, al-Mamun (r. 813–833), was also a staunch supporter of the Mutazilite point of view. And not merely a supporter: he made an effort to define it as orthodoxy and to force the traditionists to accept it as such. Unlike his caliphal predecessors, who may have punished deviance but never undertook to define orthodoxy, al-Mamun decreed that Islamic "orthodoxy" consisted in belief in the createdness of the Quran. This was the subject of the "scrutiny" (*mihna*), and those who failed it were subject to flogging or imprisonment. The theological point may strike someone not listening to religious discourse in early ninth-century Baghdad as a rather arcane one on which to construct a theological loyalty oath, but beneath it lay an enormous iceberg of philosophical argument that derived in turn from Aristotelian notions of matter, space, and time and, indeed, of God himself. Al-Mamun knew what he was about.[33]

As often seems to happen, al-Mamun caught one very large martyr in his net. Ahmad ibn Hanbal, the leader of Baghdad's traditionists, preferred jail to a created Quran, and the forces of conservatism and, on a larger plan, of decentralized religious authority had their rallying point. He was soon released, however, and the whole affair was made to seem a fiasco. Ibn Hanbal became a kind of living martyr for the traditional faith, a Galileo in reverse, so to speak: *e pur' non si muove.*

The mihna lingered on a few more years until in 848 the caliph Mutawakkil abandoned the dogma of the created Quran. But the damage had been done. What earlier caliphs of the House of Abbas had envisioned as an open society had become polarized, the rationalists versus the traditionalists and, by way of corollary, the philosophical theologians versus the lawyers. In the end the latter triumphed. Aristotelian dialectic and odds and ends of the problematic of the philosophers found some modest foothold in kalam, dialectical theology, and were allowed an untenured place on the edges of the legal curriculum, the only one that counted in Islamic higher education. But the fear of rationalism was not easily dispelled, and there was a caliphal ban on selling books dealing with kalam or philosophy in 892, which was repeated in 897.

## On Philosophy and Prophecy

The received version of philosophy (*falsafa*) in Islam was not unnaturally Greek in its origins, methodology, and problematic. It was also predictably eclectic in the manner of most philosophy in late antiquity, and its more theologically inclined contributors such as Plotinus and Proclus were disguised for the Muslim reader, as they often were earlier for the Christian, by anonymity or pseudepigraphy. But disguised or not, and whether called "first philosophy" or "metaphysics," Islam now possessed a theology, or rather another theology, to set beside the quranic portrait of God and that newly fashioned by the Mutazilite masters of kalam.[34] The very first master of falsafa, al-Kindi (d. ca. 870), a younger contemporary of al-Mamun, set out a series of disturbing positions.[35] Most ominously for many Muslims, he posited the existence of a human rational wisdom that ran parallel to the sacred wisdom of revelation. In al-Kindi the human intellect, to which the lawyers had granted some small measure of autonomy under the rubric *ijtihad* or "personal effort," was now given, in the best Hellenic fashion, direct access to God. According to al-Kindi, what the Prophet had gained without toil by God's gift, the philosopher could also attain by strenuous intellectual effort. It was a generous if somewhat grudging concession to philosophy, but the door was now open and at least one Muslim chose to walk through. The physician and philosopher al-Razi (d. 925) not only granted the philosopher access to a knowledge of God; he denied it to the prophets of revelation. Philosophy was the *only* path to wisdom.[36] This was outright apostasy and disbelief (*kufr*), and though not many other philosophers were willing to go as far as al-Razi, the extreme dangers of the rationalist position were manifest. Falsafa cannot be said to have had a brilliant career in Islam, despite the efforts of such men as al-Farabi and Avicenna to reconcile faith and reason in a more sophisticated manner than al-Kindi, and with far greater Islamic sensibilities than those displayed by al-Razi.

Unlike al-Kindi, al-Farabi (d. 950) was unwilling to write off prophetic revelation as a separate and independent means of attaining enlightenment.[37] He approached the question from the distinctive angle of political philosophy, distinctive not with regard to his mentor Plato, of course, but in the light of the history of later Greek philosophy, which betrayed no interest in political philosophy. Al-Farabi's ideal state was to be ruled by someone who combined both intellectual and practical enlightenment, the qualities of the philosopher and the prophet. The true prophet, according to al-Farabi, could take the truths shared with the philosopher by reason of surpassing intellect and convert them, through the imaginative faculty, into the figured truths of a revelation like the Quran, or into the concrete realities of a law like the sharia. But what al-Farabi said of the "prophet" was true of all prophets, and there was no apparent attempt on his part to defend the unique quality of the Islamic revelation.[38]

Avicenna (d. 1038) could explain no less than al-Farabi both the need and process of prophecy-revelation.[39] He wrote a special treatise, *On the Proof of Prophecy*.[40] How prophecy occurred could be explained easily enough within the capacious categories of Greek cognitive theories, with which Avicenna and al-Farabi were both well acquainted, but the need for revelation, if the same truths were available to unaided human reason, was considerably more problematic. On this issue, the philosophers fell back on familiar Platonic and Gnostic ground. Not everyone was capable of reflective reasoning, and so it was for the great mass of unphilosophical humankind that God, the God of both the ignorant and the learned, chose to reveal his truths through a prophet.

The argument is not unlike that found among Sufis and other mystics in pursuit of private revelation. The sharia was not for them, the bolder among them claimed; it was intended for the masses. Avicenna could understand, if not necessarily agree with, that line of reasoning, since he was not much removed from the mystical stance in his own later philosophy. Many of the Greeks in the Platonic tradition had argued that discursive reasoning had its limits, and that the final knowledge of God was not the result of some last bit of understanding falling into place but came only with a bold intuitive leap across the narrowed gap between Creator and creature, what Plotinus famously called "a flight of the alone to the Alone."[41] That moment took on great importance for Avicenna. "Illumination" (*ishraq*) or the notion of a Gnostic-type wisdom (*marifa*) does not loom large in Avicenna's philosophical encyclopedias like the *Book of Healing* or his *Book of Scientific Knowledge*, but his later mystical treatises make it clear that this intuitive union with the Divine was central to what he was beginning to conceive of as a kind of esoteric philosophy.[42]

## Kalam Matured

The distance between Avicenna and the Mutazilites of scarcely two centuries earlier is almost immeasurable. They began with the Quran; he with the first principles of reason. Their reasoning was dialectical; Avicenna had full command of the Aristotelian scientific logic. The Mutazilites had fed on some ill-digested philosophical material from disguised sources; Avicenna had educated himself on the entire range of Greek philosophical science.[43] But even the Mutazilites' modest movement in the direction of a rationalizing theology had gotten them in trouble with the traditionists, who regarded it as a dangerous innovation, particularly after al-Mamun's official support was withdrawn by his successors.

Ahmad ibn Hanbal and his followers wanted nothing to do with the newfound skill in argument that, when applied to what they regarded as the foundations of the faith, led to "innovation," which was, at best, mischief, and, at worst, heresy. Most Muslims probably agreed, and once official caliphal support for the Mutazilites was withdrawn, the Hanbalites, as they came to be called, hesitated no less in taking their anger to the streets of Baghdad and voicing their opposition to innovators and rationalists than did the fifth-century Christian monks of Alexandria, Antioch, or Constantinople. But even as they did, forces of reconciliation were at work. Tradition credits the first step to al-Ashari (d. 935), who was neither a philosopher nor, in the end, much of a dialectical theologian, a mutakallim.[44] He was at base a traditionist who was willing to vacate some of the more virulent anti-intellectualism of the Hanbalis and to accept at least some Mutazilite positions. But he could not and would not embrace a Mutazilite universe governed by the laws of natural causality or their version of God divested of his eternal quranic attributes.[45] Al-Ashari's universe was an occasionalist one of atoms and accidents in which God, a quranic God of the traditionists' understanding, intervened directly, everywhere and at all times.[46]

By the opening of the tenth century, Muslim beliefs had approached a kind of consensus, one that read the Quran somewhat literally and took as its guideline for both understanding the Quran and living a Muslim life, the sunna of the Prophet, the body of "sound" traditions reported from Muhammad. This was al-Ashari's base line of a genuine Islam, and what he proposed was what Philo had pioneered for Jews and Origen for Christians: to combine, in some fashion, what then constituted Islamic belief with the Mutazilites' rational approach to belief, in short, to construct what would be called in Christian terms a sacred theology. Thus came into existence kalam or dialectical theology.

Al-Ashari's pioneer version of kalam was notoriously heavier on hadith than on dialectic, and kalam would ever be such, but it nonetheless represents the Muslim mainstream's effort to assimilate Aristotelian rationalism, at many removes, into Islamic religious culture. Its effects from al-Ashari onward were at best unremarkable, and its most considerable practitioner, the Baghdad master al-Ghazali, found kalam sadly inferior to mysticism as a path to God.[47] The most al-Ghazali would concede was that kalam was a useful defensive weapon, "like a protective troop along the pilgrim road." The Spanish social historian Ibn Khaldun (d. 1406) later tried to phrase it more systematically: "Kalam is a science that argues from logical proofs in defense of the articles of faith and to refute innovators who deviate in their dogmas from the early Muslims and Muslim orthodoxy."[48]

Al-Ashari did not entirely convince the Hanbalis, nor did the strict traditionists prevent a version of Asharite kalam from winning a place in the spectrum of Islamic orthodoxy as a legitimate instrument for explaining and defending revelation and the traditions.[49] The opportunity for showing kalam's usefulness as a dialectical weapon arose with the aggressive growth of Ismaili Shiism, which rested its convictions on the infallible teaching (*talim*) of an Imam, but it was in fact suffused with the models and methods of Greek philosophy. Sunnism's defense was taken up by al-Ghazali, a professor of jurisprudence in Baghdad who sought to convict not only the Ismailis but also the philosophers who were their inspiration.[50] He did so not by falling back on traditionist arguments, which would have been rejected out of hand by his opponents, but by infusing kalam with sufficient rigor to meet the opposition on their own ground. Al-Ghazali took on the philosophers, chiefly al-Farabi and Avicenna, in his *Incoherence of the Philosophers*, and the Ismailis in a whole series of polemical treatises.[51] Al-Ghazali was by no means a theological reactionary. He expropriated into his own version of kalam far more of Avicenna than al-Ashari could conceivably have dreamed, and he accepted and glorified a form of Sufism whose intellectual foundations ran deep into Neoplatonism.

Why sacred theology had so mild an effect on Islamic religious culture is fairly evident. Al-Ghazali's critique of Avicenna's cosmology and of the Greek cosmology that lay behind it made it forever suspect among the mutakallimun. But the roots are deeper and more systematic. The only institutionalized form of higher education in Islam was the madrasa, which was, from its beginning to the present, unabashedly a school of Islamic law. The overwhelming majority of Islam's intelligentsia passed through that system and so, whether they practiced or not, were ulama trained in hadith-oriented jurisprudence. Asharite kalam found only a modest handhold in the madrasa curriculum, as a kind of innocuous minor pursuit; and anything more rigorous was taught, and learned, privately.[52] Thus kalam was undersubscribed, undersupported, and undervalued; and in the end it found that it had little to say. Only at the extremes of the enterprise were there signs of vitality, at the outer margins of the Greek tradition and at the outer limits of the Muslim community.

## Muslim Creeds

And yet the final triumph belonged, in a sense, to kalam. One cannot always calculate the traditionist response to the theologians since the partisans of hadith more often defended their beliefs with polemic than with staked-out positions of their own. Christianity, as we have seen, defined and redefined itself in a series of credal statements, and in the positive dogma and negative anathemas issued by the councils.[53] Islam had no comparable conciliar structure, and its closest approximation to a creed in the sense of a baptismal formula is the simple shahada: "There is no god but the God and Muhammad is his envoy."[54] By the mid–eighth century, however, longer statements in the form of a creed (aqida) began to appear anonymously in legal circles. Remarkably, they had nothing to do with the two basic elements of the shahada, which are the affirmations required of the individual Muslim, but addressed themselves to current religio-political disputes, and eventually in terms borrowed from kalam.

The ten articles of the Fiqh Akbar I took their stand against Kharijites, Shiites, and the partisans of free will, and so probably date from around 750 C.E., when these issues were current. A century and a half later, the creed called "The Testament of Abu Hanifah" had grown to twenty-seven articles. It reflected the Mutazilite controversy about the createdness of the Quran, where it took a strongly Hanbalite and traditionist stance in opposition, and was markedly more adventuresome than its predecessor in attempting to define faith and adjudicate between the relative importance of faith and good works. Technical kalam vocabulary also made its first appearance. A third document, the Fiqh Akbar II, completes the evolution. This late tenth-century creed showed clearly the penetration of kalam into traditionist thought. Like its predecessors, it was not a declaration of what one must believe to be a Muslim but rather a not very systematic Asharite statement of position on the theological arguments of its day: the corporeality of Allah, the allegorical understanding of Scripture, and the attributes of God.[55]

All these so-called creeds were manifestly not documents to live by but somewhat sectarian statements on problems troubling the early lawyers and mutakallimun. Many of the points were still in contention at the time of composition, but if one moved forward to the period of al-Ghazali and beyond, when a consensus of sorts had developed in Sunni Islam, the Muslim creeds had much the same appearance as a Christian catechism, that is, of highly stylized, albeit abbreviated and simplified treatises of scholastic theology.

## Ibn Rushd

However "philosophical" it tried to become, kalam found little favor among the ever-thinning strain of philosophers in Islam. Ibn Rushd or Averroes (d. 1198) was the most cogent Aristotelian produced in Islam.[56] He wrote his *Incoherence of the Incoherence* to refute Asharite kalam in general and al-Ghazali's sophisticated defense of it in particular.[57] Nor did he spare Avicenna in the process. The universe was not the product of a divine emanation, as al-Farabi and Avicenna thought it was, because earlier philosophers had misunderstood Aristotle; nor was it composed of atoms linked only by individual acts of God's creative will, as the kalam maintained in a misguided effort to defend God's omnipotence. In Averroes' universe, as in Aristotle's own, efficient and final causality reigned everywhere, from God, the First Cause, to humans, the moral agent.[58]

In another, briefer work, *The Decisive Treatise*, Averroes turned from the mutakallimun to a defense of philosophy against what was in twelfth-century Spain a far more powerful body of antagonists, the lawyers.[59] Al-Ghazali's works had been burned in public when they arrived in Spain for the first time; even relatively mild versions of Asharite kalam aroused the Spanish jurisprudents, who were fiercely attached to Maliki traditionism. But by the beginning of the twelfth century, there were new religious and political stirrings among the North African Berbers. In 1121, one of them, Ibn Tumart, was proclaimed Mahdi or the Rightly Guided One who would unite all humanity in the observance of Islamic law and so prepare them for the End Time. His Berber followers, who were called "Unitarians" (al-muwahhidun; in English, Almohads), eventually ruled all of North Africa from Tunis to Morocco and the southern half of Spain, and created a new religious and intellectual climate that permitted the work of the Muslim philosophers Ibn Tufayl and Averroes, while forcing the Jewish theologian Maimonides into exile.

The paradox of the divergent fates of Averroes and Maimonides simply repeats a greater one in the Mahdism of Ibn Tumart. He, a Sunni of the Sunnis, borrowed the Shiite ideology of the infallible Imam to complement his role as Mahdi. He and his followers followed the strict literalist principles of Zahiri law, forced conversion on Jews and Christians, and at the same time took up theological positions associated with Mutazilite and Asharite kalam.[60] They also encouraged a reconciliation between sharia and falsafa; Averroes had modestly asked in The Decisive Treatise, Is the study of philosophy permitted or even obligated by the Islamic law?

For Averroes, the answer was, inevitably, yes: the Quran commands a study of God's purpose in the universe, and that, Averroes demonstrated, is precisely the goal of philosophy. The principal objection to this smoothly argued conclusion is raised immediately. Philosophy, which lays its own independent claims to truth, has often been at odds with the truths of revelation. The differences, according to Averroes, are only apparent, and arise from two different modes of expression, the figurative, metaphorical language of Scripture and the scientific language of philosophy. Thus the solution lies where it had always lain from Philo onward, in the allegorical exegesis of Scripture. Averroes even pressed the point: it is the philosophers, not the mutakallimun and the lawyers, who are uniquely qualified to interpret Scripture, since they alone possess a true understanding of its "real," that is, its philosophical, meaning.

## Jewish Kalam

The lawyers were unconvinced by Averroes' *Decisive Treatise*, and after him there was no Muslim to speak so broadly and boldly for the rights of the philosopher vis-à-vis the lawyer on one hand and the mutakallim on the other. Averroes' voice continued to echo in Christian Europe but not in the Abode of Islam. Other voices, however, speaking in somewhat different accents, continued to raise the issue of reason and revelation in the Arabic-speaking world. Chief among them was that of the Jewish physician, philosopher, and talmudic scholar Moses Maimonides (d. 1204), whom Almohad persecution had driven from Spain to a long and successful career in Egypt.

Maimonides came in the midst of a long tradition of Jewish theology in the Middle Ages. The practice of speculative theology begun by Philo and suddenly abandoned was taken up once again under Islam by the gaon Saadya ibn Yusuf (d. 942). Learned in both the Scripture and the mystical tradition, Saadya was the first Jew to follow his Muslim Mutazilite contemporaries into the kalam.[61] The result was the first systematic treatise of Jewish theology, the Arabic *Book of Beliefs and Opinions*.[62] There is no mistaking who Saadya was and what he was about. In his preliminary discourse he assured his readers that his task was primarily to confirm the truths of revelation and to clear up doubts, not to establish new truths. Truth, he explained, arises generally out of the senses, reason, and intuition, to which he, as a member of "the community of monotheists," added a fourth: authentic tradition or revelation. An entire treatise of the work is devoted to a defense of the validity of prophecy in general and of the Torah in particular, and another to the redemption of Israel.[63]

Saadya clearly was not a philosopher on the Hellenic model but a theologian of the type developing within all three of the monotheistic religions of revelation. They all hastened to acknowledge that revelation was the primary source of truth. But though revelation was originally verified by miracle, it could be shaken by interior doubts and skeptical attacks from without, and so stood in need of the support of rational arguments. All the mutakallimun would agree on those propositions, and though they might differ on the necessity of rational understanding—Clement would take a more forceful position than Saadya, for example—they all cast philosophy to play Hagar to Scripture's Sarah.[64]

Even in Saadya's lifetime other Jews were discovering the attractions of falsafa as an autonomous discipline without the manacles of a bondswoman. But it was primarily in the vigorous new Jewish centers in Spain that scholars began the serious pursuit of philosophy.[65] The century between Ibn Gabirol (d. 1050 or 1070) and Ibn Ezra (d. 1164) witnessed a remarkable development of Jewish Neoplatonism.[66] It even found its own Ghazali in the person of Judah Halevi (d. 1141), whose *Khazari* or *Kuzari*, though cast in the form of a debate among a philosopher, a Muslim, a Christian, and a Jew in the presence of the king of the Khazars, had much the same intention as al-Ghazali's *Incoherence of the Philosophers*: to give the lie to the philosophers' claims to arrive at the truths that only revelation, here, specifically a Jewish, biblical revelation, could provide.[67]

## The Guide of the Perplexed

The response from philosophy ignored Judah Halevi, though not the problem he presented. Maimonides, whose important role in the evolution of Jewish law has already been remarked, was a Spanish Jew who understood the peril of being Jewish and of being a philosopher.[68] His *Guide of the Perplexed* is an apologia for philosophy and the role of reason in religious discourse, but it is much more besides.[69] Averroes and Maimonides shared a common conviction that Aristotelianism was a more rigorous and truthful account of God and the universe than the prevailing Neoplatonism, and a common "political" concern about the fate of the uninstructed believer who was caught among the unenlightened traditionism of the lawyers, the half-learned arguments of the mutakallimun, and the hard truths of philosophy. Averroes was less careful in his expression but more prudent in his proposals. Allegorical exegesis, for example, ought not be broadcast among the ordinary believers.[70] Maimonides was more cautious in the involuted *Guide*, but more willing to provide guidance for the ordinary Jew in other contexts.[71] In both his *Mishneh Torah* and his *Commentary on the Mishnah* (Sanhedrin 10.1), Maimonides set down the thirteen fundamental propositions of Jewish belief in the dogmatic form of orthodoxy rather than in the more traditional halakic mode of orthopraxy.[72] "Naked faith" was no more satisfactory for Maimonides than it had been for Clement or Origen.

The *Guide* was at least in part intended to help the Jewish believer move from simple talmudic piety to an affirmation of those propositions by patiently explaining the allegorical exegesis of Scripture, particularly those passages that might suggest that God is corporeal. But it was also designed to guide the more sophisticated student around the perplexities raised by the kalam. The mutakallimun were dangerous because they pretended to explain. They were, in fact, dialecticians rather than philosophers and their arguments were riddled with errors, as al-Farabi had pointed out two centuries earlier. And yet Maimonides would not blindly follow the philosophers. In a revealing passage he shows no hesitation in setting aside Aristotle's demonstration for the eternity of the universe as unproved; and since it was an open question, he opted to follow, without benefit of formal proof, the teaching of Scripture "which explains things to which it is not in the power of speculation to accede."[73]

Maimonides had confidence in the power of prophecy and its promulgation in a revealed Scripture, and devoted a long section of the *Guide* (2.32–48) to explaining and defending it. But unlike his mentor al-Farabi, whose arguments he followed here, Maimonides was willing to make a case, as Saadya had done, for a special Jewish revelation and to set Moses apart from the other prophets. Thus Maimonides was committed to defending the rational and philosophical basis of the Torah, a task to which al-Farabi had never to address himself with respect to the sharia. The philosophy of the Scriptures is, of course, concealed; its natural science lies within the "Work of the Creation" and its divine science in the "Work of the Chariot." The explanation of these two themes, which were favorite points of departure for Jewish mystics and the subject of frequent cautionary remarks by the rabbis, is the alleged program of the entire *Guide*.[74] Having indicated by these programmatic remarks that Scripture contains both a physics and a metaphysics, Maimonides could proceed to disengage these two sciences from the errors of the mutakallimun and their reconstitution on the basis of his own Aristotelian convictions.

Al-Ghazali and Maimonides, one arguing for kalam and one against, had much the same effect on their successors. A purely rationalist philosophy, whether from Aristotle or from al-Razi, remained unacceptable to the adherents of a revealed religion, and even the accommodations of a Farabi, an Avicenna, or an Averroes could not conceal the fact that they prized philosophical over religious wisdom, Athens over Mecca, and could make no convincing case for the unique status of the latter. Yet Maimonides, could and did make such a case for Jerusalem and so "rationalized" the law by skillfully applying a political philosophy, which the Muslim philosophers could not.[75] But the Islamic law was "rationalized" nonetheless, not by the philosopher al-Farabi but by the mutakallim al-Ghazali.

Al-Ghazali and Maimonides both argued that the conclusions of human reason did not have the final word in the process of understanding; many of them were faulty even in their own terms. Nor could human reason be ignored. Post-Ghazali kalam, Jewish, Christian, or Muslim, could no longer afford the luxury of being dialectical rather than totally demonstrative: if it was going to be the handmaiden of Scripture, it must at least be an honest woman.[76]

## Sacred Theology, Western Style

When European Christians opened the Aristotelian corpus freshly translated from the Arabic in Spain and Sicily in the mid–twelfth century, they were encountering an old, though perhaps neglected, friend. The medieval Western world had never lost contact with its Latin antecedents and, through them, with their more remote Hellenic past.[77] More, medieval Christianity possessed an early and highly persuasive theological synthesis from the hand of Augustine, which, though Augustine himself knew no Greek, had its roots in earlier Christian theologians in Antioch and Alexandria. Both the Western and Eastern Churches had already debated the complex theological issue of the Trinity, and by the fourth and fifth centuries the Western Church had acquired a large, flexible, and sophisticated Latin theological vocabulary. It also had Aristotle's *Organon* and knew how to use that powerful heuristic tool.

The twelfth-century introduction of the "new" Aristotle to the West via the Arabic versions was actually exposure to a richer and fuller Aristotle, one that now included not only the logic but the full range of the physical and metaphysical treatises, his work on the soul and on ethics. It was followed by a third wave of Hellenism in the late twelfth century when Western scholars began to translate Aristotle once again, this time directly from the Greek originals. This full encounter with Aristotelianism enabled thirteenth-century Western churchmen and intellectuals to grasp the full range of the Aristotelian worldview and to measure it against the current Platonizing Augustinianism.

This new understanding did not create a theology, as it did in Islam—Western Christendom already had a sacred theology in the Augustinian synthesis—but it provided an approach to the world and its workings that differed in consequential ways from the Platonic edifice that had been fashioned by Augustine. The encounter of the two systems threatened the intellectual foundations of Western Christendom—the East remained happy with its Christianized Plato—until the Dominican Thomas Aquinas (d. 1274), a professor of the faculty of theology at the university of Paris, successfully created out of this new Hellenic learning a Christian Aristotelianism.[78] Thomas provided an explanation of the cosmos, now in Aristotelian terms, that was both coherent and intellectually persuasive; that did justice to the scriptural givens of Christianity; and at the same time that did not appear entirely to subvert the Augustinian system on which the Western Church had grounded its teaching. The new Thomistic synthesis, laid out in all its dialectical splendor in his *Summa Theologiae*, did in fact dislodge the reigning Platonism, at least for a time, and put in its place a new theology inspired by Aristotle's epistemological and metaphysical realism and undergirded by his arguments and methods.

## The Latin Averroes

Since Thomas had before him not only the mid-twelfth-century translations of Aristotle by way of the Arabic but eventually new versions done directly from the Greek, he could proceed somewhat differently from his immediate predecessors. It was not

always possible for them to separate Aristotle from his Arab paraphrases and commentaries, to see the Greek directly rather than
through the eyes of "Alfarabius," "Avicenna," and "Averroes," as
the great Muslim philosophers were called in Latin.[79] Most problematic of all was the greatest of them, Ibn Rushd, who had a great
deal indeed to say about Aristotle. Some of it constituted perceptive
insights into the meaning of Aristotle's thought—both Aquinas
and Dante considered him *the* commentator on Aristotle—and
these became part of Latin Aristotelianism without note or re-
mark. Elsewhere, however, the explanations were his own, like his
reflections on the "agent intellect," the crucial and always operating illuminative function in human intellection that Aristotle had
cryptically and famously remarked came "from outside." Ibn
Rushd thought there was a single, universal faculty for all humankind, located in the lowest of the celestial spheres.[80] Given the
premises, this is a plausible and coherent position, but not in a
Christian context. The intellect is the talisman of the soul's immortality, and a universal intellect of any kind would render
impossible the basic Christian belief in individual immortality.
Thomas, among others, would have none of it.[81]

Ibn Rushd's speculations on the agent intellect were an attempt
to explain an obscure though critical issue of Aristotelian epistemology. Elsewhere, however, the Muslim faylasuf cut closer to the
philosophical bone. Ibn Rushd understood with perfect clarity
that God's revealed word and reason's inquiry did not lead down
the same congruent path. Rather than choose one or the other,
however, to renounce either Islam or philosophy, Ibn Rushd proposed a theory of double truth, one of revealed religion and the
other of philosophy, both equally valid, albeit in an open contradiction we are incapable of resolving.

This so-called double truth theory was by no means new. It had
been proposed before in all three religious cultures by both exegetes and mystics, among others, though in a more polite and
acceptable form, namely, that there were different levels of understanding God's truth and that they were not open to all. The ordinary believer read the Quran (or the Gospels or the Torah) and
that was enough; the philosopher, the mystic, and the adept, however, penetrated more deeply into the infinite depths of God's
Word and found in those unlit places something more profound
and perhaps, though few dared utter it, more true. One truth with

many paths to it or many levels of understanding it was an acceptable if not always comfortable notion in Judaism, Christianity, and Islam, but Ibn Rushd's dichotomous double truth was not. No one much heeded the notion of a double truth in Muslim circles because when Ibn Rushd died, Islamic falsafa died with him. But when the notion resurfaced in the thirteenth century in the faculty of arts at the university of Paris, where Ibn Rushd *was* read, it attracted a great deal of attention. The university and its right to grant its graduates licenses to teach was under the supervision of the bishop of Paris, and in 1271, and again in 1277, that bishop, by virtue of his jurisdictional powers in matters of faith and morals, issued a decree condemning not Ibn Rushd's explanations but what was perceived to be the cause of the problem, various teachings of Aristotle.

Though provocative, the Paris condemnation was a brief incident, and the Thomistic Aristotelians at Paris and elsewhere managed to make clear to the authorities that there was only one truth. Although it was undoubtedly taught in Scripture, it was universal and so accessible to—and understood by—Aristotle and other ancients. Many remained unconvinced, however. Some still thought Ibn Rushd had a point, that science or philosophy could not be reconciled with Scripture, or, as the more radical would have it, with the teachings of the Church; that faith and understanding were two different chairs that one could attempt to straddle but could never stack. Others, like the Franciscan theologians Bonaventure (d. 1274) at Paris and later Duns Scotus (d. 1309) at Oxford, were not Thomists and hence not Aristotelians, and chose to remain faithful to Augustine's Platonic synthesis.

# Epilogue: Sacred History

Historians are interested in origins and in the working of cause and intelligible effect on the slippery ground of human behavior. With the tools of comparative linguistics and archaeology they pursue the origins of Judaism in the ancient legal and epic traditions of the Middle East, in the Code of Hammurabi or the tablets of Ebla. What precisely, they want to know, were the charges on which Jesus of Nazareth was tried and executed, and under whose jurisdiction? The identity of Muhammad's Jewish or Christian teachers is sought with an iron persistence, despite the equally iron conviction that they will never know if there even were such.

The same monotheistic communities that are the objects of the historians' quest are themselves interested in history, and have been so from the beginning—not, however, in the "scientific" enterprise we call history. They read the evidence differently, through a lens exalted or reviled under the name of "sacred history."

Sacred history, like its more familiar secular counterpart, is committed to meaning and understanding, to a human understanding of God's meaning. In the Hellenic view that is the ancestor of our own, God created the world—we're no longer so sure of that—and then allowed it to evolve and operate naturally in accordance with the programs—the Greeks called them "natures"—he had embedded in them. Nothing could be more remote from the thinking of these three revelational religions, for whom God not only created the world, but continues to act in and on it, and who in the end will judge it.

It has always been thought so, and Jews, Christians, and Muslims have long collected and recorded the evidence of God's providential plan for his creation. The Greek theologians were impressed by the orderly progression of the seasons, the regular majestic movement of the heavenly bodies: "the heavens themselves proclaim the glory of God," it was said. Such thinking is not entirely alien to revelation, of course. Jesus could point to the providential raiment of the lilies of the field, and Muhammad also frequently cited the natural signs that showed that God's hand lay on the universe. But of far greater interest to Moses and Jesus and Muhammad than the cosmic glory of the heavens was God's special care of his own chosen people, a care manifested by his repeated intervention in history on their behalf.

If a miracle is the suspension of the operation of the natural causality meditated on by the Hellenes and their European successors, then sacred history is a record of the miraculous, not merely of the prodigious—like the descent of manna in the desert, or the transformation of water into wine, or the sundry other acts whereby God identifies and confirms his prophets—but of an entire divine economy whereby God undertakes to instruct and guide his people toward an end that he himself had decreed. For all three religious communities, God's intervention in human history manifests itself in two chief ways: in the revelation of his truth, whether as message, admonition, or covenant, and in his ongoing "political" guidance to the community of believers, his governance of the frail ark through the turmoil of the "nations," the *gentes*, "Gentiles," as the Jews called them, the "unbelievers" (*kafirun*) of the Muslims.

For Jew, Christian, and Muslim alike, the history of revelation and the history of the community of believers are the twin foundations of sacred history, but it is the concurrence of the matter of that history that binds them forever together. The sacred history of the Jews cares nothing for Hammurabi and knows nothing of Ebla; it is rooted in Abraham and the events of Sinai. For the early Christians, Jesus too would have been incomprehensible without Sinai and the prophets, and the Gospels have as part of their agenda a demonstration that Jesus fulfilled what was uncontrovertibly part of that revelation, the messianic promise. As a Jew, the evangelist Matthew simply assumed the authenticity of both the revelation and the promise. In Mecca Muhammad could make no such assumption: he was constrained to unfold God's earlier revelations and to demonstrate not to a Jewish but to a pagan audience that his call and his experiences were the continuation of what had begun on Sinai. It fell to the successors of the prophets, the Benei Israel, the Christians of the ekklesia, and the Muslim umma, to trace for an eternal remembrance the history of the community in its social and political context. In the recollection of the believers, the Acts of God are inevitably followed by the Deeds of Men that show them forth, in Kings and Chronicles, in the Acts of the Apostles, in the History of the Caliphs.

Each monotheistic community has validated the revealed covenant of its predecessors, even as it departed from it in the name of a new revelation that represented both the continuation and the transcendence of what had gone before. The Israelites who gathered with Moses at the foot of Sinai affirmed the truth of what had been announced to Abraham and the tribal patriarchs, and read it into the record of Scripture; indeed, in its finished version the sacred history of the Jews began with Creation itself. And though there were those who had misgivings on the subject, the early followers of Jesus, some Jews, some not, reaffirmed, like Jesus himself, the experience of the Covenant. There was, the Christians agreed, a New Covenant, but the New was inexplicable without the Old, and so the sacred history of the Jews, the history of both law and the community, became the holy past of the Christian movement.

Christianity was a revolution in Judaism in that it announced not simply a reform of the Mosaic law but its effective abrogation. It instructed the new Christians, more and more of them from among the Gentiles, that the Torah, its observance and its study, both linchpins of what rabbinic Judaism defined as a Jew, was neither obligatory nor indeed praiseworthy. Christians of strict or even regular observance were not distinguished by their voluntary embrace of the rabbinic ideal but by the pursuit of an asceticism that was radically alien to the world of the Talmud.

Islam too validated God's earlier revelatory interventions into human history—the sacred books of the Jews and Christians were true Scripture, the Quran asserts—but Muhammad claimed neither the fulfillment nor the abrogation of those revelations of earlier times. Rather, the Quran itself suggested, without undue emphasis on the question, that those other "Peoples of the Book" had misread, misunderstood, or misinterpreted the words that God had entrusted to their safekeeping. The Quran's view is somewhat closer to Jesus' than to Paul's understanding of the past of Judaism. Jesus quarreled with the Pharisees and Muhammad with the Jews of Medina about points of law, but Paul took on the very function and intent of the Mosaic law itself.

If in the sequel Jesus was, or appeared to be, a Jewish revolutionary, Muhammad was an Israelite fundamentalist. He knew the history of the prophets, with whom he closely identified himself, but he had no interest in their Books and so none in the messianic message of Jesus, who is called "Messiah" but is identified as a prophet in the Quran. As a result, none of those Books—Torah, Psalms, and Prophets—became part of the devotional life of the Muslim, as they had for the Christian. Muhammad proposed not to reread the older Scriptures with the new eyes of an enlightened faith, as the Christians did, but to return to the source, the "natural" pre-Torah religion of Abraham, the father of all believers.

There are in fact two Abrahams in the Quran. One is the well-known figure from Genesis, embroidered here and there with what appear to be Jewish legendary midrash; the other is the product of some other sensibility, the Abraham who emigrated to Arabia with his wife Hagar and son Ishmael to finally settle in Mecca, where he built the Kaaba, the "House of God," and instituted most of the ritual practices of the later Islamic pilgrimage.

Both Abrahams are the creations of sacred history, and historians stand mute before one or the other. Their silence is no great loss, perhaps, since the Muslims' and the Jews' perception of the past owes nothing to the secular historian but is grounded in God's own telling of it in Scripture: all the history that either requires is spelled out in the Bible and the Quran.

But even sacred history is no stranger to polemic. The secular historian may note that Abraham's association with Mecca appears in the Quran only after Muhammad's first confrontation with the Jews of Medina and so conclude that the invocation of Abraham as a prophetic Meccan avatar may have been a response, a retort, to the Jewish rejection of Muhammad's own prophethood. Even earlier, Abraham had been "rewritten" by the Christian Paul. Both Paul and Muhammad claimed Abraham as a believer before the fact. In both instances the "fact" was the Mosaic law or its symbol in circumcision. For Paul, Abraham's faith before circumcision made him the prototype of all believers, circumcised and uncircumcised, Jew and Gentile. For Muhammad, Abraham's belief separated *islam*, submission, from the Torah that codified it. Thus, Abraham, by his faith (according to Paul), or by his submission (according to

Muhammad), undercut Jewish claims to exclusivity and, in the long term, to the inheritance of the Covenant promise.

Paul's appeal to Abraham is made almost in passing in his Letter to the Romans, and the patriarch looms not nearly so large in Christianity as he does in the Jewish and Muslim understanding of the past. It is the person and the acts of Jesus the Messiah that are crucial to Christianity, and it is precisely Jesus who separates the typology of Christianity from that of both Judaism and Islam. Both Muslim and Jew are Covenanters for whom the path to holiness lies in fidelity of heart and observance to that Covenant. The Christian is asked not as much for fidelity as for faith, faith in Christ Jesus, who is, in his own person, the New Covenant. Jew and Muslim measure their fidelity by a deeply considered and articulated body of halakot, behavioral norms that are the touchstones of orthopraxy; the Christian measures faith by the standard instrument of orthodoxy, the creed. The archetypical figure in traditional Judaism and Islam is the legal scholar, the rabbi or the alim; in traditional Christianity it is the priest-bishop, the mediator who, like the archmediator Christ, bridges the gap between the human and the divine.

By his dual nature as God and man and by his redemptive death and resurrection, Jesus sanctified matter and set in train the Christian system of sacraments that replicate the Messiah's own conciliation of the domains of the spiritual and of the material. In Judaism and Islam the only bridge thrown across the great abyss between the transcendent God and his creation is revelation itself, the Word, the Book. The anomaly of Christianity for both Muslim and Jew is that the Word became flesh, not in the sense that the Torah or the Quran was expressed in human speech, but in a more radical understanding that the Word became man. Jesus was his own Scripture.

Muhammad was merely a man, asserts the Quran and the unanimous Muslim tradition after it, a mortal servant of God. The Jews have never thought it worth declaring the same, self-evident fact about Moses and the prophets. But Jesus is both God and man, professes the Christian, and we can be saved only through and by him. This fundamental Christian view of the nature and role of Jesus Christ in the economy of salvation gave rise to consequences alien to the sensibilities of the other two monotheists. The doctrine of the Trinity and its implied repudiation of the uniqueness of God; a priesthood that possesses not the relative magisterium of a rabbinate but the absolute and infallible magisterium of an imamate, and is moreover the sole warden and dispenser of God's sacramental grace; Eucharistic sacrifice wherein flesh becomes the Word on every altar in Christendom; and the veneration of saints and their images, all set Christianity apart from its older and younger partners in monotheism.

# *Notes*

## INTRODUCTION: THE SCRIPTURES

1. On the biblical narrative style, see Joel Rosenberg, "Biblical Narrative," in Barry W. Holtz, ed., *Back to the Sources: Reading the Classic Jewish Texts* (New York: Summit Books, 1984), 31–82. On the Quran's style, W. Montgomery Watt, *Bell's Introduction to the Qur'an* (Edinburgh: Edinburgh University Press, 1970), 69–85.

2. For a comparative approach to the notion of Scripture, see Frederick M. Denny and Rodney L. Taylor, eds., *The Holy Book in Comparative Perspective: Studies in Comparative Religion* (Columbia: University of South Carolina Press, 1985); Wilfred Cantwell Smith, *What Is Scripture?* (Minneapolis: Fortress Press, 1993); and Arthur Jeffery, *The Qur'an as Scripture* (New York: Columbia University Press, 1952).

3. Some measure of its literary complexity may be gotten from Robert Alter and Frank Kermode, *The Literary Guide to the Bible* (Cambridge: Harvard University Press, 1986).

4. The Apocrypha or books ruled out of the Jewish Bible are collected and translated in James H. Charlesworth, *The Old Testament Pseudepigrapha*, 2 vols. (Garden City: Doubleday, 1983), and of the New Testament in Wilhelm Schneemelcher and Edgar Hennecke, eds., *New Testament Apocrypha*, 2 vols. (Philadelphia: Westminster Press, 1963–1965).

5. How that process worked for both the Jewish and the Christian Scriptures is discussed (and debated) at length by the contributors to Lee Martin McDonald and James A. Sanders, *The Canon Debate* (Peabody, Mass.: Hendrickson, 2002). Also useful for the Jewish canon is Sid Z. Leiman, ed., *The Canon and Masorah of the Hebrew Bible: An Introductory Reader* (New York: Ktav, 1974).

6. See Bruce M. Metzger, *The Bible in Translation: Ancient and English Versions* (Grand Rapids: Baker Academic, 2001).

7. Modern non-Muslim scholars have considerably greater misgivings, as becomes clear from the studies collected in Stefan Wild, ed., *The*

*Qur'an as Text* (Leiden: E. J. Brill, 1996). That the skepticism goes way back is made equally clear in the older essays reprinted in Ibn Warraq, *The Origins of the Koran* (Amherst: Prometheus Books, 1998).

8. There are by now a substantial number of English translations of the Quran, prosaic and poetic, traditional and modernizing. Both prosaic and traditional—the translation is deliberately literal and reflects a traditional Muslim interpretation—is that by the convert Muhammad Marmaduke Pickthall, *The Meaning of the Glorious Qur'an*, available in several editions with or without an accompanying Arabic text. Another widely available prose version, but in this case with a distinct modernizing tendency, is that by Yusuf Ali. Two successful attempts at the Quran's difficult poetical style are by A. J. Arberry, *The Koran Interpreted* (New York: Macmillan, 1970), and particularly Michael Sells, *Approaching the Qur'an: The Early Revelations* (Ashland, Oreg.: White Cloud Press, 1999), which includes a CD of quranic recitations.

## CHAPTER ONE: THE PROMISE AND THE HEIRS

1. The pertinent biblical texts are reproduced in F. E. Peters, *Judaism, Christianity, and Islam: The Classical Texts and Their Interpretation*, 3 vols. (Princeton: Princeton University Press, 1990; henceforward Peters, *JCI Texts*), 1:1–22.

2. For the biblical covenant in comparative perspective, see Dennis J. McCarthy, *Treaty and Covenant: A Study in Form in the Ancient Near Eastern Documents and the Old Testament* (Rome: Pontifical Biblical Institute, 1981).

3. The reader may wish to become immediately acquainted with a primary resource in Islamic studies, the *Encyclopaedia of Islam*, new ed. (Leiden: E. J. Brill, 1960–). The articles are arranged alphabetically, but according to the Arabic word for the subject; hence, here the pertinent entry is "Ibrahim."

4. The pertinent texts are available in Peters, *JCI Texts*, 1:22–27.

5. All the versions of this complex story are available in Reuven Firestone, *Journeys into Holy Lands: The Evolution of the Abraham-Ishmael Legends in Islamic Exegesis* (Albany: State University of New York Press, 1990).

6. The event is viewed from a very wide-ranging Jewish perspective by Solomon Spiegel, *The Last Trial: On the Legends and Lore of the Command to Abraham to Offer Isaac as a Sacrifice—The Akedah*, trans. from the Hebrew with an intro. by J. Goldin (New York: Pantheon Books, 1967; rpt., New York: Berhman House, 1971); and more theologically by a Jesuit theologian, James Swetnam, *Jesus and Isaac: A Study of the Epistle to the Hebrews in the Light of the Aqedah* (Rome: Biblical Institute Press, 1981).

7. Where this devious path leads has been famously mapped by Jan Assmann, *Moses the Egyptian* (Cambridge: Harvard University Press, 1997).

8. Peters, *JCI Texts*, 1:44–54.

9. For an introduction to the city's complex, and contentious, history, see the studies collected in Nitza Rosovsky, ed., *City of the Great King: Jerusalem from David to the Present* (Cambridge: Harvard University Press, 1996). Particularly pertinent are the essays by Joseph Dan (60–73), Paula Fredricksen (74–92), and Angela Neuwirth (93–116), on Jerusalem's role in Jewish, Christian, and Islamic spirituality respectively. Some of the most important primary texts of Jerusalem are collected in F. E. Peters, *Jerusalem: The Holy City in the Eyes of Chroniclers, Visitors, Pilgrims, and Prophets from the Days of Abraham to the Beginnings of Modern Times* (Princeton: Princeton University Press, 1985).

10. On Solomon's temple, from a variety of perspectives, see Joseph Gutmann, ed., *The Temple of Solomon: Archeological Fact and Medieval Tradition in Christian, Islamic, and Jewish Art* (Missoula: Scholars Press, 1976). On God's presence, his *shekinah* (and the parallel Arabic *sakina*), see F. E. Peters, *The Monotheists: Jews, Christians, and Muslims in Conflict and Competition* (Princeton: Princeton University Press, 2003; henceforward Peters, *Monotheists*), vol. 2, chap. 6.

11. The straightforward narrative line is laid out in the two biblical books called Kings and in the parallel account in the two books of Chronicles.

12. Peters, *JCI Texts*, 1:59–68. On the prophets, see, among many, John Bright, *Prophecy and Promise: The Prophetic Understanding of the Future in Pre-Exilic Israel* (Philadelphia: Westminster Press, 1976); J. Lindblom, *Prophecy in Ancient Israel* (Oxford: Blackwell, 1962); David L. Petersen, *Prophecy in Israel: Search for an Identity* (Philadelphia: Fortress Press, 1987); Joseph Blenkinsopp, *A History of Prophecy in Israel*, rev. ed. (Philadelphia: Westminster/John Knox, 1996). For the continuity of the tradition, John Barton, *Oracles of God: Perceptions of Ancient Prophecy in Israel after the Exile* (London: Dartman, Longman, and Todd, 1986); and Rebecca Gray, *Prophetic Figures in Late Second Temple Palestine: The Evidence from Josephus* (Oxford: Clarendon Press 1993). There is an interesting comparative study by William Brinner, "Prophets and Prophecy in the Islamic and Jewish Traditions," in William Brinner and Stephan D. Ricks, *Studies in the Islamic and Judaic Traditions*, vol. 2 (Atlanta: Scholars Press, 1989), 63–82.

13. See Heribert Busse, *Islam, Judaism, and Christianity: Theological and Historical Affiliations*, trans. Allison Brown (Princeton: Markus Wiener, 1998), 63–112.

14. A recent collection of studies on this difficult period has been edited by Oded Lipschitz and Joseph Blenkinsopp, *Judah and the Judeans in the Neo-Babylonian Period* (Winona Lake: Eisenbrauns, 2003). The playing out of the powerful theme of exile in both Judaism and Christianity has been studied by James M. Scott, *Exile: Old Testament, Jewish and Christian Conception* (Leiden: E. J. Brill, 1997).

15. This important phase in Middle Eastern history has been treated both broadly and in detail in F. E. Peters, *The Harvest of Hellenism* (New York: Simon and Schuster, 1970; rpt., New York: Barnes and Noble, 1996). See also Susan M. Sherwin-White and Amelie Kuhrt, eds., *Hellenism in the East: Interaction of Greek and Non-Greek Civilizations from Syria to Central Asia after Alexander* (Berkeley: University of California Press, 1987). For Hellenism's effect on the Jews, see below.

16. A basic work for the latter part of the period is still Emil Schuerer, *The History of the Jewish People in the Age of Jesus Christ, 175 B.C.–A.D. 135*, rev. and ed. Geza Vermes and Fergus Millar, 2 vols. (Edinburgh: T. and T. Clark, 1973, 1979). Also instructive from the perspective of the approach here are Shaye J. D. Cohen, *From the Maccabees to the Mishnah* (Philadelphia: Westminster Press, 1987); George W. E. Nickelsburg and Michael Stone, eds., *Faith and Piety in Early Judaism: Texts and Documents* (Philadelphia: Fortress Press, 1983); Robert Kraft and George W. E. Nickelsburg, eds., *Early Judaism and Its Modern Interpreters* (Philadelphia: Fortress Press, 1986).

17. Morton Smith, *Palestinian Parties and Politics That Shaped the Old Testament*, 2d, corrected ed. (London: SCM Press, 1987), pays attention to the earlier traces. Cohen, *From the Maccabees to the Mishnah*, and Lawrence H. Schiffman, "Jewish Sectarianism in Second Temple Times," in Raphael Jospe and Stanley M. Wagner, eds., *Great Schisms in Jewish History* (New York: Ktav, 1981), 1–46, both concentrate on the late Second Temple manifestations.

18. The reappearance is explored in John Kampen, *The Hasideans and the Origins of the Pharisees: A Study in I and II Maccabees* (Atlanta: Scholars Press, 1988).

19. Our best entry into Josephus may be through the essays collected in the two volumes edited by Louis H. Feldman and Gohei Hata and published by Wayne State University Press in Detroit: *Josephus, Judaism, and Christianity* (1987) and *Josephus, the Bible, and History* (1989). For Josephus on the Pharisees, see Jacob Neusner, "Josephus' Pharisees: A Complete Repertoire," in Feldman and Hata, *Josephus, Judaism, and Christianity*, 274–292.

20. Schuerer, *History of the Jewish People*, 2:388–404; and see Jacob Neusner, *From Politics to Piety: The Emergence of Pharisaic Judaism* (New York: Ktav, 1978), esp. 1–12.

21. Schuerer, *History of the Jewish People*, 2:404–414: and see Günther Baumbach, "The Sadducees in Josephus," in Feldman and Hata, *Josephus, the Bible, and History*, 173–195.

22. A readily accessible translation is Geza Vermes, *The Dead Sea Scrolls in English*, 4th ed. (New York: Penguin, 1995). Among a great many works on the subject are Vermes, *The Dead Sea Scrolls: Qumran in Perspective*, rev. ed. (Philadelphia: Fortress Press, 1981); Joseph A. Fitzmyer, *The*

*Dead Sea Scrolls: Major Publications and Tools for Study*, rev. ed. (Atlanta: Scholars Press, 1990); and Lawrence H. Schiffman, *Reclaiming the Dead Sea Scrolls* (New York: Doubleday, 1995).

23. The literature is extensive, as may be inferred from the existence of Bernard McGinn et al., eds., *Encyclopedia of Apocalypticism* (New York: Continuum, 1998). For a running leap into the subject and its problems, two collective works will do: David Hellholm, ed., *Apocalypticism in the Mediterranean World and the Near East*, 2d ed., enlarged by supplementary bibliography (Tübingen: J. C. B. Mohr, 1989); and its follow-up, John J. Collins and James H. Charlesworth, eds., *Mysteries and Revelations: Apocalyptic Studies since the Uppsala Colloquium* (Sheffield, JSOT Press, 1991). On its long history, see Norman Cohn, *The Pursuit of the Millennium: Revolutionary Millenarians and Mystical Anarchists of the Middle Ages* (New York: Oxford University Press, 1971); and Bernard McGinn, *Visions of the End: Apocalyptic Tradition in the Middle Ages* (New York: Columbia University Press, 1997). For a comparative perspective, see John J. Collins, *The Apocalyptic Imagination: An Introduction to the Jewish Matrix of Christianity* (New York: Crossroad, 1985) and Adela Yarbro Collins, *Cosmology and Eschatology in Jewish and Christian Apocalypticism* (Leiden: E. J. Brill, 1996).

24. The point is abundantly illustrated in the essays collected and edited by James H. Charlesworth. *The Messiah: Developments in Earliest Judaism and Christianity* (Minneapolis: Fortress Press, 1992). The larger (and longer) history of the notion among Jews is traced by Gershom Scholem, *The Messianic Idea in Judaism and Other Essays on Jewish Spirituality* (New York: Schocken Books, 1971).

25. John J. Collins, *The Scepter and the Star: Jewish Messianism in the Light of the Dead Sea Scrolls* (New York: Doubleday, 1995); and Craig Evans and Peter W. Flint, eds., *Eschatology, Messianism, and the Dead Sea Scrolls* (Grand Rapids: Eerdmans, 1997).

26. See Schiffman, *Reclaiming the Dead Sea Scrolls*, part 5, "Mysticism, Messianism, and the End of Days," 315–368.

27. For a general appreciation, see Doron Mendels, *The Rise and Fall of Jewish Nationalism: Jewish and Christian Ethnicity in Ancient Palestine* (Grand Rapids: Eerdmans, 1997); and Moses Aberbach and David Aberbach, *The Roman Jewish Wars and Hebrew Cultural Nationalism* (New York: St. Martin's Press, 2000).

28. On the Jewish Diaspora generally, see John M. G. Barclay, *Jews in the Mediterranean Diaspora from Alexander to Trajan, 323 B.C.E.–117 C.E.* (Berkeley: University of California Press, 1996); and Erich S. Gruen, *Diaspora* (Cambridge: Harvard University Press, 2002). The dispersion of Hellenism in the Middle East is the general subject of Peters, *The Harvest of Hellenism*. As regards its effects on the Jews, the classic study remains Victor Tcherikover, *Hellenistic Civilization and the Jews* (New York:

Atheneum, 1959; rpt., 1970), now supplemented by Martin Hengel, *Judaism and Hellenism: Studies in Their Encounter in Palestine during the Early Hellenistic Period*, 2 vols. (London: SCM Press, 1974), and his more popular *Jews, Greeks, and Barbarians: Aspects of Hellenization of Judaism in the Pre-Christian Period* (Philadelphia: Fortress Press, 1980); as well as by Samuel Sandmel, "Hellenism and Judaism," in Stanley M. Wagner and Allen D. Breck, eds., *Great Confrontations in Jewish History* (Denver: University of Denver, 1977), 21–38; John J. Collins, *Between Athens and Jerusalem: Jewish Identity in the Hellenistic Diaspora* (New York: Crossroad, 1983); and Erich S. Gruen, *Heritage and Hellenism: The Reinvention of the Jewish Tradition* (Berkeley: University of California Press, 1998).

29. There is a grandiose, perhaps overblown, portrait of Philo and his achievement by Harry A. Wolfson, *Philo: Foundations of Religious Philosophy in Judaism, Christianity, and Islam*, 2 vols. (Cambridge: Harvard University Press, 1947); and though whittled down in Samuel Sandmel, *Philo of Alexandria: An Introduction* (Oxford: Oxford University Press, 1979), the subject is still impressive. For the perspective that most concerns us here, see Alan Mendelson, *Philo's Jewish Identity* (Atlanta: Scholars Press, 1988); David Winston, *Logos and Mystical Theology in Philo of Alexandria* (Cincinnati: Hebrew Union College Press, 1985); and Peder Borgen, *Philo, John, and Paul: New Perspectives on Early Christianity* (Atlanta: Scholars Press, 1987).

## CHAPTER TWO: A CONTESTED INHERITANCE

1. See Lawrence A. Hoffman, ed., *The Land of Israel: Jewish Perspectives* (Notre Dame: University of Notre Dame Press, 1986); and W. D. Davies, *The Territorial Dimension of Judaism* (Berkeley: University of California Press, 1982). Compare Davies's *The Gospel and the Land: Early Christianity and Jewish Territorial Doctrine* (Berkeley: University of California Press, 1974).

2. On the subject generally, see D. A. Hagner, *The Jewish Reclamation of Jesus: An Analysis and Critique of the Modern Study of Jesus* (Grand Rapids: Zondervan, 1984). The modern pioneer of Jewish scholarship on Jesus was Abraham Geiger (d. 1874), better known as an Islamicist but whose controversial contribution to Jesus research has been studied by Susannah Heschel, *Abraham Geiger and the Jewish Jesus* (Chicago: University of Chicago Press, 1998). Geiger's work was followed, after a very long interval, by Joseph Klausner's *Jesus of Nazareth: His Life, Times, and Teaching* (New York: Macmillan, 1927; rpt., New York: Menorah, 1974). Other early work is excellently summarized in Stephen Neill and Tom Wright, *The Interpretation of the New Testament, 1861–1986*, new ed. (New York: Oxford University Press, 1988), 313–359. Among the most influential contributors have been Geza Vermes, *Jesus the Jew: A Historian's Read-*

*ing of the Gospels* (London: William Collins, 1973) and *The Religion of Jesus the Jew* (Minneapolis: Fortress Press, 1993); and David Flusser, whose studies have been collected in *Judaism and the Origins of Christianity* (Jerusalem: Magnes Press, 1988).

3. *The Quest of the Historical Jesus: A Critical Study of Its Progress from Reimarus to Wrede*, trans. from the 1st German ed. by W. Montgomery and rpt. with an intro. by James M. Robinson (New York: Macmillan, 1968). Modern scholarship is not only absorbed with the historical Jesus; it is also self-absorbed and communiqués in the form of progress reports are issued at regular intervals. Reports up to 1986 are available in Neill and Wright, *The Interpretation of the New Testament*. For two of the most detailed (and argumentative) recent assessments, see Marcus J. Borg, *Jesus in Contemporary Scholarship* (Valley Forge: Trinity Press International, 1994); and Ben Witherington III, *The Jesus Quest: The Third Search for Jesus of Nazareth* (Downers Grove, Ill.: InterVarsity Press, 1995).

4. This hypothesis was put into play by Edwin Hatch, *The Influence of Greek Ideas on Christianity* (1889; rpt., New York: Harper Torchbooks, 1957).

5. See, for example, the essays collected in James H. Charlesworth, ed., *Jesus and the Dead Sea Scrolls* (New York: Doubleday, 1992).

6. For two highly detailed appreciations of these historical sources for the life of Jesus, both by accomplished biographers of Jesus, see John Dominic Crossan, *The Historical Jesus: The Life of a Mediterranean Jewish Peasant* (San Francisco: Harper, 1991); and John P. Meier, *A Marginal Jew: Rethinking the Historical Jesus*, vol. 1, *The Roots of the Problem and the Person* (New York: Doubleday, 1991); vol. 2, *Mentor, Message, and Miracles* (New York: Doubleday, 1994).

7. The classic study is by Joachim Jeremias, *Rediscovering the Parables* (New York: Scribner, 1966); but see also Norman Perrin, *Jesus and the Language of the Kingdom: Symbol and Metaphor in the New Testament* (Philadelphia: Fortress Press, 1976). For the Jewish background and foreground of the form, Claus Westermann et al., eds., *The Parables of Jesus in the Light of the Old Testament* (Edinburgh: T. and T. Clark, 1990); Harvey K. McArthur and Robert Morris Johnson, *They Also Taught in Parables: Rabbinic Parables from the First Century of the Christian Era* (Grand Rapids: Academic Books, 1990).

8. The chief Gospel texts are presented in Peters, *JCI Texts*, 1:115–154.

9. This phase of Jesus' story has received exhaustive treatment by Raymond E. Brown, *The Birth of the Messiah: A Commentary on the Infancy Narratives in the Gospels of Matthew and Luke*, new updated ed. (New York: Doubleday, 1993).

10. On this highly important figure in Jesus' life, see Joan E. Taylor, *The Immerser: John the Baptist within Second Temple Judaism* (Grand Rapids: Eerdmans, 1997).

11. The last days of Jesus are analyzed in extraordinary detail by Raymond E. Brown, *The Death of the Messiah from Gethsemane to the Grave: A Commentary on the Passion Narratives of the Four Gospels*, 2 vols. (New York: Doubleday, 1993), with matchingly complete bibliographies at every step of the way.

12. See Emil Schuerer, *The History of the Jewish People in the Age of Jesus Christ, 175 B.C.–A.D. 135*, rev. and ed. Geza Vermes and Fergus Millar (Edinburgh: T. and T. Clark, 1973, 1979), 2:547–549.

13. This crucial event in the evolution of the Jesus movement has been studied from a variety of angles by the historians, philosophers, and theologians, lay and cleric, who contributed to Stephen Davis, Daniel Kendall, and Gerald Collins, eds., *The Resurrection: An Interdisciplinary Symposium on the Resurrection of Jesus* (Oxford: Oxford University Press, 1997). Particularly useful is N. T. Wright's exhaustive study, *The Resurrection of the Son of God* (Minneapolis: Fortress Press, 2003).

14. The Gospels' postburial narratives lack the precision and continuity of the immediately preceding accounts of Jesus' arrest, trial, and execution. The endings of Mark and John in particular display a "tacked on" quality. For a textual approach to the end of Mark, see Bruce M. Metzger, *The Text of the New Testament: Its Transmission, Corruption, and Restoration*, 3rd enlarged ed. (Oxford: Oxford University Press, 1992), 226–229, 296–297; and for a contextual one to John 21, Raymond E. Brown, *The Gospel According to John*, 2 vols. paginated consecutively (New York: Doubleday, 1970), 2:1077–1082.

15. This is the so-called *Testimonium Flavianum*, a passage in *Antiquities* 18. 63–64; on it, see Shlomo Pines, *An Arabic Version of the Testimonium Flavianum and Its Implications* (Jerusalem: Israel Academy of Sciences and Humanities, 1971). Both Josephus's interpolated text and the later (uninterpolated?) Arabic version are in Peters, *JCI Texts*, 1:149.

16. The texts are displayed in Peters, *JCI Texts*, 1:150–151.

17. Neal Robinson draws a detailed and interesting comparison in his *Christ in Islam and Christianity* (Albany: State University of New York Press, 1991). The fullest treatment of references to Jesus (and Christians) in the Quran and what the Muslim commentators made of them is Jane Dammen McAuliffe, *Quranic Christians: An Analysis of Classical and Modern Exegesis* (Cambridge: Cambridge University Press, 1991). The Jesus legend, like the Muhammad legend, had a rich afterlife in Islam; see Tarif Khalidi, *The Muslim Jesus: Sayings and Stories in Islamic Literature* (Cambridge: Harvard University Press, 2001).

18. The best treatment of this complex issue is James G. Dunn, *The Parting of the Ways between Christianity and Judaism and Their Significance for the Character of Christianity* (Philadelphia: Trinity Press, 1992); and the volume edited by Dunn, *Jews and Christians: The Parting of the Ways* (Grand Rapids: Eerdmans, 1993). The early Jewish perspective on the "parting"

is traced by Lawrence H. Schiffman, "At the Crossroads: Tannaitic Perspectives on the Jewish-Christian Schism," in E. P. Sanders, ed., *Jewish and Christian Self-Definition*, vol. 2, *Aspects of Judaism in the Graeco-Roman Period* (Philadelphia: Fortress Press, 1981), pp. 115–156. The issue is by no means closed, however, as is evident from the studies collected in Adam H. Becker and Annette Yoshiko Reed, eds., *The Ways That Never Parted* (Tübingen: Mohr Siebeck, 2003), with a particularly valuable introduction by the editors, "Traditional Models and New Directions," 1–34.

19. Getting from Jesus to Paul, a mere decade perhaps, is no simple matter. Martin Hengel attempts to do so in *Between Jesus and Paul: Studies in the Earliest History of Christianity* (Philadelphia: Fortress Press, 1983); and *The Pre-Christian Paul* (Philadelphia: Trinity Press International, 1991). There is a great deal of work on Paul, an obviously crucial figure in the development of Christianity; a prudent place to begin may be Jerome Murphy-O'Connor, *Paul: A Critical Life* (Oxford: Clarendon Press, 1996). For some flavor of the controversy still surrounding him, see David Wenham, *Paul: Follower of Jesus or Founder of Christianity* (Grand Rapids: Eerdmans, 1995); and N. T. Wright, *What Saint Paul Really Said: Was Paul of Tarsus the Real Founder of Christianity?* (Grand Rapids: Eerdmans, 1997). With the progressive "rehabilitation" of Jesus in Jewish scholarship, Paul has also begun to draw more Jewish attention, not much of it positive. For a somewhat extreme example, see Hyam Maccoby, *The Mythmaker: Paul and the Invention of Christianity* (San Francisco: Harper and Row, 1986). For a more moderate one, Alan F. Segal, *Paul the Convert: The Apostolate and Apostasy of Paul the Pharisee* (New Haven: Yale University Press, 1990).

20. Jacob Neusner, *From Politics to Piety: The Emergence of Pharisaic Judaism* (New York: Ktav, 1978).

21. See chap. 1. The New Testament texts regarding the Pharisees have been collected by John Bowker, *Jesus and the Pharisees* (Cambridge: Cambridge University Press, 1973).

22. See Jacob Neusner, *Rabbinic Traditions about the Pharisees before 70*, 3 vols. (Leiden: E. J. Brill, 1970), 3:239–300. The issue is still under investigation. Recent studies approaching the problem anew include Neusner, *The Four Stages of Rabbinic Judaism* (London: Routledge, 1998); Seth Schwartz, *Imperialism and Jewish Society, 200 B.C.E. to 640 C.E.* (Princeton: Princeton University Press, 2000); and Gabriele Boccaccini, *Roots of Rabbinic Judaism* (Grand Rapids: Eerdmans, 2002).

23. Schuerer, *History of the Jewish People*, 2:199–226; Hugo Mantel, *Studies in the History of the Sanhedrin* (Cambridge: Harvard University Press, 1961; henceforward Mantel, *Sanhedrin*).

24. See Herman L. Strack and Günter Stemberger, *Introduction to the Talmud and Midrash* (Minneapolis: Fortress Press, 1992), 70–72.

25. His life, overlaid with legend, has been studied by Jacob Neusner, *A Life of Yohanan ben Zakkai* (Leiden: E. J. Brill, 1970).

26. The Mishna is discussed in more detail in chaps. 3 and 4.

27. So Neusner, *Rabbinic Traditions*, 300–319.

28. Their history under the Iranian dynasties of first the Parthians and then the Sasanians is described in detail by Jacob Neusner, *A History of the Jews in Babylonia*, 5 vols. (Leiden: E. J. Brill, 1969–1970; henceforward Neusner, *Jews in Babylonia*).

29. On the Talmuds, see chap. 4.

30. Mantel, *Sanhedrin*, 227–235.

31. Ibid., 206–221; Strack and Stemberger, *Talmud and Midrash*, 14–17.

32. These are described by Michael Avi-Yonah, *The Jews of Palestine: A Political History from Bar Kokhba to the Arab Conquest* (Oxford: Blackwell, 1976), 225–229.

33. The limits of their legal authority are set out in Neusner, *Jews in Babylonia*, 3:155–278, under the headings "The Rabbi as Administrator" and "The Rabbi as Judge." For the full extent of the interests and impact of the Babylonian rabbis, one must turn to Neusner's summary on 3:279–402 and 5:133–216.

34. For a detailed, if traditional, appreciation of the rabbis' work, see Ephraim E. Urbach, *The Sages: Their Concepts and Beliefs* (Cambridge: Harvard University Press, 1987).

35. For a Muslim critique of Western manhandling of the Quran, see S. Parvez Manzoor, "Method against Truth: Orientalism and Qur'anic Studies" (1987); rpt. in Andrew Rippin, ed., *The Quran: Style and Content* (Aldershot: Ashgate Variorum, 2001).

36. The two volumes by W. Montgomery Watt, *Muhammad at Mecca* (Oxford: Clarendon Press, 1953) and *Muhammad at Medina* (Oxford: Clarendon Press, 1956), were for long the classic life in English but there is growing skepticism concerning the sources on which Watt, and everyone else, has relied. See F. E. Peters, *Muhammad and the Origins of Islam* (Albany: State University of New York Press, 1994); and, for a taste of the scholarship (and some of the attitudes) behind that skepticism, see the important older articles reprinted in Ibn Warraq, *The Quest of the Historical Muhammad* (Amherst: Prometheus Press, 2000). For a brief but elegantly written example of a post-Watt non-Muslim life, see Michael Cook, *Muhammad* (Oxford: Oxford University Press, 1983); for a Muslim attempt at a critical life of the Prophet, written by an Egyptian in the 1950s, M. H. Haykal, *The Life of Muhammad*, trans. from the 8th Arabic ed. by I. Faruqi (N.p.: North American Trust Publications, 1976). But for what the life of Muhammad might look like to most Muslims, it is probably more realistic to consult Martin Lings's compilation of traditions in

*Muhammad: His Life Based on the Earliest Sources* (Rochester, Vt.: Inner Traditions International, 1983).

37. Available in English as *The Life of Muhammad: A Translation of Ishaq's Sirat Rasul Allah*, intro. and notes by A. Guillaume (Oxford: Oxford University Press, 1955).

38. On the earliest Arab historiographical tradition are A. A. Duri, *The Rise of Historical Writing among the Arabs*, ed. and trans. Lawrence I. Conrad (Princeton: Princeton University Press, 1983); Tarif Khalidi, *Arab Historical Thought in the Classical Period* (New York: Cambridge University Press, 1994); and Albrecht Noth, *The Early Arabic Historical Tradition: A Source–Critical Study*, 2d ed. in collaboration with Lawrence I. Conrad, trans. from the German by Michael Bonner (Princeton: Darwin Press, 1994).

39. W. A. Bijlefeld, " 'A Prophet and More Than a Prophet': Some Observations on the Qur'anic Use of the Words 'Prophet' and 'Apostle'," *Muslim World* 59 (1969):1–28.

40. See, for example, Sean Freyne, *Galilee, Jesus, and the Gospels* (Philadelphia: Fortress Press, 1988), and the studies collected in Lee I. Levine, ed., *The Galilee in Late Antiquity* (New York: Jewish Theological Seminary of America, 1992).

41. The results are immediately accessible in Michael Avi-Yonah, ed., *Encyclopedia of Archeological Excavations in the Holy Land*, 4 vols. (Jerusalem: Israel Exploration Society, 1975–1978); and Jack Finegan, *The Archeology of the New Testament*, rev. ed. (Princeton: Princeton University Press, 1992).

42. The best introduction to the Quran remains W. Montgomery Watt, *Bell's Introduction to the Qur'an* (Edinburgh: Edinburgh University Press, 1970; henceforward Watt, *Qur'an*). There is also Alford T. Welch, "Kur'an," in the *Encyclopaedia of Islam*, and his briefer article "Qur'an," in Glen Bowersock, Peter Brown, and Oleg Grabar, eds., *Late Antiquity: A Guide to the Postclassical World* (Cambridge: Belknap Press, 1999), 659–660. Finally, there is Neal Robinson's nuanced and sympathetic treatment in his *Discovering the Qur'an: A Contemporary Approach to a Veiled Text* (London: SCM Press, 1996). In progress under the general editorship of Jane Dammen McAuliffe is the *Encyclopaedia of the Quran* (Leiden: E. J. Brill, 1999– ).

43. See Watt, *Qur'an*, 108–120, and his table on 205–213. The chief biographical texts are presented in Peters, *JCI Texts*, 1:182–241.

44. What might lie behind this apparently simple expression is explored by Uri Rubin, "*Hanifiyya* and Kaba: An Inquiry into the Arabian Pre-Islamic Background of the *Din Ibrahim*," *Jerusalem Studies in Arabic and Islam* 13 (1990): 85–112.

45. See, by way of introduction, Michael Zwettler, *The Oral Tradition*

*of Classical Arabic Poetry* (Columbus: Ohio State University Press, 1978); and Gregor Schoeler, "Writing and Publishing: On the Use of Writing in the First Centuries of Islam," *Arabica* 44 (1997): 423–435.

46. Here the reader can simply be directed to two general approaches, both edited by John Esposito. *The Oxford History of Islam* (Oxford: Oxford University Press, 1999) provides a general overview by experts in the field; *The Oxford Encyclopedia of the Modern Islamic World*, 4 vols. (New York: Oxford University Press, 1995) the specifics. For one author's singularly original *tour d'horizon*, see Marshall G. S. Hodgson, *The Venture of Islam*, 3 vols. (Chicago: The University of Chicago Press, 1974).

## CHAPTER 3: COMMUNITY AND HIERARCHY

1. The boundaries of the Land for Israel are defined both broadly and narrowly in the Bible. The discrepancies appear not to have bothered either the authors or the editors of the Pentateuch, but they were of some concern to the later rabbis since the full observance of Jewish law, the statutes pertaining to agricultural tithes, for example, could be fulfilled (and were binding) only in Eretz Israel. The issue of those boundaries arose again in modern times since some Zionists are persuaded that the boundaries of the State of Israel should correspond to those of the biblical Eretz Israel.

2. The history of the Israelite community, the "tender art of living together," has been attempted by Paul D. Hanson, *The People Called: The Growth of the Community in the Bible* (San Francisco: Harper and Row, 1987).

3. The Israelite institutions are usefully and clearly surveyed in Roland de Vaux, *Ancient Israel: Its Life and Institutions* (Grand Rapids: Eerdmans, 1997).

4. For a brief overview of these historiographical issues, see the collections of essays edited by Lester L. Grabbe, *Leading Captivity Captive: "The Exile" as History and Ideology* (Sheffield: Sheffield Academic Press, 1998); and by Oded Lipschitz and Joseph Blenkinsopp, *Judah and the Judeans in the Neo-Babylonian Period* (Winona Lake: Eisenbrauns, 2003).

5. Victor Tcherikover, *Hellenistic Civilization and the Jews* (New York: Athenaeum, 1959; rpt., 1970), 269–295.

6. Ibid., 204–234.

7. Jacob Neusner, *Rabbinic Traditions about the Pharisees before 70*, 3 vols. (Leiden: E. J. Brill, 1970), 3:286–300.

8. Hugo Mantel, *Studies in the History of the Sanhedrin* (Cambridge: Harvard University Press, 1961; henceforward Mantel, *Sanhedrin*), 7–49.

9. Goran Forkman treats this issue with respect to both Judaism and early Christianity in *The Limits of Religious Community: Expulsion from the Religious Community within the Qumran Sect, within Rabbinic Judaism, and within Primitive Christianity* (Lund: Gleerup, 1972).

10. See R. Kimelman, "Birket Ha-Minim and the Lack of Evidence for an Anti-Jewish Prayer in Late Antiquity," in E. P. Sanders, ed., *Jewish and Christian Self-Definition*, vol. 2, *Aspects of Judaism in the Graeco-Roman Period* (Philadelphia: Fortress Press, 1981), 226–244.

11. Their terms and modalities are examined in Forkman, *Limits*, 92–105; and Mantel, *Sanhedrin*, 225–227.

12. Jacob Neusner, *A History of the Jews in Babylonia*, 5 vols. (Leiden: E. J. Brill, 1969–1970), 1:53–61, 103–118; 2:92–95.

13. For a comparison, see Mark R. Cohen, *Under Crescent and Cross: The Jews in the Middle Ages* (Princeton: Princeton University Press, 1994).

14. See S. D. Goitein, *Jews and Arabs: Their Contacts through the Ages* (New York: Schocken Books, 1964); Norman A. Stillman, *The Jews of Arab Lands: A History and Source Book* (Philadelphia: Jewish Publication Society of America, 1979); Bernard Lewis, *The Jews of Islam* (Princeton: Princeton University Press, 1984); Daniel Frank, ed., *The Jews of Medieval Islam: Community, Society, and Identity* (Leiden: E. J. Brill, 1995); and Steven M. Wasserstrom, *Between Muslim and Jew: The Problem of Symbiosis under Early Islam* (Princeton: Princeton University Press, 1995). These are all summary accounts. But in the great mass of documents discovered in the storehouse (*geniza*) of a Cairo synagogue, we have a detailed and firsthand view of almost all phases of Jewish life under Islam from the mid–tenth to the mid–thirteenth century. See S. D. Goitein, *A Mediterranean Society: The Jewish Communities of the Arab World as Portrayed in the Documents of the Cairo Geniza*, 5 vols. (Berkeley: University of California Press, 1967–1988).

15. A notable example is Judah Halevi (d. 1141), the Spanish physician, poet, and philosopher who left al-Andalus for Eretz Israel and who marshalled in his *Kuzari* (see chap. 8) arguments drawn from the natural sciences to demonstrate the superiority of Palestine as the home of prophecy.

16. See G. Lampe, ed., *The Cambridge History of the Bible*, vol. 2, *The West from the Fathers to the Reformation* (Cambridge: Cambridge University Press, 1970), 1–26.

17. On the role and importance of these Jewish officials under Islam, see Robert Brody, *The Geonim of Babylonia and the Shaping of Medieval Jewish Culture* (New Haven: Yale University Press, 1998).

18. Adherence to a common liturgical calendar is a common measure of orthodoxy (and sectarianism). See the case of Qumran described in Geza Vermes, *The Dead Sea Scrolls: Qumran in Perspective*, rev. ed. (Philadelphia: Fortress Press, 1981), 176–178; and the Christian dispute over the date of Easter described in the texts collected in Raniero Cantalamessa, *Easter in the Early Church: An Anthology of Jewish and Early Christian Texts* (Collegeville: Liturgical Press, 1993). See also Thomas J. Talley, *The Origins of the Liturgical Year* (Collegeville: Liturgical Press, 1986), 18–27.

19. On this obscure but obviously important figure, see Robert Eisenman, *James, the Brother of the Lord* (New York: Viking, 1997); and John Painter, *Just James: The Brother of Jesus in History and Tradition* (Minneapolis: Fortress Press, 1999).

20. The evidence of James's death is reviewed by Zvi Baras, "The *Testimonium Flavianum* and the Martyrdom of James," in Louis H. Feldman and Gohei Hata, eds., *Josephus, Judaism, and Christianity* (Detroit: Wayne State University Press, 1987), 338–348.

21. Peters, *JCI Texts*, 1:320–323. For an overview, see Glen Bowersock, Peter Brown, and Oleg Grabar, eds., *Late Antiquity: A Guide to the Postclassical World* (Cambridge: Belknap Press, 1999), s.v. "bishops."

22. Bowersock et al., *Late Antiquity*, s.v. "papa."

23. The foundation texts on the controversy are available in Peters, *JCI Texts*, 1:329–339. There is a useful historical overview of the issue by Klaus Schotz, *Total Primacy from its Origins to the Present* (Collegeville: Liturgical Press, 1996).

24. Synod texts ibid., 2:182–186. There is a far broader selection in J. Stevenson, ed., *Creeds, Councils, and Controversies* (London: SPCK, 1973). The material is historically reviewed in Leo Donald Davis, *The First Seven Ecumenical Councils 325–387: Their History and Theology* (Collegeville: Liturgical Press, 1983); and is given a topical analysis by Bernard L. Marthaler, *The Creed* (Mystic: Twenty-Third Publications, 1987).

25. Peters, *JCI Texts*, 2:330–335.

26. For the texts, see Amnon Linder, *The Jews in Roman Imperial Legislation* (Detroit: Wayne State University Press, 1987). For their interpretation in a broader historical context, R. M. Smallwood, *The Jews under Roman Rule: From Pompey to Diocletian* (Leiden: E. J. Brill, 1976); and Richard Kalmin and Seth Schwartz, eds., *Jewish Culture and Society in the Christian Roman Empire* (Louvain: Peeters, 2002).

27. Peters, *JCI Texts*, 1:342–345. On the persecutions generally, see W. C. Frend, *Martyrdom and Persecution in the Early Church* (New York: New York University Press, 1967).

28. Peters, *JCI Texts*, 1:345–346. See, amid a large literature, A. H. M. Jones, *Constantine and the Conversion of Europe* (London: Hodder and Stoughton, 1948); Ramsay MacMullen, *Constantine* (London: Croom, Helm, 1987); Garth Fowden, *Empire to Commonwealth: Consequences of Monotheism in Late Antiquity* (Princeton: Princeton University Press, 1993), chap. 4; and Samuel Lieu and Dominic Monserrat, *Constantine, History, Historiography, and Legend* (London: Routledge, 1998).

29. See Robin Lane Fox, *Pagans and Christians* (New York: Alfred A. Knopf, 1987); Fowden, *Empire to Commonwealth*; H. A. Drake, *Constantine and the Bishops: The Politics of Intolerance* (Baltimore: Johns Hopkins University Press, 2000). For a sociologist's provocative analysis of the

spread of Christianity, see Rodney Stark, *The Rise of Christianity* (San Francisco: HarperCollins, 1996).

30. The pertinent texts are in F. E. Peters, *Jerusalem: The Holy City in the Eyes of Chroniclers; Visitors, Pilgrims, and Prophets from the Days of Abraham to the Beginnings of Modern Times* (Princeton: Princeton University Press, 1985), 132–139. See also chap. 6 below.

31. The stormy relationship between Christian Church and Roman state is on full display in Peters, *JCI Texts*, 1:346–359. The consequences played out over long centuries of the European tradition. For a mere sampling of its different stages from differing perspectives: Hugo Rahner, *Church and State in Early Christianity* (San Francisco: Ignatius Press, 1992); Brien Tierney, *The Crisis of Church and State, 1050–1300* (Toronto: University of Toronto Press, 1988); Walter Ullmann, *The Growth of Papal Government in the Middle Ages: A Study in the Ideological Relation of Clerical to Lay Power* (London: Methuen, 1970); Ernst Kantorowicz, *The King's Two Bodies: A Study in Medieval Political Theology* (Princeton: Princeton University Press, 1957; rpt., 1997).

32. The standard history of the caliphate is Thomas W. Arnold, *The Caliphate* (New York: Barnes and Noble, 1966), with an appendix by Sylvia Haim, "The Abolition of the Caliphate." For a provocative analysis of the beginning of the institution, see Patricia Crone and Martin Hinds *God's Caliph: Religious Authority in the First Centuries of Islam* (Cambridge: Cambridge University Press, 1986).

33. On the origins and early development of the Shiat Ali, see S. H. M. Jafri, *The Origins and Early Development of Shi'a Islam* (New York: Longman, 1979); and the studies collected in Etan Kohlberg, *Shi'ism: Origins and Early Development* (London: Ashgate Variorum, 2003).

A highly partisan case for the authenticity of Shiite historical claims has been made by Wilfred Madelung, *The Succession to Muhammad: A Study of the Early Caliphate* (New York: Cambridge University Press, 1996). On Shiite Islam generally, see Moojan Momen, *An Introduction to Shil Islam* (New Haven: Yale University Press, 1985); Heinz Halm, *Shiism* (Edinburgh: Edinburgh University Press, 1991).

34. On Abu Hanifa in this context, the basic study remains A. J. Wensinck, *The Muslim Creed: Its Genesis and Historical Development* (London: Frank Cass and Co., 1965), 125–187.

35. The subject has attracted much attention, but the argument over the nature and application of *jihad* is inevitably a matter of texts, quranic and *hadith*, and of their interpretation. They are reviewed in Rudolph Peters, *Jihad in Classical and Modern Islam: A Reader* (Princeton: Marcus Wiener, 1996) and have been analyzed in exemplary fashion by Reuven Firestone, *Jihad: The Origin of Holy War in Islam* (New York: Oxford Uni-

versity Press, 1999). Majid Khadduri, *War and Peace in the Law of Islam* (Baltimore: Johns Hopkins University Press, 1955) is still valuable, and the comparative aspects of "holy war" among the monotheists have been the subject of two collections of essays: P. T. Murphy, ed., *The Holy War* (Columbus: The Ohio State University Press, 1976) and James Turner Johnson, ed., *The Holy War Idea in Western and Islamic Traditions* (University Park: Pennsylvania State University Press, 1997).

36. If there are shelves of studies on *jihad*, there are libraries on the Crusades. The best introduction to the subject remains Erdmann's text and Marshall Baldwin's notes in Carl Erdmann, *The Origin of the Idea of the Crusade*, translated by Marshall Baldwin (Princeton: Princeton University Press, 1977). In addition to the standard histories like the five-volume *History of the Crusades* (Madison: University of Wisconsin Press, 1969) under the general editorship of Kenneth Setton, attention will be called here only to two works from different and enlightening perspectives: James Muldoon, *Popes, Lawyers and Infidels* (Philadelphia: University of Pennsylvania Press, 1979) and Carole Hillenbrand's remarkable *The Crusades: Islamic Perspectives* (New York: Routledge, 2000).

37. The literature is extensive. Among others, see Uri Rubin and David Wasserstein, eds., *Dhimmis and Others: Jews and Christians and the World of Classical Islam* (Winona Lake: Eisenbrauns, 1997); and, for the Ottoman period, Benjamin Braude and Bernard Lewis, eds., *Christians and Jews in the Ottoman Empire: The Functioning of a Plural Society*, 2 vols. (New York: Holmes and Meir, 1982). For the growing polemic around the institution, see Bat Yeor, *The Decline of Eastern Christianity under Islam: From Jihad to Dhimmitude* (Madison, N.J.: Fairleigh Dickinson University Press, 1996).

38. On the yeshiva and the madrasa, see Daphna Ephrat and Yaakov Elman, "Orality and Institutionalization of Tradition: The Growth of the Geonic Yeshiva and the Islamic Madrasa," in Yaakov Elman and Israel Gershoni, eds., *Transmitting Jewish Traditions: Orality, Textuality, and Cultural Diffusion* (New Haven: Yale University Press, 2000), 107–137; and Peters, *Monotheists*, vol. 2, chap. 4.

CHAPTER FOUR: THE LAW

1. The topic is explored by T. J. Meek, *Hebrew Origins* (New York: Harper Torchbooks, 1964).

2. On biblical law generally, see Edward L. Greenstein, "Biblical Law," in Barry W. Holtz, ed., *Back to the Sources: Reading the Classic Jewish Texts* (New York: Summit Books, 1984), 83–104; and for what it looks like in its original setting, Baruch A. Levine, *The JPS Torah Commentary: Leviticus* (Philadelphia: Jewish Publication Society of America, 1989).

3. The term *halaka* is used in numerous different ways, but there is a

clear trajectory that passes from an effort to "derive" such statutes from the written Torah to the rabbis own, fairly open enactment of such. For an appreciation of the role of halaka in Jewish life, see Louis Ginzberg, *On Jewish Law and Lore* (New York: Atheneum, 1977), 77–126.

4. Samuel Belkin, *Philo and the Oral Law: The Philonic Interpretation of Biblical Law in Relation to the Palestinian Halaka* (New York: Johnson Reprint Corp., 1968); Lawrence H. Schiffman, *The Halakha at Qumran* (Leiden: E. J. Brill, 1975); and Schiffman, *Sectarian Law in the Dead Sea Scrolls* (Chico: Scholars Press, 1983).

5. The question of the Pharisees and the oral law is dealt with in detail by E. P. Sanders, *Jewish Law from Jesus to the Mishnah* (Philadelphia: Trinity Press International, 1990), 97–130.

6. On the identity of these individuals, see Herman L. Strack and Günter Stemberger, *Introduction to the Talmud and Midrash* (Minneapolis: Fortress Press, 1992), 69–90; and for the function of this chain of authorities, Amram Topper, "Tractate Avot and Early Christian Succession Lists," in Adam H. Becker and Annette Yoshiko Reed, eds., *The Ways That Never Parted* (Tübinger: Mohr Siebeck, 2003), 159–188, esp. 159–171, and the literature cited there.

7. See Strack and Stemberger, *Talmud and Midrash*, 35–118. The basic study remains Saul Lieberman, "The Publication of the Mishna," in his *Hellenism in Jewish Palestine* (New York: Hebrew Union College Press, 1962), 83–99. See also Birger Gerhardsson, *Memory and Manuscript: Oral Tradition and Written Transmission in Rabbinic Judaism and Early Christianity* (Grand Rapids: Eerdmans, 1998; orig. pub. 1961, rev. 1964; now rpt. with a new preface); and Jacob Neusner, *Oral Tradition in Judaism: The Case of the Mishna* (New York: Garland, 1987).

8. The Mishna is available in two English versions: Herbert Danby, *The Mishnah* (London: Oxford University Press, 1933), with many reprints; and a typographically less user-friendly version by Jacob Neusner, *The Mishna: A New Translation* (New Haven: Yale University Press, 1988). Strack and Stemberger, *Talmud and Midrash*, 124–132 provides a detailed analysis of the sixty-three tractates into which the six orders are divided. The principle of arrangement is not entirely clear, despite the fact that a great deal of exegetical energy has been expended on defining and defending the sequence of the orders and their tractates; see Danby's translation, xxiii–xvii.

9. Strack and Stemberger, *Talmud and Midrash*, 119–166.

10. For their identity, ibid., 91–108.

11. On the two Talmuds, ibid., 182–244 and the literature cited there. Also Adin Steinsaltz, *The Essential Talmud* (New York: Basic Books, 1976); Robert Goldenberg, "Talmud," in Holtz, *Back to the Sources*, 129–176. On the Jerusalem Talmud, Peter Schaefer, *The Talmud Yerushalmi and Graeco-*

*Roman Culture* (Tübingen: Mohr Siebeck, 1998); on the Babylonian, Jacob Neusner, *The Bavli: An Introduction* (Atlanta: Scholars Press, 1992).

12. See D. M. Goodblatt, *Rabbinic Instruction in Sasanian Babylonia* (Leiden: E. J. Brill, 1975); and Robert Brody, *The Geonim of Babylonia and the Shaping of Medieval Jewish Culture* (New Haven: Yale University Press, 1998), esp. 35–136.

13. On the codification of Jewish law, see Ginzberg, *On Jewish Law*, 153–186.

14. The best approach is through Isadore Twersky, *Introduction to the Code of Maimonides (Mishneh Torah)* (New Haven: Yale University Press, 1970).

15. See chap. 8.

16. Trans. Shlomo Pines, with an intro. by Leo Strauss, *Moses Maimonides: The Guide of the Perplexed* (Chicago: University of Chicago Press, 1963).

17. On Rashi, see the studies collected by H. L. Ginsberg, ed., *Rashi Anniversary Volume: Texts and Studies I* (New York: American Academy of Jewish Research, 1941); and, more briefly, Chaim Pearl, *Rashi* (New York: Grove Press, 1988).

18. See Brody, *The Geonim of Babylonia*, 185–215.

19. On the earlier attempts at codification, ibid., 216–234.

20. The easiest access to the *Shulkhan* is through one of its latter-day descendants, the *Kitzur Shulkhan Aruk* of Rabbi Solomon Ganzfried, which has been translated into English as *The Code of Jewish Law* (New York: Hebrew Publishing Co., 1961).

21. Sanders, *Jewish Law*, 1–96, is devoted to the question of Jesus' attitudes and observance.

22. E. P. Sanders, *Paul, the Law, and the Jewish People* (Philadelphia: Fortress Press, 1983). On the rabbinic debate over whether the coming of the Messiah abrogated ceremonial law, see Joseph Klausner, *From Jesus to Paul* (Boston: Beacon Press, 1961), 321 and n. 13.

23. Wayne Meeks, *The Moral World of the First Christians* (Philadelphia: Westminster Press, 1986). This is also the theme, on a much broader scale, of Robin Lane Fox, *Pagans and Christians* (New York: Alfred A. Knopf, 1987).

24. A clear and illustrative introduction is provided by *Gratian: The Treatise on Laws* (trans. Augustine Thompson) *with the Ordinary Gloss* (trans. James Gordley) (Washington D.C.: Catholic University of America Press, 1993).

25. The standard treatment is James A. Brundage, *Medieval Canon Law* (New York: Longman,1995). For broader perspectives, see Harold J. Berman, *Law and Revolution: The Formation of the Western Legal Tradition* (Cambridge: Harvard University Press, 1983), 85–119; Albert R. Jonsen and Stephen Toulmin, *The Abuse of Casuistry: A History of Moral Reasoning* (Berkeley: University of California Press, 1988), 89–136.

26. N. J. Coulson, "Qur'anic Legislation," in *A History of Islamic Law* (Edinburgh: University of Edinburgh Press, 1964), 9–20; Wael B. Hallaq, "The Qur'an as a Legal Document," in *A History of Islamic Legal Theories* (Cambridge: Cambridge University Press, 1997), 3–7.

27. See Coulson, *Islamic Law*, 21–52.

28. The *Essay* is available in English: Majid Khadduri, *Islamic Jurisprudence: Shafi'i's Risala* (Baltimore: Johns Hopkins University Press, 1961).

29. Joseph Schacht, *The Origins of Muhammadan Jurisprudence* (London: Oxford University Press, 1953), 11–18, 77–80. See, both more generally and in great detail, Muhammad Zubayr Siddiqi, *Hadith Literature: Its Origins, Development, and Special Features* (Cambridge: Islamic Texts Society, 1993); John Burton, *An Introduction to the Hadith* (Edinburgh: Edinburgh University Press, 1994), esp. 17–35; and the fundamental articles collected by Harald Motzki, ed., *Hadith: Origins and Development* (London: Ashgate Variorum, 2003).

30. On Shafii, see Coulson, *Islamic Law*, 53–61; Hallaq, *Islamic Legal Theories*, 21–35.

31. Siddiqi, *Hadith Literature*, 31–42; Burton, *Hadith*, 106–147.

32. On this important notion, Siddiqi, *Hadith Literature*, 14–27.

33. How Jesus' various images functioned in both Eastern and Western Christendom is displayed in Jaroslav Pelikan, *Jesus through the Centuries: His Place in the History of Culture* (New Haven: Yale University Press, 1985).

34. How the portrait was constructed is traced by Uri Rubin, *The Eye of the Beholder: The Life of Muhammad as Viewed by the Early Muslims* (Princeton: Darwin Press, 1995). For the length and breadth of the Muslim tradition about Muhammad, see Annemarie Schimmel, *And Muhammad Is His Messenger: The Veneration of the Prophet in Islamic Piety* (Chapel Hill: University of North Carolina Press, 1985); and the interesting essay by Earle H. Waugh, "The Popular Muhammad: Models of Interpretation of an Islamic Paradigm," in Richard Martin, ed., *Approaches to Islam in Religious Studies* (Tucson: University of Arizona Press, 1985), 41–58.

35. This has been the thrust of modern, non-Muslim criticism of the hadith, begun by Ignaz Goldziher, *Muslim Studies*, rev. trans. S. M. Stern (London: Allen and Unwin, 1971); 2:17–254; and taken up by Schacht, *Origins*, 163–175. Compare Siddiqi, *Hadith Literature*, 124–135; and Burton, *Hadith*, 148–156.

36. Siddiqi, *Hadith Literature*, 43–75.

37. Burton, *Hadith*, 157–177.

38. Danby, *The Mishnah*, 446–447. See also Judah Goldin, *The Living Talmud: The Wisdom of the Fathers and Its Classical Commentaries* (New Haven: Yale University Press, 1955).

39. Coulson, *Islamic Law*, 59–60, 76–77; Hallaq, *Islamic Legal Theories*, 117–121.

40. Rubbed, at length, in Hallaq, *Islamic Legal Theories*, 83–107.

41. Coulson, *Islamic Law*, 76–81; Hallaq, *Islamic Legal Theories*, 75–81; Burton, *Hadith*, 157–187.

42. On probabilism versus *taqlid*, "accepting on authority," in the Christian moral tradition, see John Mahoney, *The Making of Moral Theology* (Oxford: Clarendon Press, 1987), 116–174.

43. Coulson, *Islamic Law*, 36–52.

44. On Shiite law, see Coulson, *Islamic Law*, 103–119; and Moojan Momen, *An Introduction to Shii Islam* (New Haven: Yale University Press, 1985), 184–189.

45. Coulson, *Islamic Law*, 80–81.

46. Coulson, *Islamic Law*, 130–132.

47. This important development is addressed at length in the papers collected in Khalid Masud et al., eds., *Islamic Legal Interpretation: Muftis and Their Fatwas* (Cambridge: Harvard University Press, 1996).

48. See Avram Udovitch, *Partnership and Profit in Medieval Islam* (Princeton: Princeton University Press, 1970).

49. Jeanette Wakin, *The Function of Documents in Islamic Law* (Albany: State University of New York Press, 1972); compare Udovitch, *Partnership*, 9–10.

50. On hiyal, Coulson, *Islamic Law*, 139–141; and Udovitch, *Partnership*, 11–12. An entire tractate of the Mishnaic order "Festivals" is given over to the legal fiction of *erubin*, whereby one can extend the permissible limits of the domain within which Sabbath activity may be licitly carried on. See Danby, *The Mishnah*, 121–136.

51. The caliph may once have had this opportunity. See the interesting essay by S. D. Goitein, "A Turning Point in the History of the Muslim State," in *Studies in Islamic History and Institutions* (Leiden: E. J. Brill, 1968), 149–167.

52. See E. J. Rosenthal, *Political Thought in Medieval Islam* (Cambridge: Cambridge University Press, 1962), 21–112.

CHAPTER FIVE: SCRIPTURE AND TRADITION

1. The process is known generally as exegesis (see Peters, *Monotheists*, vol. 2, chap. 2; and the texts assembled in Peters, *JCI Texts*, 2:72–156). Its application in medieval Judaism, Christianity, and Islam is the subject of the papers collected in Jane Dammen McAuliffe et al., eds., *With Reverence for the Word: Medieval Scriptural Exegesis in Judaism, Christianity, and Islam* (Oxford: Oxford University Press, 2003), particularly the contribution of Stephen D. Benin, "The Search for Truth in Sacred Scripture: Jews, Christians, and the Authority to Interpret," 13–32.

2. The entire range of midrash is on display in Martin Jan Mulder, ed., *Mikra: Text, Translation, Reading, and Interpretation of the Hebrew Bible in Ancient Judaism and Early Christianity* (Philadelphia: Fortress Press, 1988), as well as in Michael Fishbane, *Biblical Interpretation in Ancient Israel* (Oxford: Clarendon Press, 1985). There are individual studies in part 2 (pp. 181–240) of John Barton, ed., *The Cambridge Companion to Biblical Interpretation* (New York: Cambridge University Press, 1998). Rabbinic midrash is the particular focus in Herman L. Strack and Günter Stemberger, *Introduction to the Talmud and Midrash* (Minneapolis: Fortress Press, 1992), 254–394; and Gary Porton, *Understanding Rabbinic Midrash: Texts and Commentary* (New York: Ktav, 1984).

3. See chap. 4.

4. On the languages of rabbinic literature, see Strack and Stemberger, *Talmud and Midrash*, 111–118.

5. See André Pelletier, "Josephus, the Letter of Aristeas, and the Septuagint," in Louis H. Feldman and Gohei Hata, eds., *Josephus, the Bible, and History* (Detroit: Wayne State University Press, 1989), 97–115. The pertinent texts, Jewish and Christian, are in Peters, *JCI Texts*, 2:14–18.

6. John Bowker, *The Targums and Rabbinic Literature* (Cambridge: Cambridge University Press, 1969); and the papers collected in Derek Robert, George Beattie, and Martin McNamara, eds., *The Aramaic Bible: Targums in Their Historical Context* (Sheffield: Journal for the Study of the Old Testament Press, 1994).

7. On the Qumran pesharim, see Maurya P. Horgan, *Pesharim: Qumran Interpretations of Biblical Books* (Washington, D.C.: Catholic Biblical Association of America, 1979).

8. These have been collected and topically arranged by Louis Ginzberg, *Legends of the Jews*, 7 vols., 10th ed. (Philadelphia: Jewish Publication Society of America, 1954).

9. As illustrated, for example, in *The Tales of the Prophets of al-Kisa'i*, trans. from the Arabic by Wheeler Thackston (Boston: Twayne, 1978). For two studies of the genre, see Khalil Athamina, "Al-Qasas: Its Emergence, Religious Origin, and Sociopolitical Impact on Early Muslim Society," *Studia Islamica* 76 (1992): 53–74; and M. J. Kister, "Legends in *Tafsir* and *Hadith* Literature: The Creation of Adam and Related Stories," in Andrew Rippin, ed., *Approaches to the History of the Interpretation of the Qur'an* (Oxford: Clarendon Press, 1988), 82–116.

10. On Hillel's *middot*, see Strack and Stemberger, *Talmud and Midrash*, 19–23.

11. Geza Vermes, "Bible and Midrash: Early Old Testament Exegesis," in P. R. Ackroyd and C. F. Evans, eds., *The Cambridge History of the Bible* vol. 1, *From the Beginnings to Jerome* (Cambridge: Cambridge Uni-

versity Press, 1970), 199–231. See also his *Scripture and Tradition in Judaism: Haggadic Studies*, 2d ed. (Leiden: E. J. Brill, 1973).

12. Vermes, "Bible and Midrash," 205–207, cites the classic instance of the biblical pronouncement on divorce (Deut. 24:1), where the grounds are described simply as a man's finding "some indecency" in his wife, hereby leaving the door open for a great deal of midrashic debate— and Jesus' own pronouncement (Matt. 5:31–32)—on what precisely constituted "indecency."

13. A reverse example is the use of images, whose biblical prohibition is, on the face of it, absolute (Exod. 20:4–5; Deut. 5:8–9), and was still understood as such at the time of Josephus. By the beginning of the second century C.E., however, attitudes were changing, and soon both secular and religious buildings of the Jews in Palestine and the Diaspora were being adorned with images of humans and animals. The exegesis of the biblical passage was adapted accordingly; see Vermes, "Bible and Midrash," 217–218. For this and the related issue of images in Islam, Peters, *Monotheists*, vol. 2, chap. 6.

14. Horgan, *Pesharim*.

15. See Louis Ginzberg, *On Jewish Law and Love* (New York: Atheneum, 1977), 127–152.

16. See Rudolph Pfeiffer, *History of Classical Scholarship, from the Beginning to the End of the Hellenistic Age* (Oxford: Clarendon Press, 1968), 210–251; Jan Whitman, *Allegory: The Dynamics of an Ancient and Medieval Technique* (Cambridge: Harvard University Press, 1987); David Dawson, *Allegorical Readers and Cultural Revision in Ancient Alexandria* (Berkeley: University of California Press, 1992).

17. On Homer in the hands of later Hellenism, see Robert Lamberton, *Homer the Theologian: Neoplatonist Allegorical Interpretation and the Growth of the Epic Tradition* (Berkeley: University of California Press, 1986).

18. Early Christian treatment of Scripture is surveyed in James L. Kugel and Rowan A. Greer, *Early Biblical Interpretation* (Philadelphia: Westminster Press, 1986); and R. P. C. Hanson, "Biblical Exegesis in the Early Church," in Ackroyd and Evans, eds., *The Cambridge History of the Bible*, 1:412–453. There is more on the longer range of Christian exegesis in part 2 (pp. 241–322) of Barton, *The Cambridge Companion to Biblical Interpretation*.

19. Trans. in M. Staniforth, *Early Christian Writings: The Apostolic Fathers* (Harmondsworth: Penguin, 1968), 193–220.

20. For a comparative study, see Marc Hirshman, *A Rivalry of Genius: Jewish and Christian Biblical Interpretation in Late Antiquity* (Albany: State University of New York Press, 1996).

21. The technique is studied in Donald Juel, *Messianic Exegesis: Christological Interpretation of the Old Testament in Early Christianity*

(Philadelphia: Fortress Press, 1988); and for a somewhat later period, Jean Daniélou, *From Shadows of Reality: Studies in the Biblical Typology of the Fathers* (London: Burns and Oates, 1960).

22. These important figures in Christian exegesis are dealt with in Ackroyd and Evans, eds., *The Cambridge History of the Bible*, 1:454–562.

23. See, for example, Aloys Grillmeier, *Christ in Christian Tradition* (London: Sheed and Ward, 1965), 338–362.

24. See Peters, *JCI Texts*, 2:157–200.

25. The relative weight of Scripture and tradition and the role of the latter in shaping the understanding of the former in the comparative context of Judaism and Catholic and Protestant Christianity have been broached by the studies collected in Frederick E. Greenspahn, ed., *Scripture in the Jewish and Christian Traditions: Authority, Interpretation, Relevance* (Nashville: Abingdon, 1982).

26. This distinction developed into a profound tension in the sixteenth century, when it became one of the central issues of the Protestant Reformation. For a brief introduction to a complex question, see Jaroslav Pelikan, *The Christian Tradition*, vol. 4, *Reformation of Church and Dogma, 1300–1700* (Chicago: University of Chicago Press, 1984), 210–212, 304–313. For the Roman counterstatement, Herbert Yedin, *A History of the Council of Trent*, vol. 2, *The First Sessions at Trent, 1545–1547*, trans. from the German by Dom Ernest Graf (St. Louis: B. Herder Book Co., 1961), 52–98.

27. This crucial development has been traced by J. N. D. Kelly, *Early Christian Doctrines* (London: Black, 1968), chap. 1; G. L. Prestige in his classic *Fathers and Heretics* (London: SPCK, 1963), chap. 1; and Hans von Campenhausen, *Ecclesiastical Authority and Spiritual Power in the Church of the First Three Centuries* (Peabody, Mass.: Hendrickson, 1997). The sources illustrating the growth of the concept are collected in Henry Bettenson, *Documents of the Christian Church* (London: Oxford University Press, 1970), 95–103. For a comparison of the Apostolic succession with the parallel phenomenon in Judaism—the connection of the oral Torah and the tradition of the Fathers back to Moses on Sinai—see Amram Tropper, "Tractate Avot and Early Christian Succession Lists," in Adam H. Becker and Annette Yoshiko Reed, eds., *The Ways That Never Parted* (Tübingen: Mohr Siebeck, 2003), 159–188.

28. So Yves Congar, *Tradition and the Traditions* (New York: Macmillan, 1966), 50–64.

29. Pelikan, *The Christian Tradition*, vol. 1, *The Emergence of the Catholic Tradition, 100–600* (Chicago: University of Chicago Press, 1971), chap. 7, "The Orthodox Consensus," 332–357. For its influence on Scripture, Congar, *Tradition and the Traditions*, 64–85.

30. On Arabic as a sacred language, see John Wansbrough, *Qur'anic Studies* (London: Oxford University Press, 1977), 99–106.

31. On quranic exegesis generally, besides the already cited Rippin, *History of Interpretation*, and the quranic contributions to McAuliffe et al., *With Reverence for the Word*, see Andrew Rippin, ed., *The Quran: Formative Interpretation* (Aldershot: Ashgate Variorum, 1999); Helmut Gaetje, *The Qur'an and the Exegesis* (Berkeley: University of California Press, 1978), and Mahmood M. Ayoub, *The Qur'an and Its Interpreters* (Albany: State University of New York Press, 1984), both with many illustrative texts; John Burton, "Qur'anic Exegesis," in M. J. L. Young et al., eds., *The Cambridge History of Arabic Literature: Religion, Learning, and Science in the Abbasid Period* (Cambridge: Cambridge University Press, 1990), 40–55; and the studies in Gerald Hawting and Abdul-Kader Shareef, eds., *Approaches to the Qur'an* (New York: Routledge, 1993).

32. See Harris Birkeland, *Old Muslim Opposition against Interpretation of the Qur'an* (Oslo: Hos. J. Dybwad, 1955); and Nabia Abbott, *Studies in Arabic Literary Papyri*, vol. 1, *Qur'anic Commentary and Tradition* (Chicago: University of Chicago Press, 1967).

33. The early evolution of the genre is traced by Fred Leemhuis, "Origins and Early Development of the *Tafsir* Tradition," in Rippin, *History of Interpretation*, 13–30.

34. Wansbrough, *Qur'anic Studies*, 122–149, esp. 145–148, where Wansbrough underlines the role of the public and popular Friday sermon in the evolution of this basic form of Muslim exegesis.

35. The radical view expressed ibid., 174–176, is in keeping with Wansbrough's even more radical thesis for a late date (eighth–ninth century) for the establishment of the text of the Quran.

36. Ibid., 177–201; and two studies by Andrew Rippin, "The Exegetical Genre *Asbab al-Nuzul*: A Bibliographical and Terminological Survey," and "The Function of the *Asbab al-Nuzul* in Qur'anic Exegesis," *Bulletin of the School of African and Oriental Studies* 48 (1985): 1–15; and 51 (1988): 1–20 respectively.

37. See Chaim Rabin, *Ancient West Arabian* (London: Taylor's Foreign Press, 1951); and Wansbrough, *Qur'anic Studies*, 85–93, for a review of the question.

38. I. Goldfeld, "The *Tafsir* of Abdullah ibn Abbas," *Der Islam* 58 (1981); 125–135.

39. Jane Dammen McAuliffe, "Quranic Hermeneutics: The Views of al-Tabari and Ibn Kathir," in Rippin, *History of Interpretation*, 46–62. Al-Tabari's commentary on sura's 1 and 2 is available in abridged English translation by John Cooper, *The Commentary on the Qur'an by al-Tabari* (Oxford: Oxford University Press, 1987).

40. The entire text and some Muslim commentary appears in Peters, *JCI Texts*, 2:144–147. On the various understandings of this difficult quranic passage, see Wansbrough, *Qur'anic Studies*, 148–151.

41. See Leon Nemoy, *Karaite Anthology* (New Haven: Yale University Press, 1952) for an introduction to Karaiteir thought and selections from their writings.

42. See Daniel J. Lasker, "Rabbanism and Karaism: The Contest for Supremacy," in Raphael Jospe and Stanley M. Wagner eds., *Great Schisms in Jewish History* (New York: Ktav, 1981), 47–72.

43. See chap. 4, n.29.

44. The debate is laid out in J. F. Peters, *God's Created Speech* (Leiden: E. J. Brill, 1976).

45. On Saadya as an exegete, see Haggai ben Shammai, "The Tension between Literal Interpretation and Exegetical Freedom: Comparative Observations on Saadia's Method," in McAuliffe et al., *With Reverence for the Word*, 33–50.

46. This approach let into dogmatic issues, namely, the essential inimitability of the Quran; see Issa Boullata, "The Rhetorical Interpretation of the Qur'an: *I'jaz* and Related Topics," in Rippin, *History of Interpretation*, 139–157. There are modern attempts at such analysis, and studies of medieval ones, collected in Issa Boullata, ed., *Literary Structures of Religious Meaning in the Qur'an* (Richmond, Surrey: Curzon Press, 2000).

47. This milieu is brilliantly displayed in María Rosa Menocal, *The Ornament of the World: How Muslims, Jews, and Christians Created a Culture of Tolerance in Medieval Spain* (New York: Little, Brown, 2002). For the Jewish literary setting in particular, see Ross Brann, *The Compunctious Poet: Cultural Ambiguity and Hebrew Poetry in Muslim Spain* (Baltimore: Johns Hopkins University Press, 1991), and his *Power in the Portrayal: Representations of Jews and Muslims in Eleventh and Twelfth Century Spain* (Princeton: Princeton University Press, 2002).

48. Studied by Benjamin Gelles, *Peshat and Derash in the Exegesis of Rashi* (Leiden: E. J. Brill, 1981). For an example of Rashi at work, Chaim Pearl, *Rashi: Commentary on the Pentateuch* (New York: Norton, 1970).

49. On medieval Jewish exegesis generally, see Edward L. Greenstein, "Medieval Bible Commentaries," in Barry W. Holtz, ed., *Back to the Sources: Reading the Classic Jewish Texts* (New York: Summit Books, 1984), 213–260; and Barry D. Walfish, "An Introduction to Medieval Jewish Biblical Interpretation," in McAuliffe et al., *With Reverence for the Word*, 3–12.

## CHAPTER SIX: THE WORSHIP OF GOD

1. Ismar Elbogen, *Jewish Liturgy: A Comprehensive History*, trans. Raymond P. Scheindlin (Philadelphia: Jewish Publication Society of America, 1993); A. Z. Idelsohn, *Jewish Liturgy and Its Development* (1932; rpt., New York: Schocken Books, 1975), chap. 3.

2. On Passover, see J. B. Segal, *The Hebrew Passover* (London: Oxford

University Press, 1963); on its calendrical (and polemical) relationship to the Christians' Easter, Paul F. Bradshaw and Lawrence A. Hoffman, *Passover and Easter: Origins and History to Modern Times* (Notre Dame: Notre Dame University Press, 1999).

3. The cult (and beliefs) of the pre-Exilic Israelites are set out, from two very different perspectives, in Yehezkel Kaufman, *The Religion of Israel: From Its Beginnings to the Babylonian Exile*, trans. and abridged by Moshe Greenberg (Chicago: University of Chicago Press, 1960); and Helmer Ringgren, *Israelite Religion* (Lanham, Md.: University Press of America, 1988 [from a 1963 German original]).

4. Menahem Haran, *Temples and Temple Service in Ancient Israel* (Winona Lake: Eisenbrauns, 1985), 58–111; and Aelred Cody, *A History of the Old Testament Priesthood* (Rome: Pontifical Biblical Institute, 1969). For the Second Temple period, E-mil Schuerer, *The History of the Jewish People in the Age of Jesus Christ, 175 B.C.–A.D. 135*, rev. and ed. Geza Vermes and Fergus Millar, 2 vols. (Edinburgh: T. and T. Clark, 1973, 1979), 2:237–291.

5. Post-Exilic temple cult is laid out in great and graphic detail in E. P. Sanders, *Judaism: Practice and Belief, 63 B.C.E.–66 C.E.* (Philadelphia: Trinity Press, 1992). There is another treatment in M. Avi-Yonah and Z. Baras, eds., *The World History of the Jewish People*, vol. 8, *Society and Religion in the Second Temple Period* (Jerusalem: Massada, 1977).

6. There is a very large literature on the subject of the early synagogue, but most of it surfaces and is discussed in Lee I. Levine, ed., *The Synagogue in Late Antiquity* (Philadelphia: American Schools of Oriental Research, 1987); and particularly in Dan Urman and Paul V. M. Flesher, eds., *Ancient Synagogues: Historical Analysis and Archaeological Survey*, 2 vols. (Leiden: E. J. Brill, 1995).

7. The various divisions of the Jewish Scriptures for liturgical purposes have been studied by J. Mann, *The Bible as Read and Preached in the Old Synagogue*, 2 vols. (New York: Hebrew Union College Press, 1940, 1966). The liturgical prayers are described in Idelsohn, *Jewish Liturgy*, 73–121.

8. See Idelsohn, *Jewish Liturgy*, 151–157, 173–187.

9. Ibid., 56–70; 89–110.

10. The complex has been studied by Joachim Jeremias, *The Eucharistic Words of Jesus* (London: SCM Press, 1966).

11. R. J. Daly, *Christian Sacrifice: The Judaeo-Christian Background before Origen* (Washington, D.C.: Catholic University of America Press, 1978).

12. The issues involved in their liturgical development are laid out in Paul F. Bradshaw, *The Search for the Origins of Christian Worship Sources and Methods for the Study of the Early Liturgy* (New York: Oxford University Press, 1992).

13. On *katechesis* and catechumen, see Michael Dujarier and Edward J. Haasl, *A History of the Catechumenate: The First Six Centuries* (New York: Sadlier, 1979); and Glen Bowersock, Peter Brown, and Oleg Grabar, eds., *Late Antiquity: A Guide to the Postclassical World* (Cambridge: Belknap Press, 1999), s.v. "catechesis."

14. C. W. Dugmore, *The Influence of the Synagogue upon the Divine Office* (Westminster: Faith Press, 1964); and Carmine De Sante, *Jewish Prayer: The Origin of the Christian Liturgy* (New York: Paulist Press, 1991).

15. The classic study remains Dom Gregory Dix, *The Shape of the Liturgy* (1945; rpt. with additional notes by Paul V. Marshall, New York: Seabury Press, 1982).

16. The standard history of the Eucharist is Hans Lietzmann, *Mass and Lord's Supper: A Study in the History of the Liturgy*, trans. with appendices, by Dorothea H. G. Reeve, intro. and further inquiry by Robert Douglas Richardson (Leiden: E. J. Brill, 1979).

17. See Richard Krautheimer, *Early Christian and Byzantine Architecture* (Harmondsworth: Penguin, 1963), 1–44; and Bowersock et al., *Late Antiquity*, s.v. "basilica."

18. The Didache is translated in M. Staniforth, *Early Christian Writings: The Apostolic Fathers* (Harmondsworth: Penguin, 1968), 227–235. Its Eucharistic evidence is studied by Johannes Betz, "The Eucharist in the Didache," in Jonathan Draper, ed., *The Didache in Modern Research* (Leiden: E. J. Brill, 1996), 244–275.

19. The Western Mass was also part of an elaborate sacramental system, on which see Pierre-Marie Gy, "Sacraments and Liturgy in Latin Christianity," in Bernard McGinn and John Meyendorff, eds., *Christian Spirituality*, vol. 1, *Origins to the Twelfth Century* (New York: Crossroad, 1987), 365–381.

20. The various liturgies are available in F. E. Brightman, *Liturgies Eastern and Western* (1896; rpt., London: Oxford University Press, 1956). On the Eastern liturgies, see also Paul Meyendorff, "Eastern Liturgical Theology," in McGinn and Meyendorff, *Christian Spirituality*, 350–364.

21. See Anton Baumstark, *Comparative Liturgy* (London: Newman Press, 1958).

22. On this difficult subject, see G. R. Hawting, "The Origins of the Islamic Sanctuary at Mecca," in G. H. A. Juynboll, ed., *Studies on the First Century of Islamic Society* (Carbondale: Southern Illinois University Press, 1982), 25–47; Uri Rubin, "The Kaba: Aspects of Its Ritual Functions and Position in Pre-Islamic and Early Islamic times," *Jerusalem Studies in Arabic and Islam* 8 (1986): 97–131.

23. See F. E. Peters, *Muhammad and the Origins of Islam* (Albany: State University of New York Press, 1994), 251–253.

24. Pertinent texts are in Peters, *JCI Texts*, 3:95–104. For possible Jewish antecedents, see the arguments adduced by S. D. Goitein, "Prayer in Islam," in *Studies in Islamic History and Institutions* (Leiden: E. J. Brill, 1968), 73–89.

25. See S. D. Goitein, "Ramadan—the Muslim Month of Fasting: Its Early Development and Religious Meaning," in *Studies*, 90–110.

26. For al-Ghazali's reflections on the subject, see Peters, *JCI Texts*, 3:106–108; and for the possible origins of the practice, S. D. Goitein, "The Origin and Nature of Muslim Friday Worship," in *Studies*, 111–125.

27. For a brief introduction, see Bowersock et al., *Late Antiquity*, s.v. "mosque"; and, for more detail, Oleg Grabar, *The Formation of Islamic Art*, rev. ed. (New Haven: Yale University Press, 1987), 99–131.

28. See F. E. Peters, *The Hajj: The Muslim Pilgrimage to Mecca and the Holy Places* (Princeton: Princeton University Press, 1994).

29. The texts are in Peters, *JCI Texts*, 3:111–114.

30. On Islamic ritual generally, see William A. Graham, "Islam in the Mirror of Ritual," in Richard G. Hovannisian and Speros Vryonis, eds., *Islam's Understanding of Itself* (Malibu: Undena Publications, 1983), 53–73; Frederick M. Denny, "Islamic Ritual: Perspectives and Theories," in Richard Martin, ed., *Approaches to Islam in Religious Studies* (Tucson: University of Arizona Press, 1985), 63–77; and the studies collected and reprinted in Gerald Hawting, ed., *The Development of Islamic Ritual* (London: Ashgate Variorum, 2004).

31. The Muslim holy days and celebrations are described in G. E. von Grunebaum, *Muhammadan Festivals* (London: Curzon Press, 1976).

32. For hadith on the subject, see Peters, *JCI Texts*, 3:108–109.

33. The subject is explored from many angles in part 2 of Peter Brown, *Society and the Holy in Late Antiquity* (Berkeley: University of California Press, 1982); and, with a focus on the Latin West, in his *Cult of the Saints: Its Rise and Function in Latin Christianity* (Chicago: University of Chicago Press, 1981).

34. Many of these shrines are described in Tewfiq Canaan, *Mohammadan Saints and Sanctuaries in Palestine* (London: Luzac, 1927; rpt., Jerusalem: Ariel, n.d.).

35. W. C. Frend, *Martyrdom and Persecution in the Early Church* (New York: New York University Press, 1967); Glen W. Bowersock, *Martyrdom and Rome* (Cambridge: Cambridge University Press, 1995); and Bowersock et al., *Late Antiquity*, s.v. "martyrs".

36. The process is traced in detail by Robert L. Wilken, *The Land Called Holy: Palestine in Christian History and Tradition* (New Haven: Yale University Press, 1992); and Güenter Stemberger, *Jews and Christians in the Holy Land: Palestine in the Fourth Century*, trans. R. Tuschling (Edinburgh: T. and T. Clark, 2000).

37. See Grace Martin Smith and Carl Ernst, eds., *Manifestations of Sainthood in Islam* (Istanbul: Isis Press, 1993); and, more particularly, Frederick M. Denny, "God's Friends: The Sanctity of Persons in Islam," in Richard Kieckhefer and George Bond, eds., *Sainthood: Its Manifestations in World Religions* (Berkeley: University of California Press, 1988), 69–97.

38. Annemarie Schimmel, *The Mystical Dimensions of Islam* (Chapel Hill: University of North Carolina Press, 1975), 213–227.

39. The first substantial study was by Ignaz Goldziher, "The Veneration of Saints in Islam," in his *Muslim Studies*, rev. trans. S. M. Stern (London: Allen and Unwin, 1971), 2:255–334. See also Schimmel, *Mystical Dimensions*, 119–213. The cult is particularly strong in North Africa: Ernst Gellner, *Saints of the Atlas* (London: Wiedenfeld and Nicolson, 1969); and Clifford Geertz, *Islam Observed* (Chicago: University of Chicago Press, 1971).

40. Peter Chelkowski, ed., *Ta'ziyeh: Ritual and Drama* (New York: New York University Press, 1979). Compare Peters, *Monotheists*, vol. 2, chap. 6.

## CHAPTER SEVEN: RENUNCIATION AND ASPIRATION

1. For the broad approach, see the studies assembled in Vincent L. Wimbush and Richard Valantasis, eds., *Asceticism* (New York: Oxford University Press, 1995).

2. The issue is discussed by Steven D. Fraade, "Ascetical Aspects of Ancient Judaism," in Arthur Green, ed., *Jewish Spirituality from the Bible through the Middle Ages* (New York: Crossroad, 1988), 253–288. On the Rechabites in particular, see James H. Charlesworth, ed. and trans., *The History of the Rechabites* (Chico: Scholars Press, 1982).

3. For Philo's view generally, see David Winston, "Philo and the Contemplative Life," in Green, *Jewish Spirituality*, 198–231.

4. See Peter Brown, *The Body and Society: Men, Women, and Sexual Renunciation in Early Christianity* (New York: Columbia University Press, 1988).

5. His biography by the equally famous bishop of Alexandria is available in *Athanasius: The Life of Anthony and the Letter to Marcellinus*, ed. Robert C. Gregg (New York: Paulist Press, 1980). More generally, see Charles Kannengiesser, "Athanasius and the Ascetic Movement of His Time," in Wimbush and Valantasis, *Asceticism*, 479–492.

6. The details are in the lives collected in Helen Waddell, *The Desert Fathers* (Ann Arbor: University of Michigan Press, 1957). The history of the Egyptian and Palestinian forms of Christian monasticism is sketched by D. J. Chitty, *The Desert a City* (Crestwood, N.Y.: St. Vladimir's Semi-

nary Press, 1977); and the Syrian form, which may have had very different indigenous roots, by Arthur Vööbus, *History of Asceticism in the Syrian Orient*, 2 vols. (Louvain: CSCO, 1958).

7. Trans. M. Monica Wagner, *Saint Basil: Ascetical Works* (Washington, D.C.: Catholic University of America Press, 1950). More generally on Basil, see the contributions to Paul Fedwick, ed., *Basil of Caesarea, Christian, Humanist, Ascetic: A Sixteen-Hundredth Anniversary Symposium* (Toronto: Pontifical Medieval Institute, 1980).

8. On Western monasticism, see Jean Leclerq, "Monasticism and Asceticism: Western Christianity," in Bernard McGinn and John Meyendorff, eds., *Christian Spirituality*, vol. 1, *Origins to the Twelfth Century* (New York: Crossroad, 1987), 113–131.

9. Text in Henry Bettenson, *Documents of the Christian Church* (London: Oxford University Press, 1970), 164–181.

10. See Timothy E. Gregory, *Vox Populi: Popular Opinion and Violence in the Religious Controversies of the Fifth Century A.D.* (Columbus: Ohio State University Press, 1979).

11. On Eastern Church monasticism, see Jean Gribomont, "Monasticism and Asceticism: Eastern Christianity," in McGinn and Meyendorff, *Christian Spirituality*, 89–112.

12. On the beginnings, see A. Louth, *The Origins of the Christian Mystical Tradition* (Oxford: Clarendon Press, 1981).

13. John Climacus, *The Ladder of Divine Ascent*, trans. Colm Luibheid and Norman Russell (New York: Paulist Press, 1983).

14. *The Prayer of Jesus*, trans. "A Monk of the Western Church" (Crestwood, N.Y.: St. Vladimir's Seminary Press, 1987). On the differences between the Eastern and Western modes of prayer in Christianity, see Kallistos Ware and Jean Leclerq, "Ways of Prayer and Contemplation," in McGinn and Meyendorff, *Christian Spirituality*, 395–426.

15. Jill Raitt, ed., *Christian Spirituality*, vol. 2, *High Middle Ages and Reformation* (New York: Crossroad, 1997), 208–222. Some basic treatises of the spiritual leader of the movement, Gregory Palamas (d. 1359), are available in English: *Gregory Palamas: The Triads*, ed. John Meyendorff, trans. Nicholas Gendle (New York: Paulist Press, 1983).

16. The best approach to Sufism is William C. Chittick, *Sufism: A Short Introduction* (Oxford: OneWorld, 2000). There is an excellent selection of early Islamic mystical texts in English in Michael A. Sells, *Early Islamic Mysticism: Sufi, Qur'an, Mi'raj, and Theological Writings* (New York: Paulist Press, 1996).

17. On Muslim mysticism generally, see Annemarie Schimmel, *The Mystical Dimensions of Islam* (Chapel Hill: University of North Carolina Press, 1975); and, in an even broader spiritual context, John Renard, *Seven Doors to Islam: Spirituality and the Religious Life of Muslims* (Berkeley:

University of California Press, 1997). Still useful is Margaret Smith, *Studies in Early Mysticism in the Near and Middle East* (1931; rpt., Amsterdam: Philo Press, 1973).

18. For a rapid survey of the Sufi literature of the Abbasid period, see Caesar E. Farah, "The Prose Literature of Sufism," in M. J. L. Young et al., eds., *The Cambridge History of Arabic Literature: Religion, Learning, and Science in the Abbasid Period* (Cambridge: Cambridge University Press, 1990), 56–75.

19. There is, of course, the exemplary (and gruesome) fate of Islam's most notorious mystic, al-Hallaj; see Louis Massignon, *The Passion of al-Hallaj: Mystic and Martyr of Islam*, trans. Herbert Mason, 4 vols. (Princeton: Princeton University Press, 1982).

20. On the tzaddiq and related types, see Arthur Green, "Typologies of Leadership and the Hasidic Zaddiq," in Green, ed., *Jewish Spirituality from the Sixteenth Century to the Present* (New York: Crossroad, 1997), 127–156.

21. See Peters, *Monotheists*, vol. 2, chap. 8. On the spirituality of the Western Christian orders, see Raitt, *Christian Spirituality*, 15–74.

22. The basic study remains J. S. Trimingham, *The Sufi Orders in Islam* (Oxford: Oxford University Press, 1971).

23. There is a particularly large literature here. The basic texts are collected in W. Foerster, ed., *Gnosticism: A Selection of Gnostic Texts* (London: Oxford University Press, 1972); and James M. Robinson, ed., *The Nag Hammadi Library in English*, rev. ed. (San Francisco: Harper and Row, 1988). Two symposia have covered almost all the issues: Ugo Bianchi, ed., *The Origins of Gnosticism* (Leiden: E. J. Brill, 1967); and Bentley Layton, ed., *The Rediscovery of Gnosticism*, 2 vols. (Leiden: E. J. Brill, 1980–1981). For a skeptical view of the entire phenomenon, Michael Allen Williams, *Rethinking "Gnosticism": An Argument for Dismantling a Dubious Category* (Princeton: Princeton University Press, 1996).

24. See A. F. J. Klijn and G. J. Reinink, *Patristic Evidence for Jewish-Christian Sects* (Leiden: E. J. Brill, 1973).

25. See Robert C. Grant, *Gnosticism and Early Christianity* (New York: Harper Torchbooks, 1966).

26. Readily accessible through Lawrence H. Schiffman, *Reclaiming the Dead Sea Scrolls* (New York: Doubleday, 1995). See, in particular, part 2, "The Community at Qumran," 63–158.

27. Jean Daniélou, *The Dead Sea Scrolls and Primitive Christianity* (New York: Mentor, 1958), 94–96.

28. See the passages translated by Jacob Neusner in his *Life of Yohanan ben Zakkai* (Leiden: E. J. Brill, 1970), 134–142.

29. On Jewish mysticism generally, there are the pioneer studies

of Gershom Scholem, *Major Trends in Jewish Mysticism* (New York: Schocken Books, 1954); and *Jewish Gnosticism, Merkabah Mysticism, and Talmudic Tradition*, 2d ed. (New York: Schocken Books, 1965). See too Ben Zion Bokser, *The Jewish Mystical Tradition* (New York: Pilgrim Press 1981); I. Chernus, *Mysticism in Rabbinic Judaism* (Berlin: Walter de Gruyter, 1982).

30. See David Halperin, *The Faces of the Chariot: Early Jewish Responses to Ezekiel's Vision* (Tübingen: J. C B. Mohr, 1988); and Joseph Dan, "The Religious Experience of the Merkavah," in Green, *Jewish Spirituality*, 289–312.

31. For its Second Temple antecedents, see Mary Dean-Otting, *Heavenly Journeys: A Study of the Motif in Hellenistic Jewish Literature* (Frankfurt: Verlag Peter Lang, 1984).

32. Gershom Scholem, *Origins of Kabbalah*, trans. from the German by Allan Arkush (Princeton: Princeton University Press; Philadelphia: Jewish Publication Society of America, 1987); and compare the very different approach of Moshe Idel, *Kabbalah: New Perspectives* (New Haven: Yale University Press, 1988).

33. Martin Samuel Cohen, *The Shiur Qomah: Liturgy and Theurgy in Pre-Kabbalistic Jewish Mysticism* (Lanham, Md.: University Press of America, 1984). The *Sefer Yetzirah* has been translated by Knut Stenring as *The Book of Formation* (New York: Ktav, 1970).

34. Texts available in English in *The Early Kabbalah*, ed. and intro. Joseph Dan, texts trans. Ronald C. Kiener (New York: Paulist Press, 1986).

35. The original is sprawling, but extensive selections are available in English in *Zohar, the Book of Enlightenment*, trans. and intro. Daniel Chanan Matt (New York: Paulist Press, 1981).

36. To get up to speed, Gershon David Hundert, ed., *Essential Papers on Hasidism* (New York: New York University Press, 1991); and, at speed, Moshe Idel, *Hasidism between Ecstasy and Magic* (Albany: State University of New York Press, 1995).

37. See Seyyed Hossein Nasr, "Ibn Sina's 'Oriental Philosophy'," in Nasr and Oliver Leaman, eds., *History of Islamic Philosophy* (London: Routledge, 1996), 247–251.

38. Avicenna reappears in chap. 8. His mysticism is treated in Henri Corbin, *Avicenna and the Visionary Recital* (Irving, Tex.: Spring Publications, 1980); and Peter Heath, *Allegory and Philosophy in Avicenna (Ibn Sina), with a Translation of the Book of the Prophet Muhammad's Ascent to Heaven* (Philadelphia: University of Pennsylvania Press, 1992). For a more general appreciation, see Seyyed Hossein Nasr, *Three Muslim Sages* (Cambridge: Harvard University Press, 1964), 20–51.

39. On Suhrawardi, see John Walbridge, *The Leaven of the Ancients: Suhrawardi and the Legacy of the Greeks* (Albany: State University of New

York Press, 2002); as well as Nasr, *Three Muslim Sages*, 52–82; and Schimmel, *Mystical Dimensions*, 259–263.

40. See part 5, "Later Islamic Philosophy," in Nasr and Leaman, *Islamic Philosophy*, 527–672.

41. There is a splendid biography by Claude Addas, *Quest for the Red Sulphur: The Life of Ibn Arabi* (Cambridge: Islamic Texts Society, 1993).

42. The easiest way in is probably through *Ibn al-Arabi: The Bezels of Wisdom*, trans. and intro. R. W. J. Austin (New York: Paulist Press, 1980).

43. The best introduction to this complex body of thought is William C. Chittick, *The Sufi Path to Knowledge: Ibn al-Arabi's Metaphysics of Imagination* (Albany: State University of New York Press, 1989).

44. On the Gnostic side of alchemy, see Titus Burckhardt, *Alchemy* (Baltimore: Penguin, 1971). The history of the occult sciences in Islam is traced in F. E. Peters, "Hermes and Harran: The Roots of Islamic Occultism," in *Intellectual Studies on Islam: Essays Written in Honor of Martin B. Dickson* (Salt Lake City: University of Utah Press, 1990), 185–218; rpt., Emilie Savage-Smith, ed., *Magic and Divination in Early Islam* (Abingdon: Ashgate, 2004). For the "practical" side of Kabbala, which comes from the same roots, see Gershom Sholem, *Kabbalah* (Utica: Meridien, 1974), 182–189.

45. On the Ismailis generally, see Farhad Daftary, *Mediaeval Ismaili History and Thought* (Cambridge: Cambridge University Press, 1996); and Heinz Halm, *Shiism* (Edinburgh: Edinburgh University Press, 1991), 162–205.

46. Azim Nanji, "Ismaili Philosophy," in Nasr and Leaman, *Islamic Philosophy*, 144–154; Ian Richard Netton, *Muslim Neoplatonists: An Introduction to the Thought of the Brethren of Purity* (London: Routledge Curzon, 2002).

47. See Farouk Mitha, *Al-Ghazali and the Ismailis: A Debate on Reason and Authority in Medieval Islam* (New York: St. Martin's Press, 2001).

48. This is available in English, along with other texts, including al-Ghazali's refutation of the Esotericists, in R. J. McCarthy, *Al-Gazali: Deliverance from Error* (New York: Twayne, 1980).

49. On the Sufi tradition of "smashing the ink-pots and tearing up the books," see Schimmel, *Mystical Dimensions*, 17–19. Thomas à Kempis (d. 1471) and many others of the Western Christian *devotio moderna* preferred to "feel compunction rather than define it."

50. Only parts of this very large work have been translated into English, but its intent and structure are explained in the introduction to book 1 of the first of the "Quarters" into which the work is divided. This has been translated by N. A. Faris, *Al-Ghazzali: The Book of Knowledge* (1962; rpt., Lahore: Sh. Muhammad Ashraf, 1970).

51. Trans. David Buchman, *Al-Ghazali: the Niche of Lights: A Parallel*

*English-Arabic Text* (Provo: Brigham Young University Press, 1998); and earlier W. H. T. Gairdner, *Al-Ghazzali's Mishkat al-Anwar: The Niche for Lights* (1915; rpt., Lahore: Sh. Muhammad Ashraf, 1952).

52. A long passage of the *Niche* is devoted to expounding the correct method of tawil (Gairdner, 122–149), and al-Ghazali severely chastised those who, like the Ismailis, thought the hidden sense abrogated the literal sense and the legal enactments authorized by the latter (Gairdner, 136–141).

53. For al-Ghazali's rogues' gallery of the "unenlightened" and those who suffered from indirect lighting, see Gairdner, *Niche*, 157–175.

## CHAPTER EIGHT: THINKING AND TALKING ABOUT GOD

1. On the nuances of *mythos* and *logos* as technical terms among the Greeks, see F. E. Peters, *A Greek Philosophical Lexicon* (New York: New York University Press, 1967), s.vv., and compare *philosophia* and *theologia* there and in Glen Bowersock, Peter Brown, and Oleg Grabar, eds., *Late Antiquity: A Guide to the Postclassical World* (Cambridge: Belknap Press, 1999).

2. On this point the pioneering study is still the best: E. R. Dodds, *The Greeks and the Irrational* (Berkeley: University of California Press, 1964).

3. Higher education in late antiquity is an important issue here. See, above all, H. I. Marrou, *A History of Education in Antiquity* (New York: Mentor, 1956), 256–308; and Bowersock et al., *Late Antiquity*, s.v. "education" and the literature cited there.

4. See Martin Hengel, *Judaism and Hellenism*, 2 vols. (London: SCM Press, 1976), 1:115–153.

5. Ibid., 1:163–169. For the intellectual climate in Alexandria at the time, P. M. Frazer, *Ptolemaic Alexandria* (London: Oxford University Press, 1972), 480–494.

6. See John Dillon, *The Middle Platonists* (London: Duckworth, 1977), 139–183.

7. The two enthusiastic volumes by Harry. A. Wolfson, *Philo: Foundations of Religious Philosophy in Judaism, Christianity, and Islam* (Cambridge: Harvard University Press, 1947), should be compared to the treatment by Henry Chadwick in A. H. Armstrong et al., eds., *The Cambridge History of Later Greek and Early Medieval Philosophy* (Cambridge: Cambridge University Press, 1967), 137–157; and that by Dillon cited above.

8. On this latter, see Armstrong et al., *Later Greek Philosophy*, 145–146.

9. See Harry A. Wolfson, *Religious Philosophy: A Group of Essays* (New York: Atheneum, 1965), 25–48.

10. W. D. Davies, *Paul and Rabbinic Judaism* (New York: Harper Torchbooks, 1967), 158–163; and Harry A. Wolfson, *The Philosophy of the Church Fathers*, 3d ed. (Cambridge: Harvard University Press, 1970), 155–167.

11. The argument is already present in Philo and in the second-century Christian Justin; see Wolfson, *Church Fathers*, 19–21.

12. Available in English as *Justin: Dialogue with Trypho*, trans. Thomas B. Falls, rev. and with a new introduction by Thomas P. Halton, ed. Michael Slusser (Washington, D.C.: Catholic University of America Press, 2003).

13. This important point was first underlined by A. D. Nock, *Conversion* (London: Oxford University Press, 1961), 164–192; see also Pierre Hadot, *Philosophy as a Way of Life: Spiritual Exercises from Socrates to Foucault*, trans. Arnold Ira Davidson (Oxford: Blackwell, 1995).

14. Texts in James M. Robinson, ed., *The Nag Hammadi Library in English*, rev. ed. (San Francisco: Harper and Row, 1988).

15. See R. C. Grant, *Gnosticism and Early Christianity* (New York: Harper Torchbooks, 1966), 120–150.

16. Tertullian's clearest statement of his position on Greek philosophy is probably in his *Prescription of Heretics*, trans. T. H. Bindley (London: SPCK, 1914). For the celebrated "I believe because it is absurd" formula, see Etienne Gilson, *A History of Christian Philosophy in the Middle Ages* (London: Sheed and Ward, 1955), 45.

17. There is a partial translation by John Ferguson, *Clement of Alexandria: The Stromateis, Books One to Three* (Washington, D.C.: Catholic University of America Press, 1991).

18. M. F. Wiles, "Origen as a Biblical Scholar," in P. R. Ackroyd and C. F. Evans, eds., *The Cambridge History of the Bible*, vol. 1, *From the Beginnings to Jerome* (Cambridge: Cambridge University Press, 1970), 454–489.

19. *Origen: On First Principles*, trans. G. W. Butterworth (New York: Harper Torchbooks, 1966).

20. See Wolfson, *Church Fathers*, 270–280, 317–321. On the early history of homoousios, see G. L. Prestige, *God in Christian Thought* (London: SPCK, 1952), chap. 10.

21. Arius's position is exhaustively analyzed in Rowan Williams, *Arius: Heresy and Tradition*, rev. ed. (London: SCM Press, 2001), and its sequel traced in Michael R. Barnes and Daniel H. Williams, eds., *Arianism after Arius: Essays on the Development of the Fourth Century Trinitarian Conflicts* (Edinburgh: T. and T. Clark, 1993).

22. This was merely the first epidemic example of the problem of *hairesis*, the "bad choice" of teaching that had dogged the local churches from early on. See the essay by Richard Lim, "Christian Triumph and Controversy," in Bowersock et al., *Late Antiquity*, 196–218, and the liter-

ature cited there. The ground between Nicea and Chalcedon is covered by Frances M. Young, *From Nicaea to Chalcedon: A Guide to the Literature and Its Background* (Philadelphia: Fortress Press, 1983); and Stuart G. Hall, *Doctrine and Practice in the Early Church* (Grand Rapids: Eerdmans, 1991).

23. The best guides to this troubled theological terrain are Aloys Grillmeier, *Christ in Christian Tradition* (London: Sheed and Ward,1965), where the emphasis is theological; and W. C. Frend, *The Rise of Monophysitism* (Cambridge: Cambridge University Press, 1972), with more detailed historical background. For the effect of these Christological disputes on the Christian Roman Empire's dream of world domination, see Garth Fowden, *Empire to Commonwealth: Consequences of Monotheism in Late Antiquity* (Princeton: Princeton University Press, 1993), chap. 5.

24. On the background for Islam, see F. E. Peters, "The Greek and Syriac Background," in Seyyed Hossein Nasr and Oliver Leaman, eds., *History of Islamic Philosophy* (London: Routledge, 1996), 40–51.

25. See W. Montgomery Watt, *The Formative Period of Islamic Thought* (Edinburgh: Edinburgh University Press, 1973), 82–118.

26. See F. E. Peters, *Aristotle and the Arabs* (New York: New York University Press, 1968); Franz Rosenthal, *The Classical Heritage in Islam* (Berkeley: University of California Press, 1975); Lenn Evan Goodman, "The Translation of Greek Materials into Arabic," in M. J. L. Young et al., eds., *The Cambridge History of Arabic Literature: Religion, Learning, and Science in the Abbasid Period* (Cambridge: Cambridge University Press, 1990), 487–491; Dimitri Gutas, *Greek Thought and Arabic Culture: The Graeco-Arabic Translation Movement in Baghdad and Early Abbasid Society* (London: Routledge, 1998).

27. "Tradition" (*hadith*) is, as we have seen, a term of art in Islam and serves as a kind of shorthand—"Prophetic tradition" is fuller and more explicit—referring to the report of a saying or deed of Muhammad. Those who transmitted, collected, or studied such reports were called "traditionists" (*muhaddith/muhaddithun*). "Traditionalist" and "traditionalism" are broader (and modern Western) terms and are used here of all those who regard the Quran, the hadith—collectively, the sunna or custom of the Prophet—and consensus as the primary basis of Muslim belief and practice. All traditionists were also traditionalists in that sense, but the latter group also included people who might more properly be thought of as theologians.

28. On these pioneers of rationalism in Islam, see Watt, *Formative Period*, 209–252.

29. On the early kalam, see ibid., 180–208; and Abdel Haleem, "Early Kalam," in Nasr and Leaman, *Islamic Philosophy*, 71–88.

30. On the later Muslim understanding of kalam, there is a brief in-

troduction by R. M. Frank, "The Science of *Kalam*," *Arabic Science and Philosophy* 2 (1992): 3–7; and a much more extensive treatment in Harry. A. Wolfson, *The Philosophy of Kalam* (Cambridge: Harvard University Press, 1976), 3–42. Maimonides' sketch of its history is discussed in Wolfson, 43–57.

31. For this distinction, commonly drawn by critical philosophers, see the passages from al-Farabi's *Enumeration of the Sciences*, trans. in R. Lerner and Muhsin Mahdi, eds., *Medieval Political Philosophy* (Ithaca: Cornell University Press, 1972), 27–30.

32. On the limits of the problematic of the kalam, see A. J. Wensinck, *The Muslim Creed: Its Genesis and Historical Development* (London: Frank Cass and Co., 1965), 58–83; and Wolfson, *Kalam*, 72–79.

33. W. M. Patton, *Ahmad ibn Hanbal and the Mihna* (London: E. J. Brill, 1897).

34. On falsafa generally, see Majid Fakhry, *History of Islamic Philosophy* (New York: Columbia University Press, 1993); Oliver Leaman, *A Brief Introduction to Islamic Philosophy* (Malden: Blackwell, 1999); and Seyyed Hossein Nasr, "The Meaning and Concept of Philosophy in Islam," in Nasr and Leaman, *Islamic Philosophy*, 21–27, and the topical articles collected there under the heading "Philosophy and Its Parts," 783–1000.

35. See Felix Klein-Franke, "Al-Kindi," in Nasr and Leaman, *Islamic Philosophy*, 165–177; and for a generous sampling of his work, Alfred Ivry, *Al-Kindi's Metaphysics* (Albany: State University Press of New York, 1974).

36. On al-Razi, see Lenn Evan Goodman, "Muhammad ibn Zakariyya al-Razi," in Nasr and Leaman, *Islamic Philosophy*, 198–215.

37. On al-Farabi, see Ian Netton, *Al-Farabi and His School* (London: Routledge, 1992); Deborah L. Black, "Al-Farabi," in Nasr and Leaman, *Islamic Philosophy*, 178–197. On the prophecy issue, Fazlur Rahman, *Prophecy in Islam: Philosophy and Orthodoxy* (Chicago: University of Chicago Press, 1978); and Richard Walzer, "Al-Farabi's Theory of Prophecy and Divination," in his *Greek into Arabic: Essays on Islamic Philosophy* (Oxford: Oxford University Press, 1962), 206–219.

38. The dangers of this position in a religious society, dangers well understood by the Platonic tradition to which al-Farabi belonged, are underscored by Leo Strauss in his *Persecution and the Art of Writing* (Glencoe, Ill.: Free Press, 1952).

39. See generally Lenn Evan Goodman, *Avicenna* (London: Routledge, 1992); and Dimitri Gutas, *Avicenna and the Aristotelian Tradition: Introduction to the Reading of Avicenna's Philosophical Works* (Leiden: E. J. Brill, 1988); and more particularly, Rahman, *Prophecy in Islam*, 30–91.

40. Trans. in R. Lerner and Muhsin Mahdi, *Medieval Political Philosophy*, 112–121.

41. See Armstrong et al., *Later Greek Philosophy*, 258–263.

42. There are selections in English in Henri Corbin, *Avicenna and the Visionary Recital* (Irving, Tex.: Spring Publications, 1980).

43. See Avicenna's autobiography, trans. and annotated by W. E. Gohlman, *The Life of Ibn Sina* (Albany: State University of New York Press, 1974).

44. Two of al-Ashari's major works are available in English: W. C. Klein, *The Elucidation of Islam's Foundation* (New Haven: Yale University Press, 1940); R. J. McCarthy, *The Theology of al-Ash'ari* (Beirut: Imprimerie Catholique, 1953).

45. See Wensinck, *Muslim Creed*, 83–101.

46. The debate between the Asharite "occasionalist" theologians and the philosophical naturalists continued well into the thirteenth century; see Wolfson, *Kalam*, 466–600; and Majid Fakhry, *Islamic Occasionalism and Its Critique by Averroes and Aquinas* (London: Allen and Unwin, 1958).

47. This judgment is most succinctly stated in his *Deliverer from Error*. See R. J. McCarthy, *Al-Gazali: Deliverance from Error* (New York: Twayne, 1980), 59–60; the text in Peters, *JCI Texts*, 3:301–302; and Richard M. Frank, *Ghazali and the Ash'arite School* (Durham: Duke University Press, 1994).

48. Ibn Khaldun's more extended remarks on the history, evolution, and function of kalam are in Peters, *JCI Texts*, 3:296–301.

49. See the fundamental article by George Makdisi, "Ash'ari and the Ash'arites in Islamic Religious History," *Studia Islamica* 17 (1962): 37–80; 18 (1963): 19–39.

50. The best English introduction to al-Ghazali is W. Montgomery Watt, *Muslim Intellectual: A Study of al-Ghazali* (Edinburgh: Edinburgh University Press, 1963); see also Massimo Campanini, "Al-Ghazzali," in Nasr and Leaman, *Islamic Philosophy*, 258–276.

51. Most of this is translated together with Averroes' counterrefutation; see n. 57 below.

52. See George Makdisi's "Conclusion" to his classical study of the madrasa, *The Rise of Colleges: Institutions of Learning in Islam and the West* (Edinburgh: Edinburgh University Press, 1981), 281–291.

53. On the Christian creed, see J. N. D. Kelly, *Early Christian Creeds*, 3d ed. (Essex: Longman Group, 1981); and Bernard L. Marthaler, *The Creed* (Mystic: Twenty-Third Publications, 1987).

54. On the history of the shahada, see Wensinck, *Muslim Creed*, 17–35.

55. All these aqidas are analyzed ibid.

56. On Ibn Rushd, see Oliver Leaman, *Averroes and His Philosophy* (Oxford: Clarendon Press,1988); Majid Fakhry, *Averroes (Ibn Rushd): His Life, Works, and Influence* (Oxford: OneWorld, 2001); Dominique Urvoy, *Ibn Rushd (Averroes)* (London: Routledge, 1991): Urvoy, "Ibn Rushd," in Nasr and Leaman, *Islamic Philosophy*, 330–345; Roger Arnaldez, *Averroes:*

*A Rationalist in Islam*, trans. David Streight (Notre Dame: University of Notre Dame Press, 2000); and in broader perspective, Klaus Braun et al., eds., *Averroes and the Aristotelian Tradition: Sources, Constitution, and Reception of the Philosophy of Ibn Rushd, 1126–1998* (Leiden: E. J. Brill, 1999).

57. His *Incoherence* has been translated, together with the appropriate sections of al-Ghazali's *Incoherence*, by S. Van den Bergh, *Averroes' Tahafut al-tahafut*, 2 vols (London: Luzac, 1954).

58. On al-Ghazali's denial of natural causality and Averroes' defense of it, see Fakhry, *Islamic Occasionalism*, 56–138.

59. Trans. with commentary by George Hourani, *Averroes on the Harmony of Religion and Philosophy: A Translation, with Introduction and Notes, of Ibn Rushd's Kitab Fasl al-Maqal* (London: Luzac, 1961).

60. See Ignaz Goldziher, *The Zahiris: Their Doctrine and History* (1884; rev. trans., Leiden: E. J. Brill, 1971).

61. See Lenn Evan Goodman, "Saadiah Gaon al-Fayyumi," in Nasr and Leaman, *Islamic Philosophy*, 696–711; Julius Guttmann, *Philosophies of Judaism* (New York: Schocken Books, 1973), 61–73; and Robert Brody, *The Geonim of Babylonia and the Shaping of Medieval Jewish Culture* (New Haven: Yale University Press, 1998), 235–332.

62. The Arabic original has been translated into English by Samuel Rosenblatt, *Saadia Gaon: The Book of Beliefs and Opinions* (1948; rpt., New Haven: Yale University Press, 1967). There is an abridged translation done in 1946 by Alexander Altman and now published with a new introduction by Daniel H. Frank in *Saadya Gaon: The Book of Doctrines and Beliefs* (Indianapolis: Hackett, 2002).

63. Rosenblatt, *Beliefs and Opinions*, 137–179, 299–322.

64. Wolfson, *Church Fathers*, 97–101.

65. See Guttmann, *Philosophies of Judaism*, 89–120.

66. See Arthur Hyman, "Jewish Philosophy in the Islamic World," in Nasr and Leaman, *Islamic Philosophy*, 677–695.

67. Barry Kogan, "Judah Halevi," in Nasr and Leaman, *Islamic Philosophy*, 718–724; and, on the *Kuzari*, N. Daniel Korobkin, *In Defense of the Despised Faith* (Northvale, N.J.: J. Aronson, 1998); and compare Yochanan Silman, *Philosopher and Prophet: Judah Halevi, the Kuzari, and the Evolution of His Thought* (Albany: State University of New York Press, 1995).

68. See Strauss, *Persecution and the Art of Writing*. There is convenient access to Maimonides the philosopher through Lenn Evan Goodman, *Rambam: Readings in the Philosophy of Moses Maimonides* (New York: Schocken Books, 1977); and compare Alexander Broadie, "Maimonides," in Nasr and Leaman, *Islamic Philosophy*, 725–738; and Guttmann, *Philosophies of Judaism*, 152–182.

69. English trans. of the Arabic original by Shlomo Pines, with an introduction by Leo Strauss, *Moses Maimonides: The Guide of the Perplexed* (Chicago: University of Chicago Press, 1963). On the larger issue of faith

and reason in medieval Judaism, see Raphael Jospe, "Faith and Reason: The Controversy over Philosophy," in Raphael Jospe and Stanley M. Wagner, eds., *Great Schisms in Jewish History* (New York: Ktav, 1981), 73–118.

70. Hourani, *Harmony*, 32–37, and trans., 63–71, 76–81.

71. See Strauss's introduction to Pines, *Guide*, and the translator's own remarks, cxvii–cxxiii.

72. See Guttmann, *Philosophies of Judaism*, 154, 178–179; and Peters, *Monotheists*, vol. 1, chap. 5.

73. *Guide* 2.17 (Pines, 294).

74. Introduction to parts 1 and 3 (Pines, *Guide*, 5–9, 415–416).

75. Ibid., lxxxix, xcviii–cxxiii.

76. On post-Ghazali kalam, see Wensinck, *Muslim Creed*, 248–276.

77. See Bernard G. Dad, "Aristoteles Latinus," in Norman Kretzmann et al., eds., *The Cambridge History of Later Medieval Philosophy* (Cambridge: Cambridge University Press, 1982), 45–79.

78. A number of the contributions to Norman Kretzmann and Eleonore Stump, eds., *The Cambridge Companion to Aquinas* (Cambridge: Cambridge University Press, 1993), lead directly into the issue that concerns us here: Joseph Owens, "Aristotle and Aquinas," 38–59; David B. Burrell, "Aquinas and Islamic and Jewish Thinkers,"60–84; and Mark D. Jordan, "Theology and Philosophy," 232–251. It should also be remarked that Thomas's other great summa, the *Contra Gentiles* (1270–1272), was written specifically as a tool for the conversion of Muslims; see Peters, *Monotheists*, vol. 1, chap. 4.

79. See C. H. Lohr's useful summary "The Medieval Interpretations of Aristotle," in Kretzmann et al., *Later Medieval Philosophy*, 80–98.

80. See Herbert A. Davidson, *Alfarabi, Avicenna, and Averroes on Intellect: Their Cosmologies, Theories of the Active Intellect, and Theories of Human Intellect* (Oxford: Oxford University Press, 1992).

81. Ralph McInerney, *Aquinas against the Averroists: On There Being Only One Intellect* (West Lafayette, Ind.: Purdue University Press, 1993); and see Edward P. Mahoney, "Sense, Intellect, and Imagination in Albert, Thomas, and Siger," in Kretzmann et al., *Later Medieval Philosophy*, 602–622. On Latin Averroism generally, see Gilson, *Christian Philosophy*, 387–409.

# Glossary

The following technical terms appear in the text transcribed from Arabic (A), Greek (G), and Hebrew-Aramaic (H). All transcription systems are unsatisfactory for those who read the original languages, and probably baffling for those who cannot. The ones used here make no special claim in that regard. I have attempted to keep diacritical marks to a minimum on the grounds that few readers will be either deceived or uninstructed by their omission. When entries appear in the form *halaka/halakot*, the first member is the singular, the second the plural. Quotation marks enclose a literal meaning of a term wherever that seemed useful.

*ab bet din* (H): junior member of the "pair" who presided over the Sanhedrin or Great Assembly;' see *bet din*.

*agape* (G): "love," "love feast"; the non-Eucharistic community meal shared by the early Christians.

*ahl al-hadith* (A): "partisans of *hadith* reports," traditionists; see *hadith, muhaddith*.

*ahl al-kalam* (A): "partisans of dialectical reasoning"; see *kalam, mutakallim*.

*Allah* (A): "the god"; the One True God.

*allegoria* (G): "other-referent"; a sense of the text different from the literal or parent meaning; see *batin, tawil*.

*amida* (H): "standing"; the series of benedictions that constitute the central part of the synagogue service.

*amir* (A): commander; *amir al-muminun*: "commander of the faithful," title of the head of the Muslim community.

*amme ha-aretz* (H): "people of the land"; "commoners"; non- or carelessly observant Jews.

*amora/amoraim* (H): "speaker"; the rabbis whose comments on the Mishna constitute the two *gemarot*.

*anachoresis* (G) withdrawal, esp. the Christian withdrawal from the world for religious motives; cf. English "anchorite."

*anamnesis* (G): "remembrance"; the recollection of Jesus' redemptive passion and death as part of the Christian liturgy.

*anaphora*(G): "lifting up"; the central part of the Eucharistic liturgy; the "canon" of the Roman mass.

*apokalypsis* (G): "unveiling," particularly of the End Time, in the form of a vision.

*apokrypha* (G): "hidden," "sequestered"; the Apocrypha are those religious writings excluded from the official canon of Scripture.

*aqeda* (H): "binding," scil. of Isaac; the intended sacrifice of Abraham's son.

*aqida* (A): creed, statement of Muslim beliefs; see *symbolon*.

*baraka* (A): "blessing"; the special favor or divine grace possessed by the "friends of God" and especially the Sufi master; see *wali, murshid, silsila*.

*batin* (A): "concealed"; the sense of Scripture concealed beneath the literal meaning and accessible only to an adept; see *tawil*.

*Bayt Allah* (A): "House of the God"; the Kaaba in Mecca; cf. Hebr.>Eng. Beth-el

*Benei Israel* (H): "Children of Israel"; Israelites; Jews.

*berit* (H): covenant, esp. the Covenant concluded between Yahweh and Abraham.

*bet din* (H): Jewish law court; the great bet din was the Sanhedrin, the chief legislative and judicial body of post-Exilic Judaism.

*bet ha-knesset* (H): "house of assembly"; congregational meeting place; the synagogue.

*bet ha-midrash* (H): "house of study"; school for the study of Jewish Scripture and law; see *midrash, yeshiva*.

*bet ha-tefilla* (H): "house of prayer"; the synagogue as a liturgical center.

*birket ha-minim* (H): "blessing over the heretics"; actually a ritual-curse of heretics introduced into synagogue worship in the first century C.E.

*Dar al-Harb* (A): "Abode of War"; those lands not under Muslim political control.

*Dar al-Islam* (A): "Abode of Islam"; the territories under Muslim political control and where, strictly speaking, the *sharia* prevails.

*dhikr* (A): "recollection," esp. of God; the external repetition of God's name in a rhythmical manner; a Sufi devotional exercise.

*dhimma* (A): the "covenant" between the Muslim community and those People of the Book who submit peaceably to its authority and so are granted the freedom to practice, within certain restrictions, their religion. Jews, Christians, and (sometimes) Zoroastrians who live under this covenant in the Abode of Islam are called *dhimmis*.

Diaspora (G): "dispersion"; the Jewish communities outside *Eretz Israel*.

*eidos/eide* (G): archetype; idea.

*ekklesia* (G): congregation; church; an individual community or the total body of Christians who constitute the "Great Church"; cf. Eng. "ecclesiastic."

*epiklesis* (G): "invocation"; the calling on the Holy Spirit to sanctify the sacrificial offering in Eastern Christian liturgies.

*episkopos* (G): "overseer"; the head of a Christian community with responsibility for their faith and morals; bishop; cf. Eng. "episcopal."

*Eretz Israel* (H): "Land of (or for) Israel"; the land promised to the Israelites in the Covenant; in law, the area where the *halakot* had to be observed in their entirety.

*erub/erubin* (H): "mixture"; by extension, the domain within which limited Sabbath activity was permissible; a tractate of the Mishnaic order of "festivals" devoted to that question.

*euangelion* (G): "good news," namely, of Jesus, a Gospel; the literary work embodying such, esp. the four canonical Gospels attributed to Matthew, Mark, Luke, and John; see *Injil* and cf. Eng. "evangelical."

*falsafa* (A): "philosophy," esp. the methods and contents of Greek philosophy transposed into Islam; a practitioner was called a *faylasuf*.

*fana* (A): "annihilation" (of self), the state antecedent to the mystic's union with God.

*faqih/fuqaha* (A): jurisprudent; one skilled in the interpretation of the *sharia*; see *fiqh*.

*fatwa* (A): an advisory judgment rendered by a competent authority on an inquiry regarding Islamic law; a responsum; see *mufti*.

*fiqh* (A): jurisprudence; the science of the principles and branches of the *sharia*.

*gaon/geonim* (H): "eminence"; the heads of the Jewish law school under Islam and the chief authorities of the Jewish communities in the Abode of Islam in medieval times.

*gemara/gemarot* (H): "completion"; an Aramaic commentary on the Mishna by the rabbis of either the Babylonian or the Palestinian academies; see *amora*.

*geniza* (H): storeroom, esp. one attached to a synagogue, where texts and documents were preserved.

*gezera/gezerot* (H): a legal enactment that extended or specified a rabbinic *halaka*.

*gnosis* (G): "knowledge," esp. the hidden knowledge of the adept, which guarantees salvation; see *hikma*.

*habura* (H): table fellowship; a common meal shared by those with common standards of ritual purity.

*hadith* (A): a report purporting to transmit the words or deeds of Muhammad on the authority of his contemporaries.

*haftara* (H): a passage of about ten verses from the Prophetic Books whose recitation followed that of the Torah in the Sabbath synagogue service.

*haggada/haggadot* (H): homily; exegesis of Scripture in the form of expositional homilies that emphasized the moral and ethical content of the text.

*hajj* (A): pilgrimage, esp. the pilgrimage to Mecca incumbent on all Muslims.

*halaka/halakot* (H): a binding legal enactment of the rabbis that either was derived from Scripture by exegetical means or appealed for its authority to the "tradition of the Fathers."

*haram* (A): "taboo"; taboo area or sanctuary; the sanctuary surrounding the Kaaba at Mecca; *Haram al-Sharif*, the "Noble

Sanctuary," Herod's platform demarcating the Temple Mount in Jerusalem; cf. Eng. "harem," the taboo section of a Muslim household, the women's quarters; see also *herem*.

*hasid/hasidim* (H): "pious"; a term used of (1) early religious supporters of the Maccabees and so the forerunners of the Pharisees; and (2) a number of groups of medieval Jewish pietists, but particularly (3) an eighteenth-century eastern European movement of popular mysticism.

*hegoumenos* (G): leader or superior, esp. of a Christian monastic community; an abbot.

*herem* (H): "taboo," "unholy"; permanent expulsion from the Jewish community; see *haram*.

*hesychia* (G): tranquility, quietude in the mystic's contemplation.

*heykal/heykalot* (H): "palace-temples"; way stations along the Jewish mystic's path to God.

*hijra* (A): "emigration," esp. Muhammad's emigration from Mecca to Medina in 622 C.E., a date that marks the beginning of the Muslim era: cf. Eng. "hegira."

*hikma* (A): wisdom; the highest level of understanding, in particular the illuminative, intuitive wisdom of the mystic, the Gnostic, or the theosopher.

*hiyal* (A): "devices," esp. legal devices or fictions used to avoid the violation of the direct letter of the law.

*homoousios* (G): "of the same substance (*ousia*)"; cf. *homoiousios*, "of a similar substance," both used of Jesus in reference to the Father.

*hyponoia* (G): "under-meaning," the latent sense of a text, which must be elicited by allegorical exegesis; see *allegoria*.

*hukm/ahkam* (A): "judgments"; quranic enactments, hence, Islamic *mitzvot*.

*hypostasis* (G): existent individual being.

*id* (A): festival, holy day; particularly *id al-fitr* at the end of Ramadan and *id al-adha* during the *hajj*.

*ijma* (A): consensus; the consensus of legal scholars of one center or school, but eventually understood to be the consensus of all Muslims.

*ijtihad* (A): "personal effort"; the application of everything from common sense to sophisticated legal reasoning to the explication of a text.

*ikhwan* (A): "brethren"; members of a religious fraternity or *tariqa*.

*ilm* (A): knowledge, esp. discursive, demonstrative knowledge and its contents; science.

*imam* (A): leader; (1) prayer leader; (2) the Imam, the charismatic leader of the Muslim community; in the Shiite view, a descendant of Ali who is so designated by his predecessor.

*iman* (A): faith; belief; the internal acceptance of God and the Prophet's mission that finds its external expression in the *shahada*; see *mumin*.

*Injil* (A): the Gospel, from the Greek *euangelion*.

*Ioudaioi* (G): "Judeans"; Jews.

*ishraq* (A): "illumination"; the intuitive understanding of the mystic or certain philosophers; see *hikma*, *marifa*.

*islam* (A): "submission," namely, to the will of God; see *muslim*.

*isnad* (A): the chain of reporters on whose authority a *hadith* is transmitted.

*ittihad* (A): identity; union, esp. the mystic's union and identification with God.

*jamaa* (A): community, esp. the Islamic community viewed as a unity; see *umma*.

*jami* (A): a place of assembly, esp. assembly for liturgical prayer in Islam; a mosque, esp. the mosque designated for the Friday congregational prayer; see *masjid*.

*jihad* (A): "striving"; striving in the way of God in either the internal or the external forum; in the latter sense, "holy war."

*kafir/kafirun* (A): an unbeliever; one who has not submitted to the will of God; a pagan; see *kufr*.

*kalam* (A): "speech"; dialectical theology, characterized by its starting from commonly accepted assumptions, its use of dialectical rather than demonstrative reasoning, and its employment as an instrument for the defense of Scripture; see *mutakallim*.

*kanon/kanones* (G): "standards" of judgment and behavior; in the latter sense, norms or laws.

*karamat* (A): spiritual blessings, esp. those given to the friends of God; see *wali*.

*kashf* (A): "unveiling"; God's self-disclosure to the mystic.

*katechesis* (G): instruction, esp. the instruction prior to Christian baptism; cf. Eng. "catechism."

*kenoma* (G): "emptiness"; the lower material and sensible world of the Gnostic; see *pleroma*.

*khalifa* (A): "deputy" or "successor"; the successor of Muhammad as the head of the community of Muslims; as Imam, the preferred Shiite term, and *amir al-muminun*; cf. Eng. "caliph."

*khutba* (A): sermon, esp. the sermon delivered at the Friday congregational prayer in the *jami*; see *minbar*. The one who delivers it is called the *khatib*.

*kohen/kohenim* (H): priest; celebrant of the Jewish sacrificial liturgy.

*koinobion* (G): community, esp. a community of Christian ascetics sharing a common life or rule; cf. Eng. "cenobitic."

*kufr* (A): disbelief; paganism; see *kafir*.

*logos/logoi* (G): word; speech; reason, human or divine, the latter sometimes personified; the mode of discourse constructed on reason; pl.: the discrete manifestations of reason inherent in the universe; cf. Eng. "logic."

*madrasa* (A): school for the advanced study of the *sharia*.

Mahdi (A): "Guided One"; an eschatological and messianic figure in Sunni Islam.

*marifa* (A): knowledge, esp. the intuitive knowledge characteristic of the mystic or Gnostic; see *hikma*.

*mashiah* (H); "anointed one"; messiah; in Greek, *Christos*.

*masjid* (A): "place of prostration"; shrine; mosque; see *jami* and cf. Eng. "mosque."

*mawla/mawali* (A): client; non-Arab convert to Islam.

*mawlid al-nabi* (A): birthday of the Prophet, a Muslim festival.

*mazalim* (A): count of complaint or appeals directed at ruler's discretionary obligation (and power) to maintain justice in the Islamic community.

*merkaba* (H): "chariot," specifically Ezekiel's, the Jewish mystic's preferred vehicle to travel to the throne of God.

*metamorphosis* (G): "re-formation," esp. of one's moral and spiritual life through grace.

*midrash/midrashim* (H): "study," esp. the study of Scripture; exegesis and the literary works devoted to such.

*mihna* (A): scrutiny, esp. of one's theological opinions.

*mihrab* (A): a niche in a mosque indicating the *qibla* or direction of prayer.

*millet* (A): a semiautonomous community within the Abode of Islam, usually constituted on religious grounds from among the People of the Book but with distinctive ethnic overtones; an organization of the *dhimmis* in the Ottoman Empire.

*min/minim* (H): generically, heretics; though possibly with more precise reference to Jewish Christians.

*minbar* (A): a raised pulpit near the *mihrab* of a mosque; the place from which the *khutba* or Friday homily is delivered.

Mishna (H): the corpus of legal and other matter compiled by the rabbis of the second and third centuries C.E., and esp. the final, authoritative version.

*mitzva/mitzvot* (H): "commandment"; a legal prescription explicitly found in the Bible.

*monachos/monachoi* (G): "solitary"; a monk.

*muadhdhin* (A): "caller"; a public summoner to prayer in Islam; cf. Eng. "muezzin."

*mufti* (A): one who is competent to render an opinion on a matter of Islamic law; see *fatwa.*

*muhaddith/muhaddithun* (A): a traditionist, a collector or expert on Prophetic traditions.

*mumin/muminun* (A): one who has faith (*iman*); a believer; a Muslim.

*murshid* (A): a spiritual guide or master; a Sufi master of novices, who possessed a particular charisma or grace (*baraka*); in Persian, a *pir.*

*muslim/muslimun* (A): "one who has submitted," namely, to the will of God; a Muslim.

*mutakallim/mutakallimun* (A): a theologian, one skilled in *kalam.*

*muwahhidun* (A): "Unitarians"; Almohads.

*mythos* (G): narrative as explanation.

*nabi* (A): prophet; the recipient of a divine revelation.

*nasi* (H): "leader," "ruler," "prince"; the senior partner of the "pair" and the chief officer of the Sanhedrin or Great Assembly; later the "patriarch," the chief representative and acknowledged head of the Jewish communities of the Roman Empire; see resh galuta.

*nazar* (A): investigation, rational inquiry.

*nidduy* (H): temporary suspension from the Jewish community; see *herem*.

*notzrim* (H): "Nazareans"? An early Jewish term for Christians.

*ousia* (G): substance.

*paradosis* (G): "handing down or over"; tradition, esp. the Christian tradition of the teachings of Jesus passed down the line of the Apostolic succession.

*parousia* (G): "presence," "coming," esp. of the Messiah; for Christians, the "Second Coming" of Jesus in the End Time.

*peshat* (H): the plain or literal sense of a scriptural passage; see *zahir*.

*pesher/pesharim* (H): commentary on Scripture, esp. those composed by the Qumran sectaries; see *midrash*.

*pesiqta* (H): the portion of the Torah and the Prophets read in the liturgical celebration of special Sabbaths and holy days.

*petiha* (H): "opening"; the verses chosen from the Prophets or the Writings by the synagogue preacher to introduce his homily; the Arabic cognate, *fatiha*, refers to the opening *sura* of the Quran.

*phainomena* (G): "that which appears"; evidence.

*pleroma* (G): "fullness" or "perfection"; the upper spiritual world of Gnosticism; the abode of God and the Aeons and the divine homeland of the divine element of humankind; see *kenoma*.

*politeia* (G): polity; form of governance; constitution.

*presbyteros/presbyteroi* (G): "elder"; the collegial heads of the Christian community; later, the subordinates of the bishop; the Christian priesthood, the celebrants of the Eucharistic liturgy.

*qabbala* (H): "that which is handed down," esp. the esoteric contents of the Jewish Gnostic traditions; cf. Eng. "Kabbala."

*qadi* (A): a government-appointed judge who was the caliph's delegate in adjudicating disputes falling under the jurisdiction of the *sharia*.

*qibla* (A): "orientation," esp. for prayer; the direction toward Mecca marked in the mosque by the *mihrab*.

*qiyama*: (A): "resurrection," esp. the universal spiritual resurrection at the Ismaili End Time.

*qiyas* (A): analogy; esp. legal reasoning using the analogical method to define or extend legal enactments; a type of *ijtihad*.

Quran (A): "recitation"; the collected revelations given by God to the Prophet Muhammad through the agency of the angel Gabriel and the text in which they were finally written down; the Muslim Scripture.

*qutb* (A): pole; pole star around whom other saints revolve.

*rasul* (A): envoy, an "apostle" of God; the Prophet Muhammad.

*resh galuta* (H): "head of the Exile," the exilarch or leader of the Jewish communities of the Iranian empires of pre-Islamic times; an office parallel to that of the nasi in the Roman Empire and antecedent of the *geonim*.

*salat* (A): prayer, esp. the five daily liturgical prayers obligatory on every Muslim.

*sama* (A): "hearing"; a Sufi ritual performance composed of acts like chanting and dancing with musical accompaniment in preparation for the ecstatic state; see *dhikr*.

*seder/sedarim* (H): one of the six "orders" into which the Mishna is divided; also used of sections into which the Torah is divided for litiurgical recitation.

*sefira/sefirot* (H): "numbers," hence, elemental principles; in the Kabbala, the primary emanations of God that constitute the *pleroma*.

*semika* (H): "ordination"; the nasi's formal delegation of his judicial powers to others.

*shahada* (A): "witnessing" or professing, esp. the Muslim profession of faith and its formulaic expression: "There is no god but the God, and Muhammad is his envoy"; see *iman*.

*shaliah/shelihim* (H): messenger; delegate; apostle.

*sharia* (A): Islamic law in general; in particular those enactments whose authority is derived from (1) the Quran, (2) the *sunna* of the Prophet, (3) the consensus of the community, or (4) the legal reasoning of jurisprudents.

*shema* (H): Deuteronomy 6:1, beginning with the phrase "Hear" (*shema*), O Lord"; in a liturgical sense, the prayer constructed around that passage.

*shia* (A): "party" or "partisans," and here particularly the *Shiat Ali*, the partisans of Ali and his descendants; those who supported the Alid claim to the imamate; Shiites.

*shirk* (A): "association," esp. of other deities with the unique God; polytheism and hence, *kufr*.

*silsila*: (A) "chain"; the line of past masters through whom the spiritual enlightenment of a Sufi order passed; see *baraka*.

*siyasa* (A): "policy"; the discretionary political powers of the caliph.

*sofer/soferim* (H): scribe, esp. the professional scribe of post-Exilic Judaism, who was also a student and exegete of the law.

Sufi (A): probably "one who wears a woolen (*suf*) cloak"; a Muslim ascetic-mystic.

*sunna* (A): "custom," "customary practice"; elliptically for *sunnat al-nabi*, the "custom of the Prophet" as reported in the *hadith*; cf. Eng. "Sunni."

*sura* (A); a chapter or traditional division of the Quran.

*symbolon* (G): statement of belief; creed.

*synaxis* (G): "gathering," "assembly," esp. for a religious service; a Christian prayer meeting on a synagogue model that was later incorporated into the Eucharistic liturgy as the preliminary to the *anaphora*.

*tafsir* (A): commentary, esp. quranic commentary; originally, perhaps, the explanation of the "plain sense" of Scripture; see *zahir*.

*tajalli* (A): "self-disclosure," God's, in the mysticism of Ibn Arabi.

*talim* (A): "teaching," esp. the authoritative and infallible magisterium of the Imam.

Talmud (H): the Hebrew Mishna of Rabbi Judah ha-Nasi accompanied by either of its Aramaic *gemarot*, the Palestinian (= Talmud Yerushalmi) or the Babylonian (= Talmud Bavli).

*tanna/tannaim* (H): "repeater" or "reciter"; the second- and third-century Jewish sages whose enactments and discussions are preserved in the Mishna.

*taqlid* (A): acceptance on the authority of another.

*taqqana/taqqanot* (H): a rabbinic legal enactment whose object was to create new institutions for the improvement of the religious, social, or economic conditions of the Jewish community.

*targum* (H): "translation," esp. the interpretative translations of the Bible into Aramaic.

*tariqa* (A): "way," esp. that of the Sufi, and eventually any one of the institutionalized "ways" that constituted the Sufi community organizations.

*tawil* (A): the explanation of obscure or ambiguous passages in the Quran; allegorical exegesis.

*Tawrat* (A): Torah.

*taziya* (A): the dramatic reenactment of the martyrdom of Ali's son, and the Prophet's grandson, Husayn.

*theologia* (G): scientific discourse about God; see *kalam*; also, the mystic's apprehension of God.

*theologoumena* (G): propositions held principally on faith.

Torah (H): the law; a term used generically of Jewish religious law or specifically of the first five books (Pentateuch) of the Bible where it is principally set forth.

*tzaddiq* (H): "just man"; a holy man characterized by both his observance of the law and his asceticism and, at times, by his possession of special spiritual powers; a Jewish saint.

*ulama* (A): "the learned"; the Islamic "rabbinate" whose prestige derived from their mastery of the religious sciences; see *faqih*.

*umma* (A): the community of Muslims.

*wali/awliya* (A): "friend," namely, of God; those who possessed special spiritual gifts; Muslim saints; see *karamat*.

*waqf* (A): land or property whose proprietorship was inalienably deeded to God and whose income was dedicated to the support of pious causes, such as the construction of a mosque or *madrasa*, and the support of its faculty and students.

*yahad* (H): community, esp. the community at Qumran.

*yeshiva/yeshivot* (H): Jewish institution for study of the Torah and Talmud; see *bet ha-midrash*.

*zahir* (A): the "open," plain, or literal sense of the text, esp. of Scripture, and so the object of *tafsir*.

*zakat* (A): a tithe obligatory on all Muslims as an offering to the poor.

*zug/zugot* (H): "pair"; the two officers, the *nasi* and the *ab bet din*, who presided over the Sanhedrin or Great Assembly of the Jewish community in Palestine.

*zuhd* (A): asceticism.

# Index